WEB MARKETING COOKBOOK

Janice M. King

Paul Knight

James H. Mason

Janice King

Jung H Mason

Paul Knight

WILEY COMPUTER PUBLISHING

JOHN WILEY & SONS, INC.

New York • Chichester • Weinheim • Brisbane • Singapore • Toronto

*For marketers in every business and nonprofit
organization who work every day to reach and communicate
with customers, members, and prospects*

Executive Publisher: Katherine Schowalter
Editor: Theresa Hudson
Associate Managing Editor: Angela Murphy
Electronic Products, Associate Editor: Mike Green
Text Design & Composition: Pronto Design & Production, Inc.

Library of Congress Cataloging-in-Publication Data:
King, Janice M.
Web marketing cookbook/Janice King, Paul Knight, James H. Mason.
p. cm.
Includes index.
ISBN 0-471-17911-6 (paper/CD-ROM)
1. Internet marketing. I. Knight, Paul, 1955- II. Mason, James H. III. Title.
HF5415. 1265.K56 1997
658.8'00285'4678--cc21   96-47738
Printed in the United States of America

10 9 8 7 6 5 4 3 2 1

Contents

Janice M. King is author of *Writing High-Tech Copy That Sells* (John Wiley & Sons, 1995) and regularly writes, speaks, and teaches on topics related to high-tech marketing communication for conferences and professional groups across the United States. Through her company MarkeTech (Bellevue, Washington), she is an independent copywriter and consultant for leading companies across North America in the telecommunications and networking industries, offering more than 15 years of marketing experience for both small business and high technology.

Paul Knight and **James H. Mason** are the founders of 64k Internet Marketing, Inc., a Seattle-based Web development firm serving more than 200 customers throughout the United States. Their company delivers comprehensive, reasonably priced development and maintenance services that enable entrepreneurs and businesses of every size to profit from a presence on the World Wide Web. These services include secure on-line credit card transactions, complex on-line database solutions, and multimedia applications such as Java, RealAudio, and Quicktime VR.

Between them, Paul and Jim offer customers more than 20 years of marketing experience and 30 years of software development experience, beginning work on the Internet in 1979. Jim also is a software development manager for The Boeing Company, and is the Webmaster for the Unitarian Universalist Association's Web site (www.uua.org). Paul was most recently an advertising executive with *The Seattle Times* newspaper, is a contributor to *Home Page* magazine, and is Board President of the Media Arts Center, a nonprofit, educational organization in Seattle that supports creative use of electronic media for communications and the arts.

 ## Visit Our Web Sites

For Janice King: http://www.writespark.com
For Paul Knight and Jim Mason: http://www.say64k.com

↳ Janice King

Any book is actually a collaboration of more people than just the named authors; all of them deserve thanks. First to Terri Hudson, my editor at John Wiley & Sons, for bringing the idea for this book to me. I continue to appreciate her confidence, creativity, and enthusiasm for my projects. My dear family and friends strengthen me with reminders of the important things in life while at the same time cheering my attempts to fly: Mom, Jo Ann, Steve, Susan, Stephanie, Carolyn, Marianne, and Dad in memory; Jim Anest, Paul Denham, Arlene Greene, Kate Harris, John Hedtke, Nancy Hoft, Katrina Ryan, and Maureen Scully. My many friends at Northlake deserve special gratitude for putting up with me through a second book.

Writing this book would not have been possible without the many hours of production assistance from Karen Lindsay, who also contributed several valuable ideas for its content. And I could not have wished for better co-authors than Paul Knight and Jim Mason. Their wisdom permeates this book, and their good humor and responsiveness kept a demanding project on track. Thanks to Jackie Mason and Margaret and Sydney Knight for being so patient.

↳ Paul Knight

Thanks to Paul Willms and Ray Derryberry, our co-workers at 64k for their patience with Jim and me when we were crabby or when they couldn't find us because we were hidden away working on this book. Also, I want to thank Paul and Ray for the valuable working knowledge of and insights into the Web communications industry they provided to me. Basically, they were good sounding boards. Thanks to Carl and Marie Knight, my mother and father for the encouragement that they have always given to me for various writing projects, including this one. Most of all, thanks to my wife Margaret for giving me the time, space, and support to write. Thanks also to my daughter Sydney who at seven years old knows a few things that those of us who work with computers for a living don't know yet. Thanks to Janice King, who is the most organized person I know. Finally, thanks to Jim Mason for originally introducing me to the World Wide Web.

Jim Mason

I want to thank Janice King for her gracious invitation to participate in the creation of this book. I had a great time working with her and Paul. I also thank my wife Jackie for letting me spend long hours exploring this new frontier.

You have probably read many books and articles about promoting your business or organization on the World Wide Web. But you may have hesitated to build your own Web site because it seems like such a major undertaking in time, expense, and effort. If you are a small business owner or manager of a nonprofit organization, you also may feel that previous discussion on Web marketing—with its focus mostly on large corporate sites—does not cover the topics and guidelines that would be most helpful to you.

Or, you may be the marketing communications or promotions manager at a larger company or organization with a year or more of experience in marketing via a Web site. Now, you want guidelines for improving its content and new ideas for information you can place on the Web.

No matter what your role or experience, you want an easy way to create Web pages—one that does not require a high level of technical skill.

For all of these reasons, *Web Marketing Cookbook* is an ideal resource for you.

How This Book Is Different

We wrote *Web Marketing Cookbook* as a practical, hands-on guide to presenting promotional materials on Web pages. By following the guidelines we offer and adapting the templates on the CD-ROM for your needs, you will be able to create an appealing, targeted, and efficient Web site with minimal investments in time, effort, and technical knowledge.

Many topics are outside the scope of this book that you will want to explore further, especially if you want to develop and maintain a Web site yourself. These topics include the following:

- General strategies for marketing on the Web or other resources of the Internet

- Implementation and project management activities for building a Web site, for example, how to find an Internet Service Provider

- Technical information on HyperText Markup Language (HTML), Common Gateway Interface (CGI), Java, Virtual Reality Markup Language (VRML), and other Web development tools

Many other books and online resources are available for these topics; check Appendix C for our recommendations.

Appendix C and the Resources page on the CD-ROM list links to specific Web sites for examples or additional detail on the topics covered here. For selected topics, we have listed keywords in the text that will lead you to relevant sites in any of the Web search tools (see Appendix C). Using the search tools will help you find not only current information, but a much broader set of sites than we could possibly reference here. You can add keywords to those we suggest in order to further target your search by topic, industry, location, or other criterion.

Who Should Read This Book

This book will be of interest to several groups of readers, including the following:

- *Small businesses owners and sales managers*. Learn how to create a site with an effective design for generating online sales, attracting qualified prospects, or supporting the in-person sales activity of representatives, dealers, telemarketers, or retail stores.

- *Promotion, fundraising, and public relations managers for nonprofit organizations and local government agencies*. Learn how to create a site that promotes your services, programs, workshops, and events to participants, donors, and the general public.

- *Marketing communication, promotion, and public relations managers in large organizations*. Discover new ideas for

Web promotion, organized by industry, and learn techniques for Web communications that balance "sizzle" with sensitivity to a visitor's interaction.

- *Webmasters and Web developers.* Understand the issues facing your marketing colleagues or clients, and learn how you can help them plan better Web sites.

- *Writers, graphic designers, and other creative staff.* Learn how to adapt print materials for presentation on a Web page and the Do's and Don'ts of Web communication.

How to Get the Most from This Book

Although we believe you will find valuable information throughout *Web Marketing Cookbook*, you don't need to read the chapters sequentially. The content is organized so you can quickly find the most relevant section for your industry, type of communication, or question about Web presentation techniques. However, if you are developing a Web site for the first time, we recommend that you read Chapters 1 through5, which present important guidelines, before beginning work with the templates. If you're ready for more advanced topics, read Chapters 6 through 11 for specific techniques that will improve the content and presentation of your information on Web pages.

We also encourage you to explore the templates on the CD-ROM (see instructions in Appendix A). Load the templates into your browser and brainstorm ideas for how you can adapt them to your promotional materials and activities. When you're ready, load the template source files into a word processor or HTML editor—you will be creating appetizing and nutritious Web pages in no time.

The CD-ROM also includes a variety of shareware and demonstration tools that will help you in developing a powerful and comprehensive Web site.

↳ Cooking Up Success

Like any meal, cooking up a successful Web site involves
quality ingredients, a skillful chef, timing, and patience. By
giving you the ingredients and techniques, we hope you will
feel prepared to invest the time and effort to realize success
with your marketing on the World Wide Web.

Janice King
Paul Knight
Jim Mason

PART I

ENTERING

THE

KITCHEN

CHAPTER ONE

WEB MARKETING: ENTREE OR APPETIZER?

Every business marketer asks the same questions: "Can my business make money on the World Wide Web?" or "Can my nonprofit organization attract members and donors on the Web?"

The answer is a simple "Yes." If you have a business that can make money using traditional communications media, you can make money using the Web. If you have a nonprofit organization that attracts members and donors using traditional marketing techniques, you can successfully draw more members and donors through effective use of the Web. Many businesses and nonprofit organizations today are transacting sales and accepting money by using technology that is readily available to Web developers.

Of course, it is unlikely that a business can make money by promoting an untested concept or undeveloped product or service on the Web. The sometimes over-hyped frenzy surrounding Web marketing has driven this misconception. A poor product will not sell, whether it is in a retail store, in a catalog, or on a Web site. However, merchandise that is competitively priced and provides good value to the customer can and is being credibly demonstrated and sold on the Web.

This chapter presents an overview of Web marketing issues and practices. Additional detail on many of these topics is presented in Chapter 4.

Bargain of the Century

Businesses are making or saving money every day using the Web to communicate information about their products and services. To predict your likely success on the Web, ask yourself these questions:

- "Can any single medium make my products or services instantly available to millions of potential customers from around the block or around the world?"

- "Can any single medium give millions of people access to my marketing materials 24 hours per day, 7 days per week?"

- "Is there any medium that offers all of these benefits, yet is affordable to the average business or organization?"

The answer clearly is the Web. It delivers information and makes sales more efficiently and inexpensively than any other medium. And unlike traditional media, marketing on the Web (at least for now) is decentralized and entrepreneurial in nature. This means anyone can market on the Web without the high cost of advertising in the traditional "big" media (newspapers, magazines, radio, and television).

Because of its limited regulation and the open nature of posting information, the Web is often described as being egalitarian. For business operators and organization managers, this openness translates into an affordable means to reach both existing and new prospects and customers.

Can I Make Direct Sales from a Web Site?

What about making money directly and immediately on the Web—is it possible? Do people actually buy products and services from Web sites? Research points to a positive response.

Data from a Neilsen survey of 4,000 North American households found that nearly 7 percent of the more than 30 million Internet users buy products and services directly from the Web.[1] Another perspective is provided by the case of Virtual Vineyards, one of the most widely publicized examples of Web marketing success. This retail-oriented Web site generated gross sales in excess of U.S. $9 million in its first year of operation.

A basic attraction of electronic commerce is that online shopping allows customers to make purchases while they view images of products and read descriptions of features and benefits. If they like what they see, and if there is an order form or electronic mechanism by which to respond, customers will make purchases online. Prominent display of a company's toll-free telephone number and other contact information further encourages sales to customers worldwide who may want to talk with a sales representative before placing an order.

The Evolution of Home Shopping

Other compelling reasons for ordering products and services on the Web are closely related to consumer demographics and psychographics. Web marketing is safe, convenient, and if one chooses, relatively anonymous. Security and anonymity make shopping electronically a comfortable and nonthreatening experience for many people.

While a case can be made for "high-touch"—the human need to be in the marketplace interacting with other human beings—when shopping, the reality is that time is more important than money to many people. The freedom to shop from home is an attractive feature of Web marketing to consumers, and one that offers tremendous commercial possibilities to businesses.

The success of television shopping networks has proven that people will buy diverse products from the convenience and privacy of their homes. The Web takes the home shopping concept several steps further by offering a greater variety of options and choices, as well as a broader degree of control that is not available with television shopping. Web shoppers can choose which products they want to view and when they want to view them. They can spend a long time reviewing information about a product, or they can instantly move to another product or Web site.

Prospective customers also can do comparison shopping without leaving their computers by visiting the Web sites of multiple vendors. Requesting additional product information is as easy as sending an e-mail message, meaning customers can get their questions answered quickly and thoroughly.

↳ Should a Business Rely on a Web Site as Its Only Marketing Medium?

Web sites work best when supported by complementary promotional materials and activities. Attempting to market a product or service solely through a Web site is unlikely to be wholly successful.

An example of the limitations of Web marketing is provided by the ways in which companies and organizations in the Internet industry use the Web for marketing. In one case, the Association of Internet Professionals (AIP)—a professional organization for Internet access providers, Web site developers, and related businesses—initially used newspaper advertisements as its primary medium to create awareness for the organization. The organization placed a series of ads promoting upcoming educational seminars in the Technology and Business sections of metropolitan newspapers, dedicating a substantial advertising budget to promote attendance at the seminars. At the end of the each seminar, the organization solicited memberships from attendees.

A sample survey of attendees at the seminars found that more than 90 percent learned of the seminar through the newspaper advertisements. However, more than 40 percent of the participants visited the AIP Web site listed in the ads before deciding to attend the event. As this example shows, the Web can be a powerful tool for enhancing promotion in other media and increasing overall results of a marketing campaign.

The AIP used this method successfully in a number of cities to build its base awareness and membership. With membership and awareness now well established, most seminars are promoted by e-mail messages sent to members and on the AIP Web site instead of newspaper advertising.

In summary, when an event is time-critical—whether a store-wide sale, a music concert, or an educational seminar—you will need to use traditional media to establish a base awareness among your prospects, which will then successfully trigger visits to the associated Web site.

Using Other Media to Promote a Web Site

Most marketers logically believe that additional traffic can be created for their Web sites if they are advertised and supported by other marketing materials. Marketers also typically plan to use Web sites as marketing tools themselves to generate new and incremental business. In this case, advertising and cross-marketing Web sites may seem to have opposite purposes, and the cross-marketing effort may seem redundant and costly.

On the contrary, Web sites are likely to attract completely new and different kinds of customers to businesses and non-profit organizations. The amount of additional traffic directed to Web sites through advertising and promotion is not incidental, but it is often significantly higher than expectations. For example, a survey of Web sites in the real estate industry found that traffic to sites that were modestly promoted in local and regional real estate publications generated more than twice the volume of visitors than comparable sites that were not promoted.[2]

The lesson from this example? Even though a Web site that is posted with the leading Web directories and search engines will attract visitors, the best way to generate traffic to a Web site is to promote it. Although limited promotion budgets are always a concern, any company or organization can easily place the site URL (Web address) on business cards and stationery. Fliers, brochures, and signage are also appropriate and relatively inexpensive media for promoting Web sites.

Potential customers using the Web are hungry for information, and they often want more details about products and services than they can get from print ads or sales fliers. By placing the URL on these materials, you encourage visits to your site.

Nonprofit Organizations on the Web

Nonprofit organizations and volunteer groups have been quick to produce Web sites, and many have been very effective at generating visits. But how successfully have they used their sites for conducting business? Many nonprofit organizations have done exceptionally well. They have used their Web sites to collect data and registration information for prospective members and sponsors, and to publicize events and activities through event calendars (see the Event Calendar template in Chapter 3).

Local and national nonprofit organizations also should examine the potential value of conducting their fund-raising activities online. With secure credit card transactions, donors can easily make pledges and contributions on the Web site.

↳ Return on Investment for Web Marketing

As with any investment in technology—whether it is the purchase of new computers or the addition of a feature-loaded fax machine—business operators want some assurance that the investment will pay for itself. Ultimately, the goal is to increase productivity or efficiencies that will drive profit to the bottom line.

Commercial Web sites should be held to these same standards to justify their investment. The good news is that Web sites easily meet the test for return on investment (ROI).

ROI in Traditional Media

Although incremental revenue can be generated by a good Web site, tracking the additional revenue is sometimes problematic. In this way, a commercial Web site most closely resembles an advertising expenditure. Determining return on investment for traditional advertising media requires accurate tracking of results. The same requirement is true for measuring the effectiveness of a Web site.

As an example, consider how you might track the results of a traditional newspaper advertisement by using a coupon. Coupons turned in at the cash register, while not documenting all incremental sales resulting from the advertisement, will provide a useful, general measurement of the advertisement's minimum effectiveness, which can then be evaluated against its cost.

Television, radio, magazines, and direct mail also offer track records and methods for measuring the cost-effectiveness of advertising. You can evaluate comparable costs for these media by using a standard, cost-per-thousand (CPM) formula. The CPM is determined by dividing the gross cost of an ad into the total figure for impressions—the number of people expected to view the ad. In newspapers and magazines, impressions are determined by total circulation; in broadcast media, the impressions are determined by the number of viewers or listeners.

ROI on the Web

These proven techniques for measuring the effectiveness of traditional media do not necessarily apply to the Web. As a result, many advertisers have been reluctant to invest substantial percentages of their marketing budgets in developing a Web site without accurate tools to measure results. To address these concerns, a subset of Web marketing disciplines has formed to document and track results for commercial Web sites. These services are typically offered by advertising and marketing agencies.

You may ask, "If large businesses are having difficulty tracking and quantifying the marketing results of their Web sites, how can a small business track its results?" One method is to use a visitor counter to measure the number of "hits" (visitor accesses) to the site. However, consider hits as a very general measurement of gross traffic to the Web site, not necessarily as a qualitative measurement of visitor interest in your company, products, or services.

In addition, a visitor counter cannot indicate how much time visitors spent on your site or why they came in the first place. A better qualitative measurement for the effectiveness of your Web site is the number and nature of e-mail messages and inquiry forms submitted by visitors to your site. This measurement can be called the contact-to-hit ratio.

Considering this ratio, a Web site might generate 1,000 hits in a three-month period. This can be a positive sign that promotion of the Web site is effective. However, if you do not receive any e-mail messages or inquiry forms during this period, you will need to determine if there is a problem with the nature or presentation of content on the site. Conversely, if your Web site experiences an abnormally low hit count, for example, 20 hits after six months, consider re-listing the site with the Web directories and search engines and increasing promotion of the site URL in your other marketing materials and activities.

Another way to evaluate ROI for Web marketing is to determine the cost per customer gained. As an example, a Web site costs U.S. $2,000 to create and maintain for a one-year period, and it generates 100 new customers. The return on investment can be calculated simply by dividing $2,000 by 100, which equals a cost per customer of $20. Although $20 per customer may be expensive to a company selling a $50 product, it would be extremely cost-effective for another company selling products that cost $5,000. You will need to determine an acceptable cost-per-customer ratio for each product or for your business as a whole.

Quality versus Quantity

Although quantitative results are easier to determine, identifying qualitative results is equally important. You must evaluate all results relating to the Web site with different expectations and perspectives than those you might have for traditional media. On the Web, your goal is quality over quantity in terms of the number of sales or leads your site generates.

The Web can deliver a customer who is ready to buy. In that way, it fills the role of a salesperson, gathering information about the customer and, in turn, delivering detailed information that allows the prospect to make a buying decision. This means prospects who complete an online form are more than just impressions created by a mass media advertisement. They are real customers who are initiating a dialogue and saying "I'm ready to buy your product or service." This is the type of qualitative result that any business or organization wants from any marketing effort.

Who Is the Web Shopper?

Even though the Web offers significant sales potential and return on your marketing dollar, currently a few hurdles exist for achieving these results. The biggest of these hurdles is obvious—not every potential prospect for your business or organization has access to the Web. And a variety of studies and surveys have indicated that Web visitors display a wide range of usage patterns. A Roper Poll conducted in 1996 indicates that Internet use is highest among Americans with total annual household incomes above $50,000.[3] This demographic is particularly advantageous for companies selling expensive items, luxury goods, or highly discretionary products and services. However, it may not reflect the characteristics of your target market, especially if you are engaged in business-to-business sales, where a higher proportion of your customers and prospects may already have convenient Web access.

As the population of Web users continues to grow, the demographics are likely to change. To find more information and current statistics on usage trends related to the Web you can use the following keywords for searches: **electronic + commerce**, **advertising + statistics**, **marketing + surveys**, or **Web + studies**.

Local Customers from an International Medium

Some retail business operators are concerned that because a Web site can be viewed internationally, it is ineffective for generating traffic to a local store or business office. We believe that a Web site can indeed increase traffic in local stores, dealers, or other facilities. By integrating your promotion across both the Web and traditional marketing media, materials, and activities—and maintaining a well-designed

Web site—you can increase in-person traffic by prospects and customers. Chapter 4 presents specific techniques to implement for this purpose.

Dialogue Marketing or "Narrowcasting"

According to a 1996 Vanderbilt University study, marketing to a potential customer on the Web is approximately one-tenth the cost of marketing in traditional media.[4] Unfortunately, most marketing and advertising companies are still using old paradigms and inapplicable quantification standards for the Web. Virtually every aspect of Web marketing differs from the traditional forms of advertising and communication that have ruled marketing for the past 50 years.

Marketers must make a fundamental shift of paradigms for how they communicate marketing information. Most traditional, mass media assume a "single-to-many" model based on gross impressions or the total reach of the particular medium or promotion. The premise of this model is that consumers are forced to come into contact with the product promotion whether they are in the market to buy the product or not.

Because traditional marketing media start out with built-in inefficiencies, another advertising term called "frequency" has evolved to describe the number of times a potential customer must be exposed to the unwanted message to illicit a response. This indiscriminate, mass-marketing model does not apply to the targeted environment that the Web provides.

A fundamental advantage of the Web for marketing and commerce is understanding that it is based on dialogue marketing. With **dialogue marketing**, the customer specifically seeks a dialogue, usually based on the need to complete a transaction at some future point.

The key to understanding the power of dialogue marketing on the Web is to acknowledge that customers have total control and choice over what information they examine. This control is in direct contrast to a newspaper advertisement for a product such as snowboards, which may be seen by numerous readers who have no interest in that product. In contrast, no one searching for a snowboard is likely to review real estate sites on the Web.

While a metropolitan newspaper might offer a circulation of one-half million readers, a Web site that draws 500 specifically interested prospects will offer greater value to the business. And when those visitors become customers by making a purchase online, the cost ratio of Web marketing becomes even more attractive for a business owner.

Media Comparisons

Calculating the ROI for Web marketing also requires a comparison of costs for the Web site relative to the costs for other marketing media. For example, the cost of a one-time advertisement in a metropolitan newspaper might be U.S. $2,000. For that same $2,000 investment, almost any small business can create a respectable presence on the Web. More importantly, the Web site will be active for a six-month to one-year period, while the single ad in the newspaper appears only on a single day.

The length of marketing exposure is often described as the promotional "shelf life." For the same cost, a Web site has an extended shelf life, while newspaper, television, and radio advertising offer an extremely short shelf life.

Web Marketing Benefits for the Business Operator

In addition to the increased sales a Web site can generate, another clear benefit for business operators is time savings. Mail-order and catalog businesses are moving to electronic commerce quickly because it is a logical extension of their current marketing and sales activity. The core competency of these businesses is already built around processing orders quickly and efficiently regardless of their source: mail, telephone, fax, or online.

The cost savings that Web marketing offers to a catalog marketing company can be tremendous when you consider the reduced labor costs achievable by processing orders online instead of by telephone. Electronic commerce requires fewer employees and can reduce ancillary overhead costs including, in many cases, physical space requirements. Why incur the cost of a customer service representative to take an order via a toll-free telephone number when the customer can complete the order form online for a fraction of the cost?

For both products and services, the labor and overhead costs of businesses selling online can be reduced through Web marketing and electronic order processing. The business operator also can deliver goods and services to the marketplace at lower cost, which can become a competitive advantage.

As a marketing medium, the efficiency of Web communication also enables businesses and organizations to reduce costs for printed materials. According to the Direct Marketing Association (DMA), the average household in the United States receives more than 88 catalogs per year; frequent shoppers may receive more than 400. The DMA also estimates annual growth of the industry at more than 7 percent per year.[5]

For any business or organization, brochures and catalogs can be costly to print, and mailing costs continue to escalate. When the material is produced and distributed on the Web, the cost of printing and distribution can be eliminated or reduced substantially.

Other cost savings can be achieved in daily communications costs, especially with international customers, for long-distance telephone calls and fax transmissions. For example, sending a 42-page faxed document from New York to Tokyo would cost an estimated U.S. $28.83.[6] Sending the same document as an e-mail message over the Internet would cost approximately U.S. $0.28. At only 1 percent of the cost, worldwide customer communications become economically feasible for even the smallest business.

Benefits to the Consumer

The most important and immediate advantages of Web marketing for customers are convenience, time savings, and an expansive selection of products and services. Potential cost savings are also possible as a result of the Web visitor's access to a greater selection of products and vendors.

The Web is a perfect medium for prospects and customers to research and compare products. Businesses can use Web sites to offer vast amounts of data on product features, structured for easy access by visitors. For example, many automobile manufacturers have developed comprehensive Web sites that provide detailed product illustrations and specifications on individual models. The customer can examine and compare many models on the Web before visiting a dealer showroom to make a test drive and negotiate the purchase.

Organic and Changing Daily

A large amount of information and data are collected daily by private and public institutions hoping to create a snapshot of who uses the Web, how often they use it, and for what purposes. Because the Web is evolving continuously, there is no single definitive and static answer to those questions. We advise practicing patience and faith in the medium and being realistic about the time required to realize the return on investment for Web marketing.

For most small and medium-sized businesses that do not enlist the services of professional media buyers and that have limited media budgets, the rationalization for building and maintaining a Web site for electronic commerce comes down to return on investment. By maintaining a realistic perspective and managing the cost of your Web site over time, it is reasonable to expect some return on that financial investment within the first year.

To illustrate, one successful real estate agent in the Seattle area documented 11 home sales in a one-year period that were directly attributable to a Web site that cost $300 to build. Her first completed sale came approximately four months after the site was posted on the Web, and her largest Web-generated home sale was valued at more than $400,000.

As this example shows, the marketing results for a Web site can be quick and substantial. The lesson is that unless your business or organization offers a well-designed and functional Web site, there is no way to know if it will be successful. Web marketing is a bit of an experiment for most companies. However, because the initial cost is relatively modest compared to other marketing tools, the question to ask yourself is "Why not make the initial investment in Web marketing and find out what results we can gain?"

The Web is more than a fad or a temporary trend. Billions of dollars have been invested worldwide by governments and private industry to build the infrastructure for continued growth of this exciting communications network. Either businesses and organizations will adopt the tools— Web sites, electronic forms, and e-mail—for thriving in this new electronic business environment, or they will be left behind.

We hope that the tools, tips, and techniques provided in this book will give you a great start toward success with your Web marketing activity.

CHAPTER TWO

WEB COMMUNICATIONS
BY INDUSTRY

The Web is a highly flexible medium, one that can accommodate a wide variety of promotional materials and activities. Yet this flexibility can make it difficult to determine which are the best choices to implement for your company or organization.

This chapter will give you many ideas for Web content and capabilities, organized by industry. Look at Figure 2.1, which identifies the templates on the CD-ROM that we recommend for your industry. Then review Figure 2.2 for ideas that apply across industries. Combine these ideas with the recommendations for your specific industry, which are presented in Figures 2.3 through 2.16. Of course, you may find ideas from other industries, or use any of the templates on the CD-ROM, as appropriate to your situation.

After gathering your ideas from this chapter, you will be ready to review the templates in Chapter 3 and begin your planning process, as described in Chapter 5.

Industry	Advertisement	Article	Brochure	Catalog Page	Catalog Contents Page	Company Profile	Contents Page	Coupon	Event Calendar	Event Registration Form	FAQ	Locator	Newsletter	Order Form	Press Release	Price/Parts Lists	Product Inquiry Form	Profile	Selection Guide	Seminar Description	Services List	Starter Page	Visitor Survey/ Registration Form	What's New Page
Agriculture																								
Equipment and Supply	X		X	X	X	X	X				X	X	X	X	X	X	X	X	X		X	X	X	X
Breeders and Veterinarians		X	X	X	X	X		X			X		X	X	X			X				X	X	X
Specialty Growers, Coops		X	X	X	X	X		X	X	X	X	X	X	X	X		X	X	X			X	X	X
Automotive																								
Dealers, Auction, Parts	X		X	X	X	X	X	X		X	X	X	X	X	X	X	X	X	X			X	X	X
Repair			X	X	X	X		X		X	X	X	X	X	X	X		X			X	X	X	X

FIGURE 2.1 Choosing templates for Web marketing.

Industry	Advertisement	Article	Brochure	Catalog Page	Catalog Contents Page	Company Profile	Contents Page	Coupon	Event Calendar	Event Registration Form	FAQ	Locator	Newsletter	Order Form	Press Release	Price/Parts Lists	Product Inquiry Form	Profile	Selection Guide	Seminar Description	Services List	Starter Page	Visitor Survey/ Registration Form	What's New Page
Creative Professionals																								
Every Creative Business	×	×	×			×					×	×	×	×	×		×	×	×	×	×	×	×	×
Writers		×	×			×			×	×	×		×	×	×	×		×			×	×	×	×
Fine Artists		×	×			×					×		×	×	×	×		×				×	×	×
Photographers, Multimedia		×	×			×			×	×	×		×	×	×			×				×	×	×
Crafts Producers		×	×			×					×		×	×	×	×		×				×	×	×
Actors/Dancers/ Models		×	×			×			×	×	×		×	×				×				×	×	×
Musicians		×	×			×			×	×	×		×	×	×			×				×	×	×

FIGURE 2.1 Continued

Industry	Advertisement	Article	Brochure	Catalog Page	Catalog Contents Page	Company Profile	Contents Page	Coupon	Event Calendar	Event Registration Form	FAQ	Locator	Newsletter	Order Form	Press Release	Price/Parts Lists	Product Inquiry Form	Profile	Selection Guide	Seminar Description	Services List	Starter Page	Visitor Survey/Registration Form	What's New Page
Education																								
Primary/Secondary Schools		×	×	×	×	×	×		×	×	×	×	×	×	×			×	×	×		×	×	×
Colleges/Universities, Adult Education		×	×	×	×	×	×		×	×	×	×	×	×	×			×	×	×		×	×	×
Financial																								
Banks, Finance Companies	×	×	×	×	×	×	×				×	×	×	×	×		×		×		×	×	×	×
Stock Brokers, Accountants		×	×		×	×					×		×	×	×		×	×	×		×	×	×	×

FIGURE 2.1 Continued

Industry	Advertisement	Article	Brochure	Catalog Page	Catalog Contents Page	Company Profile	Contents Page	Coupon	Event Calendar	Event Registration Form	FAQ	Locator	Newsletter	Order Form	Press Release	Price/Parts Lists	Product Inquiry Form	Profile	Selection Guide	Seminar Description	Services List	Starter Page	Visitor Survey/ Registration Form	What's New Page
Financial																								
Insurance Agents		×	×			×					×		×	×	×		×	×	×		×	×	×	×
Health Care																								
Hospitals, Clinics, Labs		×	×	×	×	×	×	×	×	×	×	×	×	×	×		×	×	×	×	×	×	×	×
Healthcare providers		×	×	×	×	×					×	×	×	×	×			×	×		×	×	×	×
Manufacturing																								
Consumer products	×	×	×	×	×	×	×	×	×	×	×	×	×	×	×	×	×	×	×	×	×	×	×	×
Business-to-business	×	×	×	×	×	×	×	×	×	×	×	×	×	×	×	×	×	×	×	×	×	×	×	×

FIGURE 2.1 Continued

Industry	Advertisement	Article	Brochure	Catalog Page	Catalog Contents Page	Company Profile	Contents Page	Coupon	Event Calendar	Event Registration Form	FAQ	Locator	Newsletter	Order Form	Press Release	Price/Parts Lists	Product Inquiry Form	Profile	Selection Guide	Seminar Description	Services List	Starter Page	Visitor Survey/ Registration Form	What's New Page
Media and Publishing																								
Books, Music, Software		X	X			X		X	X	X	X	X	X	X	X	X	X	X	X			X	X	X
Newsletters, Periodicals		X	X			X	X		X	X	X		X	X	X	X	X	X	X			X	X	X
Radio and television	X	X	X	X	X	X		X	X	X	X		X	X	X			X				X	X	X
Non-Profit Organizations																								
Government Agencies		X	X	X	X	X	X	X	X	X	X	X	X	X	X		X	X		X	X	X	X	X

FIGURE 2.1 Continued

Industry	Advertisement	Article	Brochure	Catalog Page	Catalog Contents Page	Company Profile	Contents Page	Coupon	Event Calendar	Event Registration Form	FAQ	Locator	Newsletter	Order Form	Press Release	Price/Parts Lists	Product Inquiry Form	Profile	Selection Guide	Seminar Description	Services List	Starter Page	Visitor Survey/ Registration Form	What's New Page
Non-Profit Organizations																								
Religious Organizations		X	X	X	X	X	X	X	X	X	X	X	X	X	X		X	X		X	X		X	X
Charities and Services		X	X	X	X	X	X	X	X	X	X	X	X	X	X		X	X		X	X	X	X	X
Arts Organizations		X	X			X	X		X	X	X	X	X	X	X		X	X		X	X	X	X	
Clubs, Social Groups		X	X	X	X	X		X	X	X	X	X	X	X	X		X	X		X	X	X	X	X
Political Organizations		X	X	X	X	X		X	X	X	X	X	X	X	X		X	X		X	X	X	X	X

FIGURE 2.1 Continued

Industry	Advertisement	Article	Brochure	Catalog Page	Catalog Contents Page	Company Profile	Contents Page	Coupon	Event Calendar	Event Registration Form	FAQ	Locator	Newsletter	Order Form	Press Release	Price/Parts Lists	Product Inquiry Form	Profile	Selection Guide	Seminar Description	Services List	Starter Page	Visitor Survey/ Registration Form	What's New Page
Non-Profit Organizations																								
Trade and Professional		×	×	×	×	×	×	×	×	×	×	×	×	×	×		×	×		×		×	×	×
Personal, Family and Home																								
Health, fashion, beauty		×	×	×	×	×		×	×	×	×	×	×	×	×		×	×	×	×		×	×	×
Health clubs		×	×	×	×	×		×			×	×	×	×	×		×	×			×	×	×	×
Home Improvement		×	×			×					×		×	×	×		×	×			×	×	×	

FIGURE 2.1 Continued

Web Communications by Industry

Industry	Advertisement	Article	Brochure	Catalog Page	Catalog Contents Page	Company Profile	Contents Page	Coupon	Event Calendar	Event Registration Form	FAQ	Locator	Newsletter	Order Form	Press Release	Price/Parts Lists	Product Inquiry Form	Profile	Selection Guide	Seminar Description	Services List	Starter Page	Visitor Survey/ Registration Form	What's New Page
Personal, Family and Home																								
Sports, recreation, hobbies		×	×	×	×	×		×	×	×	×	×	×	×	×			×	×	×	×	×	×	×
Day care, social clubs		×	×	×	×	×		×	×	×	×	×	×	×	×			×			×	×	×	×
Professional Services																								
Architects/ Technical		×	×			×					×		×		×		×	×		×	×	×	×	×
Advertising and PR		×	×			×					×		×		×		×	×		×	×	×	×	×
Attorneys		×	×			×					×		×		×		×	×		×	×	×	×	×

FIGURE 2.1 Continued

Industry	Advertisement	Article	Brochure	Catalog Page	Catalog Contents Page	Company Profile	Contents Page	Coupon	Event Calendar	Event Registration Form	FAQ	Locator	Newsletter	Order Form	Press Release	Price/Parts Lists	Product Inquiry Form	Profile	Selection Guide	Seminar Description	Services List	Starter Page	Visitor Survey/Registration Form	What's New Page
Professional Services																								
Consultants		×	×			×					×		×		×		×	×		×	×	×	×	×
Employment services		×	×			×					×		×		×		×	×		×	×	×	×	×
Event/Conference services		×	×			×			×	×	×		×		×		×	×		×	×	×	×	×
Shipping/transportation		×	×			×					×	×	×				×		×		×	×	×	×
Real Estate																								
Agents/broker firms		×	×			×					×	×	×		×		×	×	×		×	×	×	×

FIGURE 2.1 Continued

Industry	Advertisement	Article	Brochure	Catalog Page	Catalog Contents Page	Company Profile	Contents Page	Coupon	Event Calendar	Event Registration Form	FAQ	Locator	Newsletter	Order Form	Press Release	Price/Parts Lists	Product Inquiry Form	Profile	Selection Guide	Seminar Description	Services List	Starter Page	Visitor Survey/ Registration Form	What's New Page
Real Estate																								
Builders, contractors	×	×	×			×					×	×	×		×		×	×	×		×	×	×	×
Developments		×	×			×					×	×	×		×		×	×	×				×	×
Retail, Direct Mail, Online																								
Any product	×	×	×	×	×	×	×	×	×	×	×	×	×	×	×	×	×	×	×	×	×	×	×	×
Travel																								
Travel/reservation services			×			×		×	×	×	×	×	×	×	×		×	×	×		×	×	×	×

FIGURE 2.1 Continued

Industry	Advertisement	Article	Brochure	Catalog Page	Catalog Contents Page	Company Profile	Contents Page	Coupon	Event Calendar	Event Registration Form	FAQ	Locator	Newsletter	Order Form	Press Release	Price/Parts Lists	Product Inquiry Form	Profile	Selection Guide	Seminar Description	Services List	Starter Page	Visitor Survey/Registration Form	What's New Page
Travel																								
Tour operators			×			×		×	×	×	×	×	×	×	×	×	×	×	×			×	×	×
Lodging	×	×	×			×		×	×	×	×	×	×		×	×	×	×				×	×	×
Area tourism programs	×	×	×			×		×	×	×	×	×	×	×	×		×	×				×	×	×
Attractions/entertainment	×		×			×		×	×	×	×	×	×	×	×		×	×				×	×	×
Restaurants				×	×	×		×	×	×		×	×	×	×	×	×	×				×	×	×

FIGURE 2.1 Continued

Every Business or Organization

	Promotional Ideas	Ideas for Links
Every Business or Organization	• Contact information: toll-free, telephone and fax numbers; postal and e-mail addresses • Location map, directions, store/branch/office locator • Business hours: sales, service, departments, stores, offices • Business profile, history, philosophy, achievements, financial information • Personal profiles: founders, owners, executives, salespeople, other employees with customer, member, or public contact • Customer or participant testimonials • Product and service information: basic and specialized • Special promotions, contests, giveaways, activities, events, services • Current newsletter • Events and activities calendar	• Related businesses, publications, organizations • Chambers of Commerce, industry association, community sites • Manufacturer sites • Members and affiliates • Topic sites related to products, services, expertise • Target market sites

FIGURE 2.2 Every business or organization.

Every Business or Organization

	Promotional Ideas	Ideas for Links
Service Providers, Consultants, Self-Employed Professionals	• Products and services offered; specialties • Online services or advice • Personal profile or resume • Lists of presentations, workshops, seminars • Lists of books, articles, other publications • Certifications, licenses, affiliations, awards, honors • Education and training • Client list or description of markets served • Customer testimonials • Online portfolio, samples, or excerpts of typical work, audio or video clips • Fee information and typical contract terms	• Related service providers, publications, businesses • Professional associations • Customer/client sites • Topic sites related to products, services, expertise • Target market sites

FIGURE 2.2 Continued

Agriculture

See Figures 2.1 and 2.2 and ideas for these industries: Retail, Direct Mail, and Online Stores; Personal, Family, and Home Interests

	Promotional Ideas	Ideas for Links
Farm and Garden Equipment Dealers, Supply Companies	• Product Finder (make, model, options) • Inventory information • Repair services • Parts availability • Specialty products and services • Request form for print catalog	• Dealer networks
Breeders and Veterinarians	• Animal specialties and availability • Farm, kennel, office facilities • Credentials • Lineage information • Animal husbandry information	• Business sites with related products and services • Owner's associations
Specialty Growers, Coops, Subscription Farms	• Products offered and current availability • Land, growing conditions, harvest information • Retail and wholesale sales information • Seasonal promotions • Facilities, equipment, services information	• Coops: individual members • Cooking sites • Regional networks • Government sites • Weather sites

FIGURE 2.3 Agriculture.

Automotive, Other Vehicles, and Equipment

See Figures 2.1 and 2.2 and ideas for these industries:
Manufacturing; Retail, Direct Mail, and Online Sales

	Promotional Ideas	Ideas for Links
Dealers, Auction, Parts Distributors	• Product Finder Service (make, model, year, equipment) • Service and parts department packages, promotions, coupons • Specialty products and services • Inventory information • Appointment scheduling form • Finance, lease, fleet programs • Parts locator service	• Dealer Networks
Repair	• Types of repairs/ specialties • Service packages, promotions, coupons • Mechanic and technician profiles/certifications • Insurance and warranty program information • Online diagnostic questionnaire	• Collector sites

FIGURE 2.4 Automotive, other vehicles, and equipment.

Creative Professionals

See Figures 2.1 and 2.2 and ideas for these industries: Professional Services; Retail, Direct Mail, and Online Stores

	Promotional Ideas	Ideas for Links
Every Creative Business	• Services and products offered: basic and specialties • Lists: clients, projects, exhibits, commissions, awards • Online portfolio, excerpts, or samples • Resume or Profile: personal photograph • Electronic media services: audio, video, Quicktime VR, Shockwave, animated GIF, etc.	• Genre or media sites • Industry association sites • Art technology sites
Writers	• Genres (fiction, nonfiction articles, corporate communications, screenplays) • Bookstore appearances, lectures, readings, other events • Published works: bibliography, excerpts, reviews • Ordering information • Trivia or topical quizzes	• Publisher and bookseller sites • Writer's networks • Client and sponsor sites

FIGURE 2.5 Creative professionals.

Creative Professionals

See Figures 2.1 and 2.2 and ideas for these industries: Professional
Services; Retail, Direct Mail, and Online Stores

	Promotional Ideas	Ideas for Links
Fine Artists (Graphic Designers: See Professional Services)	• Genres or media • Calendar of future exhibits • Gallery/agent information • Products and services • Studio facilities and equipment for custom work • Published works: bibliography, excerpts, reviews	• Gallery and artists' representative sites
Photographers, Filmmakers, Multimedia Producers	• Products and services • Specialties • Equipment and facilities; technical capabilities • Exhibit/screening calendar • Video excerpts of projects	• Gallery, studio, production, artist's representative sites • Entertainment and technology sites
Crafts Producers	• Published works • Equipment and facilities for custom work • Calendar of future exhibits and fairs • List of galleries and stores where products are sold	• Gallery and festival sites • Craft sites

FIGURE 2.5 Continued

Creative Professionals

See Figures 2.1 and 2.2 and ideas for these industries: Professional Services; Retail, Direct Mail, and Online Stores

	Promotional Ideas	Ideas for Links
Actors, Models, Dancers, Performance Groups	• Excerpts from published reviews • Calendar of future appearances • Availability/booking information • Online photo gallery • Audio or video clips	• Venue, sponsor, client sites • Agent site • Fan Club • Entertainment sites • Promotion sites for films or other performances
Musicians and Groups	• Musician and band profile • Recordings and merchandise • Calendar of future performances • Availability/booking information • Online excerpts from a recording or performance • Contest for free tickets or album • Reviews of recordings or performances	• Record company • Fan club • Concert venues and promoters • Opening acts and affiliated performers

FIGURE 2.5 Continued

Education

See Figures 2.1 and 2.2 and ideas for these industries:
Non-Profit Organizations

	Promotional Ideas	**Ideas for Links**
Primary and Secondary Schools (public or private)	• Facilities description (special classrooms, labs, athletics) • Events calendar (athletics, dances, club meetings, theater and music performances) • Teacher and staff portfolios; e-mail and telephone lists • Annual report and school newsletter • Volunteer opportunities • Parent-Teacher Association information • School lunch menu • Fun page with educational games or resources • Bus/transportation information and routes • Kindergarten/transfer student registration information	• District and regional sites • Education associations • Alumni association • Learning resources • Child-oriented sites

FIGURE 2.6 Education.

Education

See Figures 2.1 and 2.2 and ideas for these industries:
Non-Profit Organizations

	Promotional Ideas	**Ideas for Links**
Colleges and Universities, Adult Education Programs, Private Seminars	• On-line course catalog: descriptions and schedules • Prospective student information and guidelines • Request form for application package and print catalog • Events calendar (athletics, lectures, performing arts, exhibitions) • Faculty and instructor profiles • Special program offerings • Campus and facilities information • Online registration form and instructions • College, department, or program Fact Sheet • New Student FAQ document	• Alumni associations • Student groups and newspaper • Department pages • Educational associations • Sponsor and instructor sites

FIGURE 2.6 Continued

Financial

See Figures 2.1 and 2.2 and ideas for these industries:
Professional Services

	Promotional Ideas	Ideas for Links
Banks, S&Ls, Credit Unions, Finance Companies, Mortgage Brokers	• Branch office and teller machine locator • Current interest rates • Loan and savings account selection guide • Special account promotions • New account information • Prequalification form for loans • Loan officer profiles	• Financial planning sites • Business development sites • Government sites
Stock Brokers, Investment Firms, Financial Planners, Accountants	• Fee information • Specialties • Certifications, licenses, affiliations • Services and programs • "How to Choose a . . ." Selection Guide	• Financial planning sites • Investment information sites • Parent brokerage firm site

FIGURE 2.7 Financial.

Financial

See Figures 2.1 and 2.2 and ideas for these industries:
Professional Services

	Promotional Ideas	Ideas for Links
Insurance agents	• Explanation of different insurance types • "How to choose the Best Policy" Selection Guide • Instructions for submitting claims • Information on local or national regulatory issues • Products and services • Self-qualifying form for policies • Safety tips: auto, fire, security	• Insurance company, financial planning, investment information sites

FIGURE 2.7 Continued

Health Care

See Figures 2.1 and 2.2 and ideas for these industries:
Professional Services, Non-Profit Organizations

	Promotional Ideas	Ideas for Links
Hospitals, Clinics, Laboratories, Care Centers	• Facilities (labs, childbirth centers, hospice) • Events: classes, health fairs, fundraisers • Staff profiles • Insurance, payment, billing information • List of affiliated providers • Office hours and locator • Appointment request form • Emergency services availability • Volunteer opportunities • Foundation and fundraising programs	• Health information sites • Public health agencies • Hospice and social service agencies
Physicians, Dentists, Other Healthcare Providers, Alternative Providers, Counselors	• Services and specialization • Insurance, payment and billing information • Education and experience (resume) • Training, certifications, licenses • Office hours and locations • Appointment request form • Philosophy statement on patient care • Staff profiles • Patient testimonials	• Hospital and clinic sites • Health information sites • Affiliated providers

FIGURE 2.8 Health care.

Manufacturing

See Figures 2.1 and 2.2 and ideas for these industries: Retail, Direct Mail, and Online Stores; Industries related to your target markets

	Promotional Ideas	Ideas for Links
Consumer products	• Online product catalog, price lists, order form • Service, repair, parts information • Product brochures • Company information • Demonstrations and events • Dealer or store locator • Coupons and special promotions	• Manufacturer sites for related products and services • Dealer and retail store sites
Business-to-business products	• Online product catalog, price lists, order form • Service, repair, parts information • Product brochures • Company information • Trade shows, seminar, event calendar • Customer group information • Articles and background information • Dealer or sales office locator • Special promotions	• Manufacturer sites for related products and services • Dealer sites

FIGURE 2.9 Manufacturing.

Media and Publishing

See Figures 2.1 and 2.2 and ideas for these industries:
Creative Professionals

	Promotional Ideas	Ideas for Links
Books, Music, Tapes, Video, Games, Software (online or print/media sales)	• Description; features and benefits list • Contents list • Author or performer profile • Catalog of related products and services • Online order form • Calendar of readings, performances, other events • Store or dealer locator • Video or audio excerpts	• Author, performer, studio, company sites • Entertainment sites
Newsletters, Periodicals, and Update Services	• Online sample and indexes • Subscription and back issue information and online form • Profiles of columnists and contributors • Related products and services • Editorial calendar • Editor profiles, contact information	• Sponsor or contributor sites • Industry, topic, community sites
Radio and television	• Program listings • Profiles of on-air staff • Event calendar • Advertising information • Product sales (promotional merchandise) • Phone numbers for call-in request lines, talk shows	• Network and individual program sites • Entertainment and news sites • Community sites

FIGURE 2.10 Media and publishing.

Nonprofit Organizations

See Figures 2.1 and 2.2 and ideas for these industries: Retail, Direct Mail, and Online Stores; Creative Professionals; Recreation and Leisure

	Promotional Ideas	Ideas for Links
Government Agencies	• Mission and responsibilities information • Services, program, facilities information • Office, court, and other facility locator • Public meetings and events calendar • Department, board, commission information • Annual reports, meeting minutes, rulings information • Profiles of staff and elected officials • Agency statistics and financial information	• Regional and higher-level government sites • Community networks
Religious and Spirituality Organizations	• Worship services information • Clergy and lay leader profiles • Adult and child education program descriptions • Community outreach information • Locator, facilities information, office hours • Articles and study materials • Membership information • Newsletters and bulletins • Events calendar • Prayer request form	• Affiliated churches and groups • Denomination sites • Religious information and spirituality sites

FIGURE 2.11 Nonprofit organizations.

Nonprofit Organizations

See Figures 2.1 and 2.2 and ideas for these industries: Retail, Direct Mail, and Online Stores; Creative Professionals; Recreation and Leisure

	Promotional Ideas	Ideas for Links
Charities and Service Organizations	• Services, class, program information • Event calendar and registration form • Client and donor newsletter • Fundraising information and product catalog • Offices, service center, other facilities information • Office/program locator • Profiles of staff and board of directors • Volunteer opportunities	• Affiliated agencies • Directory sites
Arts Organizations	• Events calendar • Ticket, subscription, membership information • Facilities description, floor plans, gallery guides, seating charts • Retail store information • Ticket order form • Hours and locator • Artist and staff profiles • Volunteer opportunities	• Artist and performer sites • Art Directory sites • Genre sites • Affiliated organization sites
Interest Groups, Clubs, Social Groups	• Services offered to members and the public • Meeting and conference information • Chapter information	• Parent organization site • Affiliated organizations

FIGURE 2.11 Continued

Nonprofit Organizations

See Figures 2.1 and 2.2 and ideas for these industries: Retail, Direct Mail, and Online Stores; Creative Professionals; Recreation and Leisure

	Promotional Ideas	Ideas for Links
Interest Groups, Clubs, Social Groups (continued)	• Profile of members, staff, leaders • Events and activity calendar • Fundraising information • Publications available • Online membership form • Volunteer opportunities	
Political organizations	• Issue, campaign, party information • Voter registration information • Event and appearance calendar • Volunteer opportunities • Position statements • Newsletters and reports • Fundraising information • Press information and contacts • Candidate profile	• Election information sites • Affiliated campaigns and candidates • Issues information sites • News organization sites
Trade and Professional Associations; Business and Community Networks	• Services offered to members and the public • Meeting and conference information • Chapter information • Profile of members, staff, leaders • Events and activities calendar • Fundraising information • Publications available • Online membership form • Volunteer opportunities	• Local chapter, group, member sites • Higher-level group sites • Related organization sites

FIGURE 2.11 Continued

Personal, Family, and Home Interests

See Figures 2.1 and 2.2 and ideas for these industries: Retail, Direct Mail, and Online Stores; Professional Services; Agriculture

	Promotional Ideas	Ideas for Links
Health, fashion, beauty (salons, consultants, services, stores)	• Staff profiles • Store locator • Facilities and equipment information • Online appointment form • Customer newsletter • Event calendar • Pricing and fee information • Special promotions	• Topic sites • Manufacturer sites
Health clubs and fitness services	• Facilities and equipment information • Membership information, fees, online sign-up • Class and event information • Reservation/appointment form • Special promotions • Fitness and health tips	• Health and sports information sites • Affiliated clubs • Related products and services

FIGURE 2.12   Personal, family, and home interests.

Personal, Family, and Home Interests

See Figures 2.1 and 2.2 and ideas for these industries: Retail, Direct Mail, and Online Stores; Professional Services; Agriculture

	Promotional Ideas	Ideas for Links
Home maintenance, gardening, interior design	• Staff profiles; licenses and certification, credentials • Emergency services information • Facilities and equipment information • Geographic availability • Seasonal and special promotions • Project portfolio • Client list • Online estimation form	• Business partner and referral sites • Topic publication sites • Manufacturer sites
Sports, Recreation, Hobbies and Leisure Activities, Groups and Venues	• Activities, programs, services information • Membership information • Fees, pricing, payment information • Locator and operating hours • Facilities and equipment information • Class, event, tournament calendar • Retail shop information • Accommodations and transportation	• Area tourism sites • Industry association and interest group sites • Local business sites • Activity-related publication and information sites

FIGURE 2.12 Continued

Personal, Family, and Home Interests

See Figures 2.1 and 2.2 and ideas for these industries: Retail, Direct Mail, and Online Stores; Professional Services; Agriculture

	Promotional Ideas	Ideas for Links
Day care providers, Camps, Social Clubs, Activity Groups	• Philosophy statement • Program and membership information • Facilities and equipment information • Event calendar • Staff profiles; licenses and certifications • Hours and fees	• Children or seniors topic sites • Regional organization sites • Accreditation/licensing agency sites

FIGURE 2.12 Continued

Professional Services

See Figures 2.1 and 2.2 and ideas for these industries: Creative Professionals; Retail, Direct Mail and Online Sales

	Promotional Ideas	Ideas for Links
Architects, Engineers, Technical Professionals	• Project portfolio: photos or sketches and descriptions • Staff profiles • Specialties and custom services • Geographic availability • Project management philosophy • Equipment and facilities information • Certifications, awards, special training	• Client sites • Business partner sites • Design, development, construction information sites • Industry/professional association sites
Advertising and Public Relations Agencies, Graphic Designers, Printing and Publishing Services	• Services and specialization • Lists of clients and projects • Online portfolio • Staff profiles • Equipment and facilities information	• Client and business partner sites • Media sites
Attorneys	• Services and bar association memberships • Specializations and case experience • Fees, billing, payment information • Staff profiles • List of publications and presentations • Online newsletter • Practice mission statement or philosophy	• Bar association sites • Legal reference and information sites

FIGURE 2.13 Professional services.

Professional Services

See Figures 2.1 and 2.2 and ideas for these industries: Creative
Professionals; Retail, Direct Mail and Online Sales

	Promotional Ideas	Ideas for Links
Consultants (Management, technical, creative services)	• Services and specialties • Project portfolio: description and images • Profile or resume • Client list • Project management philosophy • List of published works (books, articles) • Calendar of future seminars and speeches • Online advice newsletter • Firm history • Office locations and contact information	• Client, publisher, sponsor sites • Industry/professional association sites
Employment Agencies, Recruiters, Career Counselors	• Services and specialties • Staff profiles • Fee, billing, payment information • Philosophy or mission statement • Publications list • Product information (books, tapes) • Classes and event calendar	• Employment and career information sites

FIGURE 2.13 Continued

Professional Services

See Figures 2.1 and 2.2 and ideas for these industries: Creative
Professionals; Retail, Direct Mail and Online Sales

	Promotional Ideas	Ideas for Links
Event and Conference Services	• Services: standard and customized • Geographic and schedule availability • Staff profile • Client list and project descriptions • Event calendar • Insurance, bond, license information	• Event sponsors • Business partners
Shipping and Courier Companies, Transportation	• Shipping guidelines • Schedule and geographic availability information • Packaging instructions • Services: standard and special handling • Insurance information • Pickup and delivery locations and hours (locator) • Facilities and equipment information • Online tracking for shipments	• Industry sites • Government sites for regulatory information

FIGURE 2.13 Continued

Real Estate

See Figures 2.1 and 2.2 and ideas for these industries:
Professional Services

	Promotional Ideas	Ideas for Links
Agents and broker firms	• Sales specialties and expertise • Available properties; descriptions, maps, floor plans • Credentials; license and certification information • Area information • Personal profile	• Regional property listing sites • Mortgage and bank sites • Real estate and home activity information sites
Builders, Contractors, Property Management Services	• Project descriptions and experience • Specialized expertise, equipment, facilities • Staff profiles; licenses, bonding • Client list • Services and product information • Pricing/bidding information	• Real estate and construction information sites • Business partner sites • Manufacturer sites
Developments (Office and commercial buildings, homes, apartments, condominiums)	• Facilities and amenities description • Site maps and floor plans • Available units information • Lease or purchase rates and terms • Customization options • Security services	• Community information sites • Relocation service sites

FIGURE 2.14 Real estate.

Retail, Direct Mail, and Online Sales

See Figures 2.1 and 2.2 and ideas for these industries:

Industries related to your target markets

	Promotional Ideas	Ideas for Links
Any product	• Online product catalog and order form • Shipping and payment information • Services information • Store locator and hours • Coupons and special promotions • Classes, demonstrations, and in-store event calendar • Gift suggestions and reminders; new product notification service • Request form for printed catalogs and brochures • Inquiry form for specific products, services, price quotes • Comment forms for collecting customer testimonials	• Manufacturer sites • Activity, interest, topic sites

FIGURE 2.15 Retail, direct mail, and online sales.

Travel

See Figures 2.1 and 2.2 and ideas for these industries:
Retail, Direct Mail, and Online Sales; Non-Profit Organizations

	Promotional Ideas	Ideas for Links
Travel agencies and reservation services	• Specialty services • Seasonal travel advice and promotions • Traveler profile form • Tour, cruise, lodging inquiry form • Online reservation form	• Area tourism sites • Tour operator sites • Travel publications and information sites
Tour operators	• Details on available tours (description, date, itinerary, price) • Other products and services • Reservation instructions and online form • Request form for print brochure • Traveler profile form	• Area tourism sites • Travel publications and information sites • Lodging and attraction sites related to the tour
Lodging: hotels, inns, vacation home rentals, resorts, retreat centers, campgrounds	• Description of rooms, suites, facilities • Restaurant menu items; food service hours • Programs and events; seasonal activities • Meeting rooms and other group facilities and services • Local attractions and activities • Online reservation and request forms • Rates and payment information • Event calendar	• Local attraction sites • Area tourism sites • Hospitality network sites • Travel publication and information sites

FIGURE 2.16 Travel.

Travel

See Figures 2.1 and 2.2 and ideas for these industries:
Retail, Direct Mail, and Online Sales; Non-Profit Organizations

	Promotional Ideas	Ideas for Links
Area tourism programs	• Local attractions (museums, parks, recreation) • Events calendar and seasonal activities • Membership information • Currency exchange • Transportation information • International visitor information	• Member, community, and local government sites • Travel publication and information sites
Attractions: Museums, parks, historical sites; entertainment and concert venues	• Description of facilities, activities, fees • Events calendar, classes, seasonal activities • Membership and fundraising information • Ticket availability and online order form • Virtual tour, online map	• Area tourism sites • Affiliated organizations • Performer/artist site • Travel, history, entertainment, leisure publications and information sites

FIGURE 2.16 Continued

Travel

See Figures 2.1 and 2.2 and ideas for these industries:
Retail, Direct Mail, and Online Sales; Non-Profit Organizations

	Promotional Ideas	Ideas for Links
Restaurants	• Excerpts from published reviews • Menus: actual or example • Chef profile • Seasonal dinners, wine tastings, other events • Special promotions • Catering information and inquiry form • Banquet room and private party information • Online reservation and request form • Retail shop, delivery, or take out information • Online product catalog	• Area tourism sites • Business partner sites • Food, wine, cooking publication and information sites

FIGURE 2.16 Continued

CHAPTER THREE

WEB MARKETING TEMPLATES

Even though you may be very familiar with the process for creating and publishing print materials, you may have little, if any, experience with Web publishing. The templates on the CD-ROM are designed to make Web publishing easier for you. They offer fully developed Web pages, ready for your text, images, and multimedia elements.

This chapter provides a complete description and illustration of each template and its underlying HTML code. It also covers numerous ideas for achieving the most effective use of these templates on your site.

↳ Working with the Templates

The templates in this book accommodate the most common promotional materials and forms for businesses, consultants, and nonprofit organizations (see Figure 3.1). They can be adapted easily to a wide range of content and marketing activities.

You can also adapt the templates for many types of documents and forms that are not described in this book, yet are suitable for publication on your Web site. For example, you may want to place the content of an annual report online, or you may want to accept memberships on your Web site. Use these templates as a starting point, adding and revising content and presentation techniques to suit the needs of your communication. In particular, the Starter Page template offers the basic ingredients to create a Web page for almost any content.

You can change any aspect of each template: adding or deleting text, images, and multimedia elements, or changing the page layout. To begin, start your browser, load a template from the CD-ROM, and find its section in this chapter. When viewing the template's HTML code in a word processor, the text presented in red in the RTF file for each template gives you a starting point for making content changes. See Appendices A and B for complete instructions on working with the template files on the CD-ROM.

Promotional Activity	Primary Templates	Secondary Templates
Selling a product online through a catalog or brochure.	• Brochure • Catalog Page • Product Order Form	• Selection Guide • Price/Parts List
Announcing a new product or service.	• Brochure • Press Release	
Promoting a course, workshop, or event.	• Event Calendar • Event Registration Form • Seminar Description	• Product Inquiry Form • Profile (for Instructor)
Attracting clients for a consulting or service business.	• Brochure • Profile • Services List	
Encouraging visits to a dealer or retail store.	• Coupon • Locator	• Brochure • Product Inquiry Form
Recruiting members or donors.	• Brochure • Services List • Newsletter	• Event Calendar • Order Form (adapt for memberships or contributions)
Providing general company or organization information.	• Company Profile • FAQ • Newsletter	• Press Release • Profile • What's New
Gathering feedback from prospects and customers.	• Visitor Survey	

FIGURE 3.1 Matching templates to promotional activities.

The templates contain example text for four fictitious organizations. We chose these examples to help you understand the types of content and promotion techniques that can be applied to each template. The example organizations are as follows:

• *Global Products Co.*, a product manufacturer

- *Everything You Need Catalog Co.*, a mail-order business

- *Fun Events Association*, a nonprofit organization

- *Web Marketing Consultants Co.*, a consulting business

Remember that any template can be adapted for any business or organization—not just the example companies shown here. The following tips are also important to remember while working with the templates:

- The templates assume a graphical browser with capabilities comparable, at a minimum, to those of Netscape 1.2 or above.

- The template files are designed to be compatible with all Web development platforms: Windows 3.1, Windows 95, Windows NT, Macintosh, and any UNIX operating system. Filenames use a maximum of eight characters with three-character extensions.

- Not all browsers support e-mail ("mailto:") links; when you use such a link, show the full e-mail address. It is also a good idea to list all contact information—phone, fax, and postal mail—to enable the visitor to reach you through these methods as well.

- The <TAB> key is the standard in browsers for moving among fields on a form. The <ENTER> key is generally not used on forms, except for fields that allow entries with multiple lines.

- The templates use a <TABLE> construct to create a two-column layout: One row using the <TR> tag and two columns within that row using <TD> tags.

↳ Advertisement

A "click-through" banner advertisement for your site that appears on another Web site is usually a GIF or JPEG image, which is easily created using a graphics program or from a graphics file in TIFF or other common format. The Advertisement template, in the form of a GIF file, contains a space for placing your own logo or product image and call-to-action text that will encourage visitors to click on the ad and enter your site.

You can edit this image with a graphics program such as *Lview* (see Appendix C), Paintshop Professional, or Adobe Photoshop. You can also use these programs to create a new banner advertisement by scanning an existing printed ad into a GIF file or designing a new image. See Figure 3.2.

Online Promotion Tips

These tips will help you adapt this template for your promotions:

- Present a special promotion such as an online sale or product of the day.

- Announce new products.

- Promote contests (see Chapter 10 for a discussion of legal considerations).

- Create separate ads for each site where you advertise to focus on the market attracted to that site. Consider linking each ad to a different page on your site as a way to track the effectiveness of that external site for reaching your prospects. A different page can be as simple as a standard Welcome Page that is modified with a small amount of text customized to each audience.

FIGURE 3.2 Advertisement template.

Presentation Tips

These tips will enhance the presentation of your information in this template:

1. Minimize the amount of copy, as shown in Figure 3.2. Remember, you are just trying to entice the reader to click on the ad and link to your site. You do not need to make the complete sale here.

2. Identify your company, product, or promotion clearly so visitors can immediately determine their interest.

3. Focus on a single message, product, or promotion.

4. Include a specific, benefit-oriented call to action such as *Click here for savings!*

5. When the advertisement appears on the external site, you can ensure that the name of your Web site is contained within the banner <IMG> tag itself by including the statement ALT="Global Products Co." This will show the name of your Web site in the image area for the ad, even if visitors have turned off image display. (See Figure 3.3.)

Development Tips

Use simple, eight-bit colors to minimize the number of bytes required for your banner. This also will ensure that it displays correctly (non-dithered) on older monitors.

Related templates: None

Alternative templates: None

Navigation guidelines: Not applicable

Advanced implementation and design guidelines: You may want to create an animated GIF banner. This is a GIF image that contains a sequence of images that the browser automatically displays in sequence, creating an animation effect (see the animation examples on the CD-ROM). You can create very effective and eye-catching logos and banners using this relatively simple technique. A recommended resource is *GIF Construction Set* software from Alchemy Mindworks (see Appendix C).

```
<html><head><title>Banner Advertisment Page</title></head>

<body bgcolor="#ffffff">

<p><br>
<center>
 <IMG SRC="ad.jpg " WIDTH=600 HEIGHT=122 ALT="Banner
Advertisement">
</center>

</body>
</html>
```

FIGURE 3.3 Advertisement HTML code.

Article

The Article template (see Figure 3.4) is designed to present a magazine or newsletter article, but can be adapted to many documents and purposes. White papers, text-heavy brochures, essays, and reports are examples of other documents suited for this template.

Online Promotion Tips

These tips will help you adapt this template for your promotions:

- Link to pages that present more information on any product, people, or organizations mentioned in the

FIGURE 3.4 Article template.

article. These links can be embedded in the text or images such as a product photograph.

- Link to a glossary page for any words that may be unfamiliar to visitors.

TIP:

Page names shown in **bold** have a corresponding template in this chapter.

Presentation Tips

These tips will enhance the presentation of your information in this template (see corresponding callouts in Figure 3.4):

1. Link to a **Profile** page or an e-mail form the visitor can use to send a message to the author(s) of the article.

2. Break text into short paragraphs to ease online reading.

3. Include a biographical statement that lists the author's employer and job title, academic degrees, or other expertise related to the topic of this article.

4. Use this image placeholder for a photo of the author.

Development Tips

Figure 3.5 presents the HTML code for the Article template.

Related templates: Newsletter, Profile

Alternative templates: Brochure

Navigation guidelines: If using this template as part of an online newsletter, include links to other articles and the newsletter contents page. (See the Newsletter template for details on this navigation.)

Advanced implementation and design guidelines:

- Use video clips to show an event, activity, or product demonstration.

- Use audio clips for interview excerpts, lengthy quotes, or speeches.

- Consider using a two-column table. Leave one column blank and place text in the other column, making a shorter line length. (See Chapter 7 for details and an illustration.)

```
<HTML><HEAD><TITLE>Article</TITLE></HEAD>

<BODY BGCOLOR="#ffffff">

<TABLE>
<TR>
<TD NOWRAP>
<IMG SRC="artban.jpg"  WIDTH=350 HEIGHT=50 ALT="Article">
<IMG SRC="wmclogo.jpg " ALT="Logo" WIDTH=261 HEIGHT=100>
</TD>
</TR>
</TABLE>


<CENTER><FONT SIZE="+3">Web Marketing Wisdom</FONT>
<BR><FONT SIZE="+2">by <A HREF="../exprof/exprof.htm">Expert
Consultant</A>
</FONT>

<P>
<I><FONT SIZE="+1">Valuable insights that will help you real-
ize excellent results from your Web site.</FONT></I>

<TABLE BORDER=0 CELLPADDING=10 CELLSPACING=10 ALIGN=CENTER>

<TR>
<TD VALIGN=TOP>
<IMG SRC="catitm1.gif"  WIDTH=200 HEIGHT=316 VALIGN=TOP
ALT="Catalog Page Screen Shot" BORDER=1></A>

</TD>
<TD  VALIGN=TOP>
Every business marketer asks the same question: "Can my busi-
ness make money on the World Wide Web?" or "Can my non-profit
organization attract members and donors on the Web?"

<P>Creating and maintaining a site on the World Wide Web can
bring many valuable benefits to your business or non-profit
organization. These include: reaching your prospects anywhere,
```

FIGURE 3.5 Article HTML code.

```
anytime; updating information quickly and easily; and pre-
senting your information with exciting multimedia elements.

</TD>
</TABLE>

<TABLE BORDER=0 CELLPADDING=10 CELLSPACING=10 ALIGN=CENTER>

<TR><TD VALIGN=TOP><IMG SRC="king.jpg"  WIDTH=144 HEIGHT=206
VALIGN=TOP ALT="Expert Consultant" BORDER=0></A><P><FONT
SIZE="+1">About the Author</FONT>
<BR><A HREF="../exprof/exprof.htm">Expert Consultant</A> is a
marketing consultant who helps businesses create a high-
impact presence on the World Wide Web.

</TD>
<TD  VALIGN=TOP><FONT SIZE="+1">Creating an Appealing Web
Site</FONT><BR>

<P>If you're new to online marketing, an excellent resource
is <I>The Web Marketing Cookbook</I> by Janice King, Paul
Knight, and Jim Mason. This book is packed with useful guid-
ance for creating a good Web site. The included CD-ROM con-
tains numerous templates for Web pages that will have you
creating an exciting and informative site in very little
time!

</TD>
</TABLE>

</CENTER>

<P><BR>

<P><HR SIZE=3>
<CENTER>
http://www.webmarketco.com/article.htm
<BR>Copyright &copy; 1997 <A HREF="dummy.htm"> Web Marketing
Consultants Co.</A>
<BR>Questions and comments to: <A
HREF="mailto:emailname@domain.name">emailname@domain.name</A>
<P><A HREF="dummy.htm"><IMG SRC="back.gif" WIDTH=80 HEIGHT=40
BORDER=0></A> 
<A HREF="dummy.htm"><IMG SRC="forward.gif" WIDTH=80 HEIGHT=40
BORDER=0></A> 
<A HREF="dummy.htm "> <IMG SRC="home.gif" WIDTH=80 HEIGHT=40
```

FIGURE 3.5 Continued

```
BORDER=0></A> 
<A HREF="dummy.htm"> <IMG SRC="contents.gif" WIDTH=80
HEIGHT=40 BORDER=0></A> 
<A HREF="mailto:emailname@domain.name"> <IMG SRC="email.gif"
WIDTH=80 HEIGHT=40 BORDER=0></A>
<BR><FONT SIZE=-1><A HREF="dummy.htm">Back</A> ||
<A HREF="dummy.htm">Forward</A> ||
<A HREF="dummy.htm">Home</A> ||
<A HREF="dummy.htm">Contents</A> ||
<A HREF="mailto:emailname@domain.name">E-Mail</A></FONT>
</BODY>
</HTML>
```

FIGURE 3.5 Continued

 # Brochure

The Brochure template (see Figure 3.6) is highly adaptable for promoting a product, service, event, course, individual, or organization.

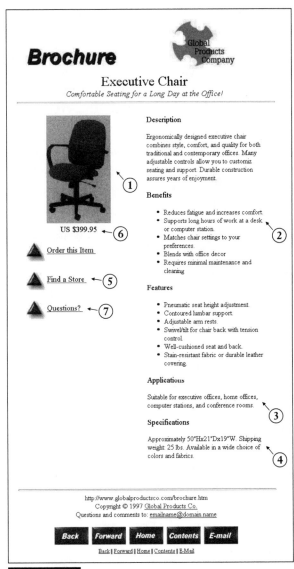

FIGURE 3.6 Brochure template.

Web Marketing Templates

75

Online Promotion Tips

These tips will help you adapt this template for your promotions:

- Link to other Brochure or **Catalog** pages for related products or accessories to create cross-sell and up-sell opportunities.

- Link to a **Price/Parts List** page for the product(s) described in the brochure.

- Link to pages with gift suggestions, a **Coupon**, **Product Inquiry Form**, or a **Selection Guide** to encourage a visitor's further exploration of products and services offered by your business, both on and off the Web.

- Always include a call-to-action such as "Order this item!" If the action can be completed online, link to an **Order Form** or other page as shown here. If the action must be completed offline, include all instructions and information necessary for the visitor to take the action (see Chapter 4).

Presentation Tips

You can adapt this template to accommodate the content and organization of your printed brochure by adding or eliminating any elements. However, if you are marketing multiple products or services, this template gives you a consistent and well-structured way to present key information on a Web page. These tips will enhance the presentation of your information in this template (see corresponding callouts in Figure 3.6):

1. Include one or more images related to the subject of this brochure (photos, diagrams, or illustrations).

2. Bullet lists make your Features and Benefits easy to see and read. Presenting features and benefits in a two-column table is an alternative approach.

3. Use narrative text or bullets to describe possible uses or environments for the product or adapt this section for additional product information.

4. List product details such as size, weight, and technical requirements. If the list is lengthy, place it on a separate Web page and link to that page from this point.

5. Describe the locations for purchasing the product or link to a **Locator** page if appropriate.

6. Specify price and other sales information; describe special promotions. Link to a **Coupon** page if appropriate.

7. Link to an e-mail message, a **Product Inquiry Form**, or a **Selection Guide**.

Development Tips

Figure 3.7 presents the HTML code for the Brochure template.

Related templates: Company Profile, Services List, Coupon

Alternative templates: Catalog Page

Navigation guidelines: If using this template as part of a catalog, include links to other **Catalog Pages** and the **Catalog Contents**.

Advanced implementation and design guidelines: Include a video clip showing an event or product demonstration or an audio clip with a presentation or performance sample.

If you are adapting a multipage brochure, consider presenting the text and images on several Web pages as well. However, this does *not* mean the brochure's appearance on the Web should be identical to its print form. Instead, determine how you can restructure the content to be more readable and easier to navigate across several Web pages (see discussion and examples in Chapter 6).

```
<HTML><HEAD><TITLE>Brochure</TITLE></HEAD>

<BODY BGCOLOR="#ffffff">

<TABLE>
<TR>
<TD NOWRAP>
<IMG SRC="broban.jpg"  WIDTH=350 HEIGHT=50  ALT="Brochure">
<IMG SRC="glblogo.jpg " WIDTH=154 HEIGHT=122 ALT="Logo" >
</TD>
</TR>
</TABLE>


<CENTER><FONT SIZE="+3">Executive Chair</FONT>
<BR><FONT SIZE="+1"><I>Comfortable Seating for a Long Day at
the Office!
</I></FONT>
<HR SIZE=3>

<TABLE BORDER=0 CELLPADDING=10 CELLSPACING=10 ALIGN=CENTER>

<TR>
<TD VALIGN=TOP>
<IMG SRC="chair.gif"  WIDTH=151 HEIGHT=246 VALIGN=TOP
ALT="Chair Photo" BORDER=0>
<BR>


<FONT SIZE=+1>
US $399.95
<P><A HREF="../order/order.htm"><IMG SRC="bluearrow.gif"
ALIGN=MIDDLE BORDER=0></A><A HREF="../order/order.htm">Order
this Item </A>
<P><A HREF="../locator/locator.htm"><IMG SRC="bluearrow.gif"
ALIGN=MIDDLE BORDER=0></A><A
HREF="../locator/locator.htm">Find a Store </A>
<P><A HREF="../inquiry/inquiry.htm"><IMG SRC="bluearrow.gif"
ALIGN=MIDDLE BORDER=0></A><A
HREF="../inquiry/inquiry.htm">Questions? </A>
</FONT>

</TD>
<TD VALIGN=TOP>
```

FIGURE 3.7 Brochure HTML code.

```
<P><FONT SIZE="+1">Description
</FONT>
<P>Ergonomically designed executive chair combines style, com-
fort, and quality for both traditional and contemporary
offices. Many adjustable controls allow you to customize
seating and support. Durable construction assures years of
enjoyment.

<P><FONT SIZE="+1">Benefits</FONT><UL><LI>Reduces fatigue and
increases comfort.<LI>Supports long hours of work at a desk
or computer station.
<LI>Matches chair settings to your preferences.
<LI>Blends with office decor
    <LI>Requires minimal maintenance and cleaning
</UL>

<P><FONT SIZE="+1">Features
</FONT><UL>
<LI>  Pneumatic seat height adjustment.
<LI>Contoured lumbar support.
<LI>Adjustable arm rests.
<LI>Swivel/tilt for chair back with tension control.
<LI>Well-cushioned seat and back.
<LI>Stain-resistant fabric or durable leather covering.</UL>

<P><FONT SIZE="+1">Applications
</FONT>
<P>Suitable for executive offices, home offices, computer
stations, and conference rooms.

<P><FONT SIZE="+1">Specifications
</FONT>
<P>Approximately 50"Hx21"Dx19"W. Shipping weight: 25 lbs.
Available in a wide choice of colors and fabrics.




</TD>
</TR>
</TABLE>


</CENTER>
```

FIGURE 3.7 Continued

```
<P><BR>


<P><HR SIZE=3>
<CENTER>
http://www.globalproductsco.com/brochure.htm
<BR>Copyright &copy; 1997 <A HREF="dummy.htm">Global Products
Co.</A>
<BR>Questions and comments to: <A
HREF="mailto:emailname@domain.name">emailname@domain.name</A>
<P><A HREF="dummy.htm"><IMG SRC="back.gif" WIDTH=80 HEIGHT=40
BORDER=0></A> 
<A HREF="dummy.htm"><IMG SRC="forward.gif" WIDTH=80 HEIGHT=40
BORDER=0></A> 
<A HREF="dummy.htm "> <IMG SRC="home.gif" WIDTH=80 HEIGHT=40
BORDER=0></A> 
<A HREF="../contents/contents.htm"> <IMG SRC="contents.gif"
WIDTH=80 HEIGHT=40 BORDER=0></A> 
<A HREF="mailto:emailname@domain.name"> <IMG SRC="email.gif"
WIDTH=80 HEIGHT=40 BORDER=0></A>
<BR><FONT SIZE=-1><A HREF="dummy.htm">Back</A> ||
<A HREF="dummy.htm">Forward</A> ||
<A HREF="dummy.htm">Home</A> ||
<A HREF="../contents/contents.htm">Contents</A> ||
<A HREF="mailto:emailname@domain.name">E-Mail</A></FONT>
</BODY>
</HTML>
```

FIGURE 3.7 Continued

 # Catalog Contents

The Catalog Contents Page (see Figure 3.8) gives visitors a convenient list of all products available in your online catalog. With an active link for each product name, a visitor can navigate directly to the catalog page that presents detailed information and an image for that item.

Online Promotion Tips

These tips will help you adapt this template for your promotions:

- Use this page if you sell numerous products on your Web site. Link to it from the home page, **Contents**

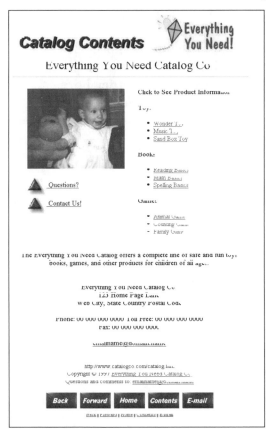

FIGURE 3.8 Catalog Contents template.

page, or any other page on your site that contains a catalog link.

- Create a link to a **Catalog Page** for a "featured" product or holiday/seasonal products.

Presentation Tip

Using tables is an effective way to segment lists of related products into categories or groups.

Development Tips

See the Catalog Contents HTML code in Figure 3.9. Use the <TABLE> tag to organize your product information in a readable format.

Related templates: Brochure, Catalog Page

Alternative templates: None

Navigation guidelines: This is the first template in a sequence for making an online sale. The next templates are the **Catalog Page** or **Brochure** and the **Order Form**.

Advanced implementation and design guidelines: None

```
<HTML><HEAD><TITLE>Catalog Contents Page</TITLE></HEAD>

<BODY BGCOLOR="#ffffff">

<TABLE>
<TR>
<TD NOWRAP>
<IMG SRC="contban.jpg" WIDTH=350 HEIGHT=50 ALT="Catalog
Contents">
<IMG SRC="catlogo1.jpg " WIDTH=210 HEIGHT=100 ALT="Logo" >
</TD>
</TR>
</TABLE>


<CENTER><FONT SIZE="+3">Everything You Need Catalog Co.</FONT>

<HR SIZE=3>
```

FIGURE 3.9 Catalog Contents HTML code.

```
<TABLE BORDER=0 CELLPADDING=10 CELLSPACING=10 ALIGN=CENTER>

<TR>
<TD VALIGN=TOP>
<IMG SRC="catitm1.jpg"  WIDTH=252 HEIGHT=202 VALIGN=TOP
ALT="Product Image" BORDER=0></A>
<P><FONT SIZE=+1>
<A HREF="../inquiry/inquiry.htm"><IMG SRC="bluearrow.gif"
ALIGN=MIDDLE BORDER=0> Questions?</A>
<BR><A HREF="mailto:emailname@domain.name"><IMG SRC="bluear-
row.gif" ALIGN=MIDDLE BORDER=0> Contact Us!</A>
</FONT>
</TD>

<TD VALIGN=TOP>
<P><FONT SIZE="+1">Click to See Product Information
</FONT>

<P><FONT SIZE="+1">Toys
</FONT><UL>
<LI><A HREF="catitm1.htm">Wonder Toy</A>
<LI><A HREF="dummy.htm">Music Toy</A>
<LI><A HREF="dummy.htm">Sand Box Toy</A>
</UL>

<P><FONT SIZE="+1">Books
</FONT><UL>
<LI><A HREF="dummy.htm">Reading Basics</A>
<LI><A HREF="dummy.htm">Math Basics</A>
<LI><A HREF="dummy.htm">Spelling Basics</A>
</UL>

<P><FONT SIZE="+1">Games
</FONT><UL>
<LI><A HREF="dummy.htm">Animal Game</A>
<LI><A HREF="dummy.htm">Counting Game</A>
<LI><A HREF="dummy.htm">Family Game</A>
</UL>


</TD>
</TR>
</TABLE>

<FONT SIZE=+1>
The Everything You Need Catalog offers a complete line of
```

FIGURE 3.9 Continued

```
safe and fun toys,<BR> books, games, and other products for
children of all ages.

</CENTER>

<P><BR>
<CENTER>
<P>
Everything You Need Catalog Co.
<BR>123 Home Page Lane
<BR>Web City, State Country Postal Code
<P>Phone: 00 000 000 0000 Toll Free: 00 000 000 0000
<BR>Fax: 00 000 000 0000
<P><A HREF="mailto:emailname@domain.name">emailname@domain.
name</A>
</FONT>
</CENTER>


<P><HR SIZE=3>
<CENTER>
http://www.catalogco.com/catalog.htm
<BR>Copyright &copy; 1997 <A HREF="dummy.htm">Everything You
Need Catalog Co.</A>
<BR>Questions and comments to: <A
HREF="mailto:emailname@domain.name">emailname@domain.name</A>
<P><A HREF="dummy.htm"><IMG SRC="back.gif" WIDTH=80 HEIGHT=40
BORDER=0></A> 
<A HREF="dummy.htm"><IMG SRC="forward.gif" WIDTH=80 HEIGHT=40
BORDER=0></A> 
<A HREF="dummy.htm "> <IMG SRC="home.gif" WIDTH=80 HEIGHT=40
BORDER=0></A> 
<A HREF="../contents/contents.htm"> <IMG SRC="contents.gif"
WIDTH=80 HEIGHT=40 BORDER=0></A> 
<A HREF="mailto:emailname@domain.name"> <IMG SRC="email.gif"
WIDTH=80 HEIGHT=40 BORDER=0></A>
<BR><FONT SIZE=-1><A HREF="dummy.htm">Back</A> ||
<A HREF="dummy.htm">Forward</A> ||
<A HREF="dummy.htm">Home</A> ||
<A HREF="../contents/contents.htm">Contents</A> ||
<A HREF="mailto:emailname@domain.name">E-Mail</A></FONT>
</BODY>
</HTML>
```

FIGURE 3.9 Continued

Catalog Page

The Catalog Page (see Figure 3.10) presents information on individual items in a product catalog. Even though you can easily adapt the information from a printed catalog to this template, consider taking advantage of the lower cost for Web documents to add longer text descriptions, more images, video demonstrations, or audio samples. (See Chapter 4 for a discussion of other capabilities and issues related to online sales.)

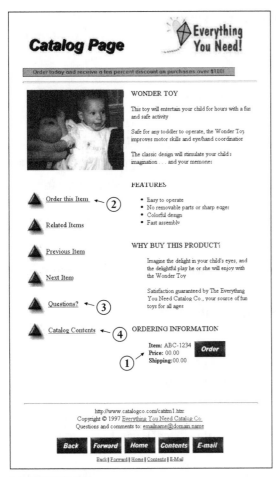

FIGURE 3.10 Catalog Page template.

Online Promotion Tips

These tips will help you adapt this template for your promotions:

- Add links to the catalog pages for other models, accessories, and related products to create cross-sell and up-sell opportunities or include that information on this page.

- Link to pages with gift suggestions, a **Coupon**, **Product Inquiry Form**, or a **Selection Guide**.

- Always include a call-to-action such as "Order this item!" with a link that takes the visitor to an online **Order Form** or a Web page that presents instructions for taking the action. More ideas for the call to action are covered in Chapter 6.

Presentation Tips

These tips will enhance the presentation of your information in this template (see corresponding callouts in 3.10):

1. If you sell to an international market, accepting multiple currencies and applying different shipping rates, consider using the **Price/Parts List** template to present that detail. Link to that page from Price here.

2. Link to an **Order Form** page.

3. Link to a **Product Inquiry Form**, **FAQ**, or **Selection Guide** page.

4. Link to a **Catalog Contents** page.

Development Tips

Figure 3.11 presents the HTML code for the Catalog Page template.

Related templates: Catalog Contents, Coupon, Product Inquiry Form, Selection Guide, Price/Parts List, Order Form.

```
<HTML><HEAD><TITLE>Catalog Page</TITLE></HEAD>

<BODY BGCOLOR="#ffffff">

<TABLE>
<TR>
<TD NOWRAP>
<IMG SRC="catban.jpg"  WIDTH=350 HEIGHT=50 ALT="Catalog
Page">
<IMG SRC="catlogo1.jpg " WIDTH=210 HEIGHT=100 ALT="Logo" >
</TD>
</TR>
</TABLE>
<BR><IMG SRC="catbar.gif" WIDTH=549 HEIGHT=20 BORDER=1>
<HR SIZE=3 >

<TABLE BORDER=0 CELLPADDING=5 CELLSPACING=5>
<TR>
<TD VALIGN=TOP>
<IMG SRC="catitm1.jpg"  WIDTH=252 HEIGHT=202 VALIGN=TOP
ALT="Product Image" BORDER=0>

<PRE>

</PRE>
<FONT SIZE=+1>
<P><A HREF="../order/order.htm"><IMG SRC="bluearrow.gif"
ALIGN=MIDDLE BORDER=0></A><A HREF="../order/order.htm">Order
this Item </A>
<P><A HREF="dummy.htm"><IMG SRC="bluearrow.gif" ALIGN=MIDDLE
BORDER=0></A><A HREF="dummy.htm">Related Items</A>
<P><A HREF="dummy.htm"><IMG SRC="bluearrow.gif" ALIGN=MIDDLE
BORDER=0></A><A HREF="dummy.htm">Previous Item</A>
<P><A HREF="dummy.htm"><IMG SRC="bluearrow.gif" ALIGN=MIDDLE
BORDER=0></A><A HREF="dummy.htm">Next Item</A>
<P><A HREF="../faq/faq.htm"><IMG SRC="bluearrow.gif"
ALIGN=MIDDLE BORDER=0></A> <A
HREF="../faq/faq.htm">Questions?</A>
<P><A HREF="../catalog/catalog.htm"><IMG SRC="bluearrow.gif"
ALIGN=MIDDLE BORDER=0></A> <A
HREF="../catalog/catalog.htm">Catalog Contents</A>
</FONT>


</TD>
```

FIGURE 3.11 Catalog Page HTML code.

```
<TD  VALIGN=TOP>
<FONT SIZE=+1>WONDER TOY</FONT>
<P>This toy will entertain your child for hours with a fun
and safe activity.

<P>Safe for any toddler to operate, the Wonder Toy improves
motor skills and eye/hand coordination.

<P>The classic design will stimulate your child's imagination
. . . and your memories.

<P><BR><FONT SIZE=+1>FEATURES</FONT>
<UL>
<LI>Easy to operate
<LI>No removable parts or sharp edges
<LI>Colorful design
<LI>Fast assembly
</UL>

<P><BR><FONT SIZE=+1>WHY BUY THIS PRODUCT?</FONT>
<UL>Imagine the delight in your child's eyes, and the
delightful play he or she will enjoy with the Wonder Toy.

<P>Satisfaction guaranteed by The Everything You Need Catalog
Co., your
source of fun toys for all ages.

</UL>
<P><BR><FONT SIZE=+1>ORDERING INFORMATION</FONT>
<UL>
<TABLE BORDER=0 WIDTH=0 HEIGHT=0>
<TR>
<TD VALIGN=TOP>
<B>Item:</B> ABC-1234
<BR><B>Price:</B> 00.00
<BR><B>Shipping:</B>00.00
<P><BR>
</TD>
<TD VALIGN=TOP>
<A HREF="../order/order.htm"><IMG SRC="order.gif" WIDTH=80
HEIGHT=40 BORDER=0></A>
</TD>
</TABLE>
</TD>
</TR>
</TABLE>
```

FIGURE 3.11 Continued

```
<P><BR>


<P><HR SIZE=3>
<CENTER>
http://www.catalogco.com/catitm1.htm
<BR>Copyright &copy; 1997 <A HREF="dummy.htm">Everything You
Need Catalog Co.</A>
<BR>Questions and comments to: <A
HREF="mailto:emailname@domain.name">emailname@domain.name</A>
<P><A HREF="dummy.htm"><IMG SRC="back.gif" WIDTH=80 HEIGHT=40
BORDER=0></A> 
<A HREF="dummy.htm"><IMG SRC="forward.gif" WIDTH=80 HEIGHT=40
BORDER=0></A> 
<A HREF="dummy.htm "> <IMG SRC="home.gif" WIDTH=80 HEIGHT=40
BORDER=0></A> 
<A HREF="../contents/contents.htm"> <IMG SRC="contents.gif"
WIDTH=80 HEIGHT=40 BORDER=0></A> 
<A HREF="mailto:emailname@domain.name"> <IMG SRC="email.gif"
WIDTH=80 HEIGHT=40 BORDER=0></A>
<BR><FONT SIZE=-1><A HREF="dummy.htm">Back</A> ||
<A HREF="dummy.htm">Forward</A> ||
<A HREF="dummy.htm">Home</A> ||
<A HREF="../contents/contents.htm">Contents</A> ||
<A HREF="mailto:emailname@domain.name">E-Mail</A></FONT>
</BODY>
</HTML>
```

FIGURE 3.11 Continued

Alternative templates: Brochure

Navigation guidelines: If using this template as part of a catalog, you will need to determine how you want to sequence the <u>Previous Item</u> and <u>Next Item</u> links: alphabetically by item name or to related items within a category.

Advanced implementation and design guidelines:

- Use video clips to show a product demonstration.

- Use an audio clip for a sound demonstration or music excerpt.

- Implement a "shopping basket" program to automatically track a visitor's selections and enter the data on the **Order Form** (see Chapter 4).

 Company Profile

The Company Profile (see Figure 3.12) presents basic information about your company, organization, or group.

Online Promotion Tips

These tips will help you adapt this template for your promotions:

- Include the mission statement or statement of purpose in the Overview section.

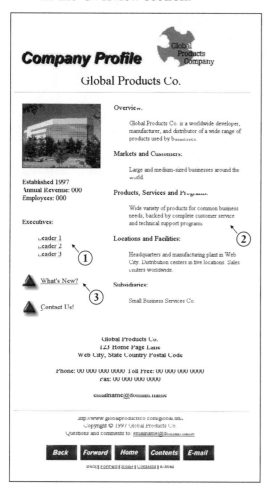

FIGURE 3.12 Company Profile template.

- Adapt the content of this template to match an existing Fact Sheet or to present the most relevant data about your organization.
- Link to a **FAQ** page to provide additional information that would interest visitors.

Presentation Tips

These tips will enhance the presentation of your information in this template (see corresponding callouts in Figure 3.12):

1. Link to pages that present more information on any products, people, or organizations mentioned in the Company Profile (see the **Profile** template). These links can be embedded in the text or images.

2. Link to a glossary page for any words that may be unfamiliar to visitors.

3. Link to a **What's New** page to encourage visitors to view the latest news about your organization or current promotions on your Web site.

Development Tips

Figure 3.13 presents the HTML code for the Company Profile template.

Related templates: What's New Page
Alternative templates: Brochure
Navigation guidelines: Not applicable
Advanced implementation and design guidelines: None

```
<HTML><HEAD><TITLE>Company/Organization Profile
Page</TITLE></HEAD>

<BODY BGCOLOR="#ffffff">

<TABLE>
<TR>
<TD NOWRAP>
```

FIGURE 3.13 Company Profile HTML code.

```
<IMG SRC="coban.jpg" WIDTH=350 HEIGHT=50  ALT="Company
Profile">
<IMG SRC="glblogo.jpg " ALT="Logo" WIDTH=154 HEIGHT=122>
</TD>
</TR>
</TABLE>

<CENTER><FONT SIZE="+3">Global Products Co.</FONT>
<HR SIZE=3>

<TABLE BORDER=0 CELLPADDING=10 CELLSPACING=10 ALIGN=CENTER>

<TR>
<TD VALIGN=TOP>
<IMG SRC="building.jpg"  WIDTH=200 HEIGHT=160 VALIGN=TOP
ALT="Corporate Building" BORDER=1></A>
<FONT SIZE=+1>
<P>Established 1997
<BR>Annual Revenue: 000
<BR>Employees: 000
<P><BR>
<P>Executives:
<UL><A HREF="../exprof/exprof.htm">Leader 1</A>
<BR><A HREF="../exprof/exprof.htm">Leader 2</A>
<BR><A HREF="../exprof/exprof.htm">Leader 3</A>
</UL>
<P><BR>
<A HREF="dummy.htm"><IMG SRC="bluearrow.gif" ALIGN=MIDDLE
BORDER=0>What's New?</A>
<P><A HREF="mailto:emailname@domain.name"><IMG
SRC="bluearrow.gif" ALIGN=MIDDLE BORDER=0>Contact Us!</A>
</A>
</FONT>
</TD>
<TD VALIGN=TOP>

<P><FONT SIZE="+1">Overview:
</FONT>
<UL>Global Products Co. is a worldwide developer, manufac-
turer, and distributor of a wide range of products used by
businesses.</UL>

<P><FONT SIZE="+1">Markets and Customers:
</FONT><UL>Large and medium-sized businesses around the
world.</UL>
```

FIGURE 3.13 Continued

```
<P><FONT SIZE="+1">Products, Services and Programs:
</FONT> <UL>Wide variety of products for common business
needs, backed by complete customer service and technical sup-
port programs.</UL>

<P><FONT SIZE="+1">Locations and Facilities:
</FONT><UL> Headquarters and manufacturing plant in Web City.
Distribution centers in five locations. Sales  centers world-
wide.</UL>

<P><FONT SIZE="+1">Subsidiaries:
</FONT><UL>Small Business Services Co.</UL>


</TD>
</TR>
</TABLE>

<FONT SIZE=+1>
<CENTER>
<P>
Global Products Co.
<BR>123 Home Page Lane
<BR>Web City, State Country Postal Code
<P>Phone: 00 000 000 0000 Toll Free: 00 000 000 0000
<BR>Fax: 00 000 000 0000
<P><A HREF="mailto:emailname@domain.name">emailname@domain.
name</A>
</FONT>
</CENTER>

<P><HR SIZE=3>
<CENTER>
http://www.globalproductsco.com/global.htm
<BR>Copyright &copy; 1997 <A HREF="dummy.htm">Global Products
Co.</A>
<BR>Questions and comments to: <A
HREF="mailto:emailname@domain.name">emailname@domain.name</A>
<P><A HREF="dummy.htm"><IMG SRC="back.gif" WIDTH=80 HEIGHT=40
BORDER=0></A> 
<A HREF="dummy.htm"><IMG SRC="forward.gif" WIDTH=80 HEIGHT=40
BORDER=0></A> 
<A HREF="dummy.htm "> <IMG SRC="home.gif" WIDTH=80 HEIGHT=40
BORDER=0></A> 
<A HREF="../contents/contents.htm"> <IMG SRC="contents.gif"
```

FIGURE 3.13 Continued

```
WIDTH=80 HEIGHT=40 BORDER=0></A> 
<A HREF="mailto:emailname@domain.name"> <IMG SRC="email.gif"
WIDTH=80 HEIGHT=40 BORDER=0></A>
<BR><FONT SIZE=-1><A HREF="dummy.htm">Back</A> ||
<A HREF="dummy.htm">Forward</A> ||
<A HREF="dummy.htm">Home</A> ||
<A HREF="../contents/contents.htm">Contents</A> ||
<A HREF="mailto:emailname@domain.name">E-Mail</A></FONT>
</BODY>
</HTML>
```

FIGURE 3.13 Continued

↳ Contents Page

The Contents page (see Figure 3.14) can list and link to all pages or topics on your site. Create a link for each page or topic listed in the Contents.

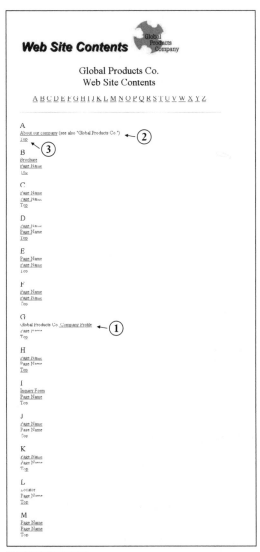

FIGURE 3.14 Contents Page template.

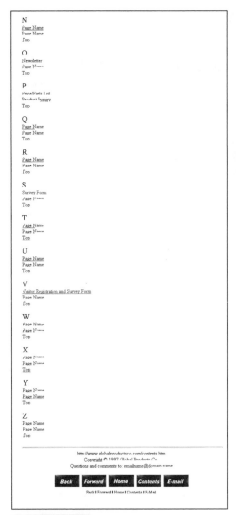

FIGURE 3.14 Continued

Online Promotion Tips

These tips will help you adapt this template for your promotions:

- Make the listing sufficiently descriptive to allow the visitor to determine the type of information or function on the page before clicking on the link.

- List each page in several areas, considering the different terms a visitor might use to seek that information.

Presentation Tips

These tips will enhance the presentation of your information in this template (see corresponding callouts in Figure 3.14):

1. Link on the key word(s) in the listing.

2. Cross-reference related topics with "See Also" listings.

3. Use a <u>Top</u> or <u>Index</u> link to allow the visitor to return to the list of letters and search for another topic. This helps the visitor avoid scrolling through a lengthy Contents page.

Development Tips

Figure 3.15 presents the HTML code for the Contents page template.

Related templates: None

Alternative templates: None

Navigation guidelines: For a very large site, you may want to reduce loading and scrolling times by implementing the content over multiple Web pages—one for each letter or group of letters.

Advanced implementation and design guidelines: You can implement a search script that enables the visitor to enter a keyword or phrase to find any page in the site. The script presents to the browser a list of the pages on your site that contain the specified words or phrases.

```
<HTML><HEAD><TITLE>Web Site Contents Page</TITLE></HEAD>

<BODY BGCOLOR="#ffffff">

<TABLE>
<TR>
<TD NOWRAP>
<IMG SRC="globan.jpg"  WIDTH=350 HEIGHT=50 ALT="Web Site
Contents">
<IMG SRC="glblogo.jpg " ALT="Logo" WIDTH=154 HEIGHT=122>
</TD>
```

FIGURE 3.15 Contents Page HTML code.

```
</TR>
</TABLE>

<CENTER>
<P>
<FONT SIZE=+3>Global Products Co.
<BR>Web Site Contents
</FONT>
<P><FONT SIZE=+2>
<A NAME="top"></A>
<A HREF="#A">A</A>
<A HREF="#B">B</A>
<A HREF="#C">C</A>
<A HREF="#D">D</A>
<A HREF="#E">E</A>
<A HREF="#F">F</A>
<A HREF="#G">G</A>
<A HREF="#H">H</A>
<A HREF="#I">I</A>
<A HREF="#J">J</A>
<A HREF="#K">K</A>
<A HREF="#L">L</A>
<A HREF="#M">M</A>
<A HREF="#N">N</A>
<A HREF="#O">O</A>
<A HREF="#P">P</A>
<A HREF="#Q">Q</A>
<A HREF="#R">R</A>
<A HREF="#S">S</A>
<A HREF="#T">T</A>
<A HREF="#U">U</A>
<A HREF="#V">V</A>
<A HREF="#W">W</A>
<A HREF="#X">X</A>
<A HREF="#Y">Y</A>
<A HREF="#Z">Z</A>
 </FONT>
</CENTER>
<BR><HR SIZE=3>

<A NAME="A"></A>
<P><FONT SIZE=+2>A</FONT>
<BR><A HREF="../coprof/coprof.htm">About our company</A> (see
also "Global Products Co.")
<BR><A HREF="#top">Top</A>
```

FIGURE 3.15 Continued

```
<A NAME="B"></A>
<P><FONT SIZE=+2>B</FONT>
<BR><A HREF="../brochure/brochure.htm">Brochure</A>
<BR><A HREF="webpage.htm">Page Name</A>
<BR><A HREF="#top">Top</A>

<A NAME="C"></A>
<P><FONT SIZE=+2>C</FONT>
<BR><A HREF="webpage.htm">Page Name</A>
<BR><A HREF="webpage.htm">Page Name</A>
<BR><A HREF="#top">Top</A>

<A NAME="D"></A>
<P><FONT SIZE=+2>D</FONT>
<BR><A HREF="webpage.htm">Page Name</A>
<BR><A HREF="webpage.htm">Page Name</A>
<BR><A HREF="#top">Top</A>

<A NAME="E"></A>
<P><FONT SIZE=+2>E</FONT>
<BR><A HREF="webpage.htm">Page Name</A>
<BR><A HREF="webpage.htm">Page Name</A>
<BR><A HREF="#top">Top</A>

<A NAME="F"></A>
<P><FONT SIZE=+2>F</FONT>
<BR><A HREF="webpage.htm">Page Name</A>
<BR><A HREF="webpage.htm">Page Name</A>
<BR><A HREF="#top">Top</A>

<A NAME="G"></A>
<P><FONT SIZE=+2>G</FONT>
<BR>Global Products Co.<A HREF="../coprof/coprof.htm"> Company
Profile</A>
<BR><A HREF="webpage.htm">Page Name</A>
<BR><A HREF="#top">Top</A>

<A NAME="H"></A>
<P><FONT SIZE=+2>H</FONT>
<BR><A HREF="webpage.htm">Page Name</A>
<BR><A HREF="webpage.htm">Page Name</A>
<BR><A HREF="#top">Top</A>

<A NAME="I"></A>
<P><FONT SIZE=+2>I</FONT>
```

FIGURE 3.15 Continued

```
<BR><A HREF="../inquiry/inquiry.htm">Inquiry Form</A>
<BR><A HREF="webpage.htm">Page Name</A>
<BR><A HREF="#top">Top</A>

<A NAME="J"></A>
<P><FONT SIZE=+2>J</FONT>
<BR><A HREF="webpage.htm">Page Name</A>
<BR><A HREF="webpage.htm">Page Name</A>
<BR><A HREF="#top">Top</A>

<A NAME="K"></A>
<P><FONT SIZE=+2>K</FONT>
<BR><A HREF="webpage.htm">Page Name</A>
<BR><A HREF="webpage.htm">Page Name</A>
<BR><A HREF="#top">Top</A>

<A NAME="L"></A>
<P><FONT SIZE=+2>L</FONT>
<BR><A HREF="../locator/locator.htm">Locator</A>
<BR><A HREF="webpage.htm">Page Name</A>
<BR><A HREF="#top">Top</A>

<A NAME="M"></A>
<P><FONT SIZE=+2>M</FONT>
<BR><A HREF="webpage.htm">Page Name</A>
<BR><A HREF="webpage.htm">Page Name</A>
<BR><A HREF="#top">Top</A>

<A NAME="N"></A>
<P><FONT SIZE=+2>N</FONT>
<BR><A HREF="webpage.htm">Page Name</A>
<BR><A HREF="webpage.htm">Page Name</A>
<BR><A HREF="#top">Top</A>

<A NAME="O"></A>
<P><FONT SIZE=+2>O</FONT>
<BR><A HREF="../newsltr/newsltr.htm">Newsletter</A>
<BR><A HREF="webpage.htm">Page Name</A>
<BR><A HREF="#top">Top</A>

<A NAME="P"></A>
<P><FONT SIZE=+2>P</FONT>
<BR><A HREF="../pricelst/pricelst.htm">Price/Parts List</A>
<BR><A HREF="../inquiry/inquiry.htm">Product Inquiry</A>
<BR><A HREF="#top">Top</A>
```

FIGURE 3.15 Continued

```
<A NAME="Q"></A>
<P><FONT SIZE=+2>Q</FONT>
<BR><A HREF="webpage.htm">Page Name</A>
<BR><A HREF="webpage.htm">Page Name</A>
<BR><A HREF="#top">Top</A>

<A NAME="R"></A>
<P><FONT SIZE=+2>R</FONT>
<BR><A HREF="webpage.htm">Page Name</A>
<BR><A HREF="webpage.htm">Page Name</A>
<BR><A HREF="#top">Top</A>

<A NAME="S"></A>
<P><FONT SIZE=+2>S</FONT>
<BR><A HREF="../survey/survey.htm">Survey Form</A>
<BR><A HREF="webpage.htm">Page Name</A>
<BR><A HREF="#top">Top</A>

<A NAME="T"></A>
<P><FONT SIZE=+2>T</FONT>
<BR><A HREF="webpage.htm">Page Name</A>
<BR><A HREF="webpage.htm">Page Name</A>
<BR><A HREF="#top">Top</A>

<A NAME="U"></A>
<P><FONT SIZE=+2>U</FONT>
<BR><A HREF="webpage.htm">Page Name</A>
<BR><A HREF="webpage.htm">Page Name</A>
<BR><A HREF="#top">Top</A>

<A NAME="V"></A>
<P><FONT SIZE=+2>V</FONT>
<BR><A HREF="../survey/survey.htm">Visitor Registration and
Survey Form</A>
<BR><A HREF="webpage.htm">Page Name</A>
<BR><A HREF="#top">Top</A>

<A NAME="W"></A>
<P><FONT SIZE=+2>W</FONT>
<BR><A HREF="webpage.htm">Page Name</A>
<BR><A HREF="webpage.htm">Page Name</A>
<BR><A HREF="#top">Top</A>

<A NAME="X"></A>
<P><FONT SIZE=+2>X</FONT>
```

FIGURE 3.15 Continued

```
<BR><A HREF="webpage.htm">Page Name</A>
<BR><A HREF="webpage.htm">Page Name</A>
<BR><A HREF="#top">Top</A>

<A NAME="Y"></A>
<P><FONT SIZE=+2>Y</FONT>
<BR><A HREF="webpage.htm">Page Name</A>
<BR><A HREF="webpage.htm">Page Name</A>
<BR><A HREF="#top">Top</A>

<A NAME="Z"></A>
<P><FONT SIZE=+2>Z</FONT>
<BR><A HREF="webpage.htm">Page Name</A>
<BR><A HREF="webpage.htm">Page Name</A>
<BR><A HREF="#top">Top</A>

<P><HR SIZE=3>
<CENTER>
http://www.globalproductsco.com/contents.htm
<BR>Copyright &copy; 1997 <A HREF="dummy.htm">Global Products
Co.</A>
<BR>Questions and comments to: <A
HREF="mailto:emailname@domain.name">emailname@domain.name</A>
<P><A HREF="dummy.htm"><IMG SRC="back.gif" WIDTH=80 HEIGHT=40
BORDER=0></A> 
<A HREF="dummy.htm"><IMG SRC="forward.gif" WIDTH=80 HEIGHT=40
BORDER=0></A> 
<A HREF="dummy.htm "> <IMG SRC="home.gif" WIDTH=80 HEIGHT=40
BORDER=0></A> 
<A HREF="../contents/contents.htm"> <IMG SRC="contents.gif"
WIDTH=80 HEIGHT=40 BORDER=0></A> 
<A HREF="mailto:emailname@domain.name"> <IMG SRC="email.gif"
WIDTH=80 HEIGHT=40 BORDER=0></A>
<BR><FONT SIZE=-1><A HREF="dummy.htm">Back</A> ||
<A HREF="dummy.htm">Forward</A> ||
<A HREF="dummy.htm">Home</A> ||
<A HREF="../contents/contents.htm">Contents</A> ||
<A HREF="mailto:emailname@domain.name">E-Mail</A></FONT>
</BODY>
</HTML>
```

FIGURE 3.15 Continued

 # Coupon

Given that every consumer enjoys saving money, what better way to encourage sales than with a Coupon? You can use Web coupons (see Figure 3.16) for online sales or to print paper coupons the visitor can use when visiting a store or event or when placing an order by telephone or postal mail.

Online Promotion Tips

These tips will help you adapt this template for your promotions:

- Verify that coupon terms and rules for use comply with all applicable laws and commerce regulations, or clearly state limitations, prerequisites, expiration date, and other conditions for use.

- Add a barcode symbol to the coupon image if appropriate.

FIGURE 3.16 Coupon template.

Presentation Tips

These tips will enhance the presentation of your information in this template (see corresponding callouts in Figure 3.16):

1. This sample coupon is a scan of a printed coupon, saved as a GIF file.

2. Link to an online **Order Form**. Applying the coupon automatically requires a unique order form that is programmed for this purpose; see the template **Coupon Order Form** on the CD-ROM for an example.

3. If the coupon is for a product the visitor can purchase online, include a link to the **Catalog Page** for that product. Remember, the visitor may not view the product information before seeing the coupon (depending on the navigation paths defined in your site).

Development Tips

Figure 3.17 shows the HTML code for the Coupon template. If you create a coupon using a <TABLE> construct the time required to download the page will decrease. However, a scanned coupon image has the advantage of continuity with your printed coupons.

Related templates: Catalog Page (for coupons related to an online purchase)

Alternative templates: None

Navigation guidelines: Consider the role of the coupon in encouraging an online sale, and define the navigation path for the sale process accordingly. To do this, include a link to this Coupon page from a **Catalog Page**, **Brochure**, or **Order Form**.

Advanced implementation and design guidelines: None

```
<HTML><HEAD><TITLE>Coupon Page</TITLE></HEAD>

<BODY BGCOLOR="#ffffff">

<TABLE>
<TR>
<TD NOWRAP>
<IMG SRC="coupban.jpg"  WIDTH=350 HEIGHT=50 ALT="Coupons">
<IMG SRC="catlogo1.jpg " WIDTH=210 HEIGHT=100 ALT="Logo" >
</TD>
</TR>
</TABLE>

<TABLE BORDER=0 CELLPADDING=10 CELLSPACING=10 ALIGN=CENTER>

<TR>
<TD VALIGN=TOP WIDTH=50%>
<FONT SIZE=+1>
<P><A HREF="../order/order.htm"><IMG SRC="bluearrow.gif"
ALIGN=MIDDLE BORDER=0>Order with Coupon</A>
<P><A HREF="../catalog/catitm1.htm"><IMG SRC="bluearrow.gif"
ALIGN=MIDDLE BORDER=0>Catalog Page</A>
<P><A HREF="dummy.htm"><IMG SRC="bluearrow.gif" ALIGN=MIDDLE
BORDER=0>More Promotions</A>
</FONT>
</TD>
<TD WIDTH=50% VALIGN=TOP ALIGN=CENTER>

<P><IMG SRC="coup.gif" WIDTH=200 HEIGHT=290 ALT="Coupon">
<P><A HREF="coupord.htm"><IMG SRC="order.gif" WIDTH=80
HEIGHT=40 BORDER=0 BORDER=0 ALT="Order Now!"></TD>
</TR>
</TABLE>

</A>
</CENTER>


<P><HR SIZE=3>
<CENTER>
http://www.catalogco.com/coupon.htm
<BR>Copyright &copy; 1997 <A HREF="dummy.htm">Everything You
Need Catalog Co.</A>
<BR>Questions and comments to: <A
HREF="mailto:emailname@domain.name">emailname@domain.name</A>
```

FIGURE 3.17 Coupon HTML code.

```
<P><A HREF="dummy.htm"><IMG SRC="back.gif" WIDTH=80 HEIGHT=40
BORDER=0></A> 
<A HREF="dummy.htm"><IMG SRC="forward.gif" WIDTH=80 HEIGHT=40
BORDER=0></A> 
<A HREF="dummy.htm "> <IMG SRC="home.gif" WIDTH=80 HEIGHT=40
BORDER=0></A> 
<A HREF="dummy.htm"> <IMG SRC="contents.gif" WIDTH=80
HEIGHT=40 BORDER=0></A> 
<A HREF="mailto:emailname@domain.name"> <IMG SRC="email.gif"
WIDTH=80 HEIGHT=40 BORDER=0></A>
<BR><FONT SIZE=-1><A HREF="dummy.htm">Back</A> ||
<A HREF="dummy.htm">Forward</A> ||
<A HREF="dummy.htm">Home</A> ||
<A HREF="dummy.htm">Contents</A> ||
<A HREF="mailto:emailname@domain.name">E-Mail</A></FONT>
</BODY>
</HTML>
```

FIGURE 3.17 Continued

 Event Calendar

An Event Calendar (see Figure 3.18) is a convenient way to promote classes, performances, trade shows, and other activities of interest to visitors.

Online Promotion Tips

These tips will help you adapt this template for your promotions:

- Link to a **Coupon** to offer discounted tickets.

- Link to additional pages for event information: **Registration Form**; **Locator**; **Newsletter** with post-event news, photos, wrap-ups, proceedings; speaker handouts with links to the speaker's Web site or a **Profile** page.

- Link to a **Seminar Description** page to present detailed information on courses and workshops.

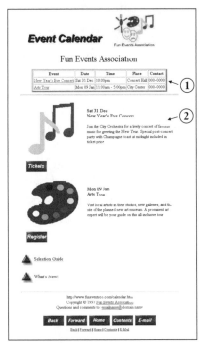

FIGURE 3.18 Event Calendar template.

Presentation Tips

These tips will enhance the presentation of your information in this template (see corresponding callouts in Figure 3.18):

1. Use the table for a quick summary of multiple events within a month, year, or other time period.

2. Use this section to present details on the event. As an alternative, you can link to a separate page that presents an event **Brochure** or **Seminar Description** from its listing in the table.

Development Tips

Figure 3.19 shows the HTML code for the Event Calendar template. These tips will help you with additional development:

1. Use the <TABLE> tag to present event information in a well-organized format.

2. Add action buttons to encourage visitor interaction.

Related templates: Event Registration Form, Brochure (adapt to present event information); Locator (for a map to the venue); Seminar Description

Alternative templates: None

Navigation guidelines: Link to the event description from the event name in the table, or link directly to an **Event Registration Form**.

Advanced implementation and design guidelines: If you have many events, create a monthly or weekly calendar grid, with links on each day when an event is scheduled. These links can lead to this **Event Calendar**, which would present information for only the selected date.

```
<HTML><HEAD><TITLE>Event Calendar</TITLE></HEAD>

<BODY BGCOLOR="#ffffff">

<TABLE>
<TR>
<TD NOWRAP>
<IMG SRC="calban.jpg"  WIDTH=350 HEIGHT=50   ALT="Event
Calendar">
<IMG SRC="fealogo.jpg " ALT="Logo"  WIDTH=154 HEIGHT=122>
</TD>
</TR>
</TABLE>

<CENTER>
<BR><FONT SIZE=+3>Fun Events Association</FONT>
<P>

<TABLE BORDER=5>   ←①
<TR><TH>Event</TH><TH>Date</TH><TH>Time</TH><TH>Place</TH><TH>
Contact</TH></TR>
<TR><TD><A HREF="#newyears">New Year's Eve
Concert</A></TD><TD>Sat 31 Dec</TD><TD>10:00pm </TD>
<TD>Concert Hall</TD><TD>000-0000</TD>
<TR><TD><A HREF="#artstour">Arts Tour</A></TD><TD>Mon 09
Jan</TD><TD>11:00am - 5:00pm</TD><TD>City Center</TD><TD>000-
0000</TD>
<P>
</TABLE>

<HR SIZE=3>

<TABLE BORDER=0 CELLPADDING=10 CELLSPACING=10 ALIGN=CENTER>
<TR>
<TD VALIGN=TOP>
<IMG SRC="music.gif"  WIDTH=184 HEIGHT=194 VALIGN=TOP
ALT="Music Gala!" BORDER=0>
<P><A HREF="../event/eventfrm.htm"><IMG SRC="tickets.gif"
WIDTH=80 HEIGHT=40 BORDER=0></A>
</TD>

<TD VALIGN=TOP>
<FONT SIZE=+1>
<A NAME="newyears"></A>
<P><BR>Sat 31 Dec
```

FIGURE 3.19 Event Calendar HTML code.

```
<BR>New Year's Eve Concert</FONT>
<P>Join the City Orchestra for a lively concert of favorite
music for greeting the New Year. Special post-concert party
with Champagne toast at midnight included in ticket price.
</FONT>
</TD>
</TR>

<TR>

<TD VALIGN=TOP>
<IMG SRC="palette.gif"  WIDTH=200 HEIGHT=166 VALIGN=TOP
ALT="Arts Tour" BORDER=0>
<P><A HREF="../event/eventfrm.htm"><IMG SRC="register.gif"
WIDTH=80 HEIGHT=40 BORDER=0></A>
</TD>

<TD VALIGN=TOP>
<FONT SIZE=+1>
<A NAME="artstour"></A>
<P><BR>Mon 09 Jan
<BR>Arts Tour</FONT>
<P>Visit local artists in their studios, new galleries, and
the site of the planned new art museum. A prominent art
expert will be your guide on this all-inclusive tour.


</FONT>
</TD>
</TR>

</TABLE>

</CENTER>

<FONT SIZE=+1>
<P><A HREF="../guide/guide.htm"><IMG SRC="bluearrow.gif"
WIDTH=49 HEIGHT=46 ALIGN=MIDDLE BORDER=0 ALT="*">Selection
Guide
</A>
<P><A HREF="../whatsnew/whatsnew.htm"><IMG SRC="bluearrow.gif"
WIDTH=49 HEIGHT=46 ALIGN=MIDDLE BORDER=0 ALT="*">What's New!
</A></FONT>
<P><HR SIZE=3>
<CENTER>
```

②

FIGURE 3.19 Continued

```
http://www.funeventsco.com/calendar.htm
<BR>Copyright &copy; 1997 <A HREF="dummy.htm">Fun Events
Association</A>
<BR>Questions and comments to: <A
HREF="mailto:emailname@domain.name">emailname@domain.name</A>
<P><A HREF="dummy.htm"><IMG SRC="back.gif" WIDTH=80 HEIGHT=40
BORDER=0></A> 
<A HREF="dummy.htm"><IMG SRC="forward.gif" WIDTH=80 HEIGHT=40
BORDER=0></A> 
<A HREF="dummy.htm "> <IMG SRC="home.gif" WIDTH=80 HEIGHT=40
BORDER=0></A> 
<A HREF="dummy.htm"> <IMG SRC="contents.gif" WIDTH=80
HEIGHT=40 BORDER=0></A> 
<A HREF="mailto:emailname@domain.name"> <IMG SRC="email.gif"
WIDTH=80 HEIGHT=40 BORDER=0></A>
<BR><FONT SIZE=-1><A HREF="dummy.htm">Back</A> ||
<A HREF="dummy.htm">Forward</A> ||
<A HREF="dummy.htm">Home</A> ||
<A HREF="dummy.htm">Contents</A> ||
<A HREF="mailto:emailname@domain.name">E-Mail</A></FONT>
</BODY>
</HTML>
```

FIGURE 3.19 Continued

Event Registration Form

Use the Event Registration Form template (see Figure 3.20) to accept an online registration or ticket purchase for a class, program, performance, or other event. The template can be adapted for other purposes, such as a restaurant or hotel reservation form or appointment form.

FIGURE 3.20 Event Registration Form template.

Online Promotion Tip

Always provide instructions for submitting the form via fax, postal mail, or telephone for visitors who want to use these methods.

Presentation Tip

If the form is lengthy, place navigation buttons and links at both the top and bottom of the page.

Development Tips

Figure 3.21 presents the HTML code for the Event Registration Form template.

1. Use the <FORM> construct to capture the visitor's registration information. When the visitor clicks the Send button, the browser sends the form to the *mail-form.cgi* script on your Web server. This script invokes an e-mail program on the server to send this information in an e-mail message to any address(es) you specify in the form's hidden variables. The script then returns a "thank you" page (as specified by the filename entered in the VALUE variable) to the browser as a confirmation for the visitor.

   A general-purpose "thank you" page (thnx.htm) is included on the CD-ROM. It displays the text "Thanks from Janice King. Thanks for sending your inquiry. We'll be in touch." You can modify this text to fit your needs, then save the file with the same name or a different name. Remember to change the file directory and name entered for the VALUE field in the form's HTML file so the script will display the correct "thank you" page.

   The purpose of the THNX.HTM file is to confirm to your visitor that the form has been processed successfully. If you leave the mailformURL variable blank, the browser will simply return to the form and the visitor may be confused about whether the form was processed.

```
<HTML><HEAD><TITLE>Event Registration Form</TITLE></HEAD>

<BODY BGCOLOR="#ffffff">
<TABLE>
<TR>
<TD NOWRAP>
<IMG SRC="eventban.jpg"  WIDTH=350 HEIGHT=50  ALT="Event
Calendar">
<IMG SRC="fealogo.jpg " ALT="Logo"  WIDTH=154 HEIGHT=122>
</TD>
</TR>
</TABLE>

<CENTER>
<P>
<FONT SIZE=+3>Fun Events Association</FONT>
</CENTER>
<HR SIZE=3>
Complete all items on this form, then click on Send to sub-
mit. <A HREF="eventfax.htm">
<BR>Click Here</A> if you prefer to fill out the form and
mail or fax it to us.

<FORM ACTION="/cgi-local/mailform.cgi" METHOD="POST">  ← ①, ②
 <INPUT TYPE="hidden" NAME="mailformFromEmail" VALUE="Event
Registrant">
 <INPUT TYPE="hidden" NAME="mailformFromName" VALUE="Event
Registrant">

 <INPUT TYPE="hidden" NAME="mailformToEmail" VALUE="email-
name@domain.name">

 <INPUT TYPE="hidden" NAME="mailformToName" VALUE="Your Name">

 <INPUT TYPE="hidden" NAME="mailformSubject" VALUE="Event
Registration">

 <INPUT TYPE="hidden" NAME="mailformURL"
VALUE="http://www.funeventsco.com/eventthx.htm">

 <INPUT TYPE="hidden" NAME="mailformBcc" VALUE="">


<P>Last Name
<BR><INPUT TYPE="text" NAME="1-lastname" SIZE="20">
 <BR>First Name
```

FIGURE 3.21 Event Registration Form HTML code.

```
<BR><INPUT TYPE="text" NAME="1a-firstname" SIZE="20">
<P>Address
<BR><TEXTAREA NAME="1b-address" ROWS="3" COLS="30"></TEXTAREA>
<P>Phone
<BR><INPUT TYPE="text" NAME="2-phone" SIZE="20">
 <BR>Fax
<BR><INPUT TYPE="text" NAME="3-fax" SIZE="20">
 <P>E-Mail address
<BR><INPUT TYPE="text" NAME="4-email" SIZE="20">

<P>Event Name
<BR><INPUT TYPE="text" NAME="5-eventname" SIZE="40">
<BR>Date(s)
<BR><INPUT TYPE="text" NAME="6-dates" SIZE="15">
<P>Location
<BR><INPUT TYPE="text" NAME="7-location" SIZE="40">
 <BR># Attending
<BR><INPUT TYPE="text" NAME="8-number" SIZE="5">
<P>Comments
<BR><TEXTAREA NAME="9-comments" ROWS="3" COLS="40"></TEXTAREA>


<P><INPUT TYPE="SUBMIT" VALUE="Send"> <INPUT TYPE="RESET"
VALUE="Reset">

 </FORM>


<CENTER>
<FONT SIZE=+1><A HREF="../calendar/calendar.htm">Events
Calendar </A></FONT>


<P>Fun Events Association
<BR>123 Home Page Lane
<BR>Web City, State  Country  Postal Code

<P>Phone: 00 000 000 0000 Toll-Free: 00 000 000 0000
<BR>Fax: 00 000 000 0000
</CENTER>

<P><HR SIZE=3>
<CENTER>
http://www.funeventsco.com/eventfrm.htm
<BR>Copyright &copy; 1997 <A HREF="dummy.htm">Fun Events
Association</A>
```

FIGURE 3.21 Continued

```
<BR>Questions and comments to: <A
HREF="mailto:emailname@domain.name">emailname@domain.name</A>
<P><A HREF="dummy.htm"><IMG SRC="back.gif" WIDTH=80 HEIGHT=40
BORDER=0></A> 
<A HREF="dummy.htm"><IMG SRC="forward.gif" WIDTH=80 HEIGHT=40
BORDER=0></A> 
<A HREF="dummy.htm "> <IMG SRC="home.gif" WIDTH=80 HEIGHT=40
BORDER=0></A> 
<A HREF="dummy.htm"> <IMG SRC="contents.gif" WIDTH=80
HEIGHT=40 BORDER=0></A> 
<A HREF="mailto:emailname@domain.name"> <IMG SRC="email.gif"
WIDTH=80 HEIGHT=40 BORDER=0></A>
<BR><FONT SIZE=-1><A HREF="dummy.htm">Back</A> ||
<A HREF="dummy.htm">Forward</A> ||
<A HREF="dummy.htm">Home</A> ||
<A HREF="dummy.htm">Contents</A> ||
<A HREF="mailto:emailname@domain.name">E-Mail</A></FONT>
</BODY>
</HTML>
```

FIGURE 3.21 Continued

2. A printable version of this form is on the CD-ROM; see the template **Event Registration FAX Form**.

Related templates: Event Calendar
Alternative templates: None
Navigation guidelines: As shown here, always provide a direct link back to the **Event Calendar** or **Brochure** that sent the visitor to this page.

Advanced implementation and design guidelines: Your script can be set up to enter data automatically into selected fields, based on a visitor's choices in previous fields. For example, the script could automatically enter event details if it was programmed to capture the visitor's selection. This automation saves the visitor from needing to enter the information twice.

↳ FAQ Page

One advantage of the World Wide Web is that it can give visitors fast answers to their most common questions about your organization, products, or services. Although a well-structured Web site can help visitors find targeted information quickly, sometimes they need a higher-level perspective or guidance on where to start. A FAQ page (see Figure 3.22) does exactly what its component words imply: it answers Frequently Asked Questions about your site, company, products, events or other topics.

FAQ is an Internet-specific acronym that may have no meaning for your visitors. You may want to use other phrases such as "About XYZ Organization," or "About This Site" in the banner and headline for this page.

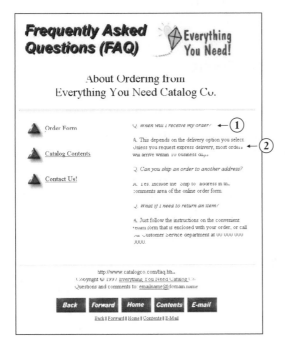

FIGURE 3.22 FAQ Page template.

Online Promotion Tips

These tips will help you adapt this template for your promotions:

- Choose a focus for the FAQ: your company, products, services, or the Web site. If your FAQ list is small, you can cover all of these topics in one document, but group related questions together and identify each group with a subhead.

- Don't try to answer every possible question. Use an e-mail link or the **Product Inquiry Form** to encourage the visitor to contact you with complex or unique questions.

- Keep your answers short. Link to other pages on your site where the visitor can find detailed information about the product or topic.

- Check the content regularly to ensure that it remains current and to add or delete questions based on the inquiries you receive from visitors.

Presentation Tips

These tips will enhance the presentation of your information in this template (see corresponding callouts in Figure 3.22):

1. Use a bold or italic font style to distinguish question text from answer text.

2. If the text is brief, consider using a two-column table, with questions in one column and answers in the other, with one Q & A pair per row.

Development Tips

Figure 3.23 shows the HTML code for the Frequently Asked Questions template.

Related templates: None
Alternative templates: None

Navigation guidelines: Consider adding links at the bottom of the page to move the visitor to the next page in the sales process or navigation path you have defined for the site.

Advanced implementation and design guidelines: None

```
<HTML><HEAD><TITLE>Frequently Asked Questions
Page</TITLE></HEAD>
<BODY BGCOLOR="#ffffff">

<TABLE>
<TR>
<TD NOWRAP>
<IMG SRC="faqban.jpg"  WIDTH=350 HEIGHT=100 ALT="Frequently
Asked Questions">
<IMG SRC="catlogo1.jpg " WIDTH=210 HEIGHT=100 ALT="Logo" >
</TD>
</TR>
</TABLE>

<CENTER>

<BR><FONT SIZE=+3>About Ordering from <BR>Everything You Need
Catalog Co.</FONT>
</CENTER>
<BR><HR SIZE=3 >

<TABLE BORDER=0 CELLPADDING=10 CELLSPACING=10 ALIGN=CENTER>

<TR>
<TD VALIGN=TOP WIDTH=40%>
<FONT SIZE=+1>
<P><A HREF="../order/order.htm"><IMG SRC="bluearrow.gif"
ALIGN=MIDDLE BORDER=0>Order Form</A>
<P><A HREF="../catalog/catalog.htm"><IMG SRC="bluearrow.gif"
ALIGN=MIDDLE BORDER=0>Catalog Contents</A>
<P><A HREF="mailto:emailname@domain.name"><IMG SRC="bluear-
row.gif" ALIGN=MIDDLE BORDER=0>Contact Us!</A>

</FONT>
</TD>
<TD VALIGN=TOP WIDTH=60%>
```

FIGURE 3.23 FAQ Page HTML code.

```
<P>Q. <I>When will I receive my order?</I>
<P>A. This depends on the delivery option you select. Unless
you request express delivery, most orders will arrive within
10 business days.


<P>Q. <I>Can you ship an order to another address?</I>

<P>A. Yes. Include the "Ship to" address in the comments area
of the online order form.


<P>Q. <I>What if I need to return an item?</I>

<P>A. Just follow the instructions on the convenient return
form that is enclosed with your order, or call our Customer
Service department at 00 000 000 0000.

</TD>
</TR>
</TABLE>
<BR><P>
<P><HR SIZE=3>
<CENTER>
http://www.catalogco.com/faq.htm
<BR>Copyright &copy; 1997 <A HREF="dummy.htm">Everything You
Need Catalog Co.</A>
<BR>Questions and comments to: <A
HREF="mailto:emailname@domain.name">emailname@domain.name</A>
<P><A HREF="dummy.htm"><IMG SRC="back.gif" WIDTH=80 HEIGHT=40
BORDER=0></A> 
<A HREF="dummy.htm"><IMG SRC="forward.gif" WIDTH=80 HEIGHT=40
BORDER=0></A> 
<A HREF="dummy.htm "> <IMG SRC="home.gif" WIDTH=80 HEIGHT=40
BORDER=0></A> 
<A HREF="dummy.htm"> <IMG SRC="contents.gif" WIDTH=80
HEIGHT=40 BORDER=0></A> 
<A HREF="mailto:emailname@domain.name"> <IMG SRC="email.gif"
WIDTH=80 HEIGHT=40 BORDER=0></A>
<BR><FONT SIZE=-1><A HREF="dummy.htm">Back</A> ||
<A HREF="dummy.htm">Forward</A> ||
<A HREF="dummy.htm">Home</A> ||
<A HREF="dummy.htm">Contents</A> ||
<A HREF="mailto:emailname@domain.name">E-Mail</A></FONT>
</BODY>
</HTML>
```

FIGURE 3.23 Continued

 Locator

The Locator template (see Figure 3.24) can guide visitors to a nearby retail store, dealer, program office, service center, or other facility.

Online Promotion Tip

Organize the content consistently to help visitors find the information quickly.

Presentation Tip

The table simplifies your tasks for creating and maintaining this information.

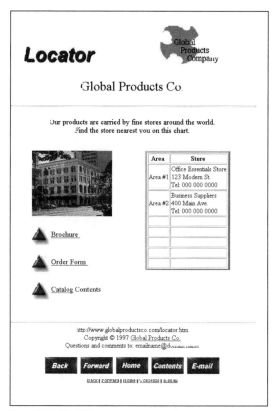

FIGURE 3.24 Locator template.

Development Tips

See Figure 3.25 for the HTML code for the Locator template.

Use the <TABLE> tag to organize your location information in an easily readable format.

Related templates: Company Profile

Alternative templates: None

Navigation guidelines: Link to this page from the home page, a **Catalog Page**, or **Company Profile** page.

Advanced implementation and design guidelines: If you have numerous locations spread across a broad geographical area, you may want to create a separate page that presents a graphical map to target the visitor's region or town. From that page, create a link to this Locator page that leads directly to the section with locations in that area (see the discussion of geographic maps in Chapters 10 and 11).

```
<HTML><HEAD><TITLE>Locator Page</TITLE></HEAD>

<BODY BGCOLOR="#ffffff">


<TABLE>
<TR>
<TD NOWRAP>
<IMG SRC="locban.jpg" WIDTH=350 HEIGHT=50  ALT="Locator ">
<IMG SRC="glblogo.jpg " ALT="Logo" WIDTH=154 HEIGHT=122>
</TD>
</TR>
</TABLE>


<CENTER>
<BR>
<FONT SIZE=+3>Global Products Co.</FONT>
<P>
<HR SIZE=3>
<BR><FONT SIZE=+1>Our products are carried by fine stores
around the world. <BR>Find the store nearest you on this
chart.</FONT>
<P>

<TABLE BORDER=0 CELLPADDING=10 CELLSPACING=10 ALIGN=CENTER
WIDTH=90%>
<TR>
<TD VALIGN=TOP WIDTH=50%>

<IMG SRC="store.jpg"  WIDTH=200 HEIGHT=160 VALIGN=TOP
ALT="Storefront" BORDER=0></A>

<FONT SIZE=+1>

<P><A HREF="../brochure/brochure.htm"><IMG SRC="bluearrow.gif"
WIDTH=49 HEIGHT=46 ALIGN=MIDDLE BORDER=0 ALT="*">Brochure
<P><A HREF="../order/order.htm"><IMG SRC="bluearrow.gif"
WIDTH=49 HEIGHT=46 ALIGN=MIDDLE BORDER=0 ALT="*">Order Form
<P><A HREF="../catalog/catalog.htm"><IMG SRC="bluearrow.gif"
WIDTH=49 HEIGHT=46 ALIGN=MIDDLE BORDER=0 ALT="*">Catalog
Contents

</FONT>
</TD>
```

FIGURE 3.25 Locator HTML code.

```
<TD VALIGN=TOP WIDTH=50%>
<TABLE BORDER=5 ><TR><TH><B>Area </B></TH> <TH>Store
</TH></TR>
<TR><TD  >Area #1</TD><TD>Office Essentials Store<BR>123
Modern St.<BR>Tel: 000 000 0000</TD>
<TR><TD  >Area #2</TD><TD>Business Suppliers<BR>400 Main
Ave.<BR>Tel: 000 000 0000</TD>
<TR><TD> </TD><TD> </TD></TR>
<TR><TD> </TD><TD> </TD></TR>
<TR><TD> </TD><TD> </TD></TR>
<TR><TD> </TD><TD> </TD></TR>
<TR><TD> </TD><TD> </TD></TR>
</TABLE>

</TD>
</TR>
</TABLE>

</CENTER>

<P><HR SIZE=3>
<CENTER>
http://www.globalproductsco.com/locator.htm
<BR>Copyright &copy; 1997 <A HREF="dummy.htm">Global Products
Co.</A>
<BR>Questions and comments to: <A
HREF="mailto:emailname@domain.name">emailname@domain.name</A>
<P><A HREF="dummy.htm"><IMG SRC="back.gif" WIDTH=80 HEIGHT=40
BORDER=0></A> 
<A HREF="dummy.htm"><IMG SRC="forward.gif" WIDTH=80 HEIGHT=40
BORDER=0></A> 
<A HREF="dummy.htm "> <IMG SRC="home.gif" WIDTH=80 HEIGHT=40
BORDER=0></A> 
<A HREF="../contents/contents.htm"> <IMG SRC="contents.gif"
WIDTH=80 HEIGHT=40 BORDER=0></A> 
<A HREF="mailto:emailname@domain.name"> <IMG SRC="email.gif"
WIDTH=80 HEIGHT=40 BORDER=0></A>
<BR><FONT SIZE=-1><A HREF="dummy.htm">Back</A> ||
<A HREF="dummy.htm">Forward</A> ||
<A HREF="dummy.htm">Home</A> ||
<A HREF="../contents/contents.htm">Contents</A> ||
<A HREF="mailto:emailname@domain.name">E-Mail</A></FONT>
</BODY>
</HTML>
```

FIGURE 3.25 Continued

↳ Newsletter

Use the Newsletter template (see Figure 3.26) to present a complete online edition on a single Web page. This template also can serve as a Contents or Front Page that links to individual articles that are implemented on separate pages using the **Article** template.

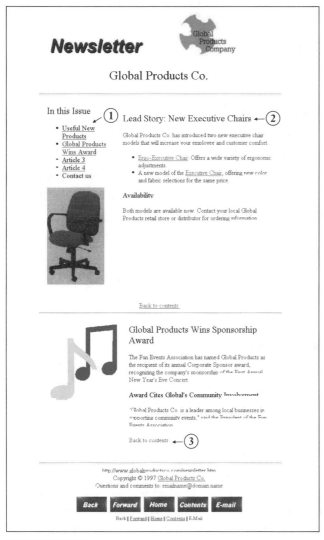

FIGURE 3.26 Newsletter template.

Online Promotion Tips

These tips will help you adapt this template for your promotions:

- Adapt your print newsletter for this Web page, or create a separate online edition.

- Link to pages that present more information on any product, people, or organizations mentioned in an **Article**. These links can be embedded in the text or images.

- Link to a glossary page for any words that may be unfamiliar to visitors.

Presentation Tips

These tips will enhance the presentation of your information in this template (see corresponding callouts in Figure 3.26):

1. List links to all articles, even if they are placed on the same page. This gives the visitor a fast way to jump to the topic of interest.

2. Use consistent headlines and text styles for presenting articles.

3. Give visitors a quick way to return to the "In This Issue" list.

Development Tips

See Figure 3.27 for the HTML code for the Newsletter template.

At the top of the front page, build an index of links to each article in the newsletter. The links can lead to articles within the same page or on multiple pages.

Related templates: Article

Alternative templates: None

Navigation guidelines: Choose whether you want to place the complete newsletter on a single Web page for fast loading, or place the articles on individual pages if they are lengthy and include many images. In this case, use the

Newsletter template to display a Table of Contents or "front page" with links to the articles.

Advanced implementation and design guidelines: None

```
<HTML><HEAD><TITLE>Newsletter Page</TITLE></HEAD>

<BODY BGCOLOR="#ffffff">


<TABLE>
<TR>
<TD NOWRAP>
<IMG SRC="newsban.jpg" WIDTH=350 HEIGHT=50  ALT="Newsletter">
<IMG SRC="glblogo.jpg " ALT="Logo" WIDTH=154 HEIGHT=122>
</TD>
</TR>
</TABLE>


<CENTER>

<BR>
<FONT SIZE=+3>Global Products Co.</FONT>
<P>
<HR SIZE=3>


<TABLE BORDER=0 CELLPADDING=10 CELLSPACING=10 ALIGN=CENTER
WIDTH=100%>
<TR>
<TD VALIGN=TOP WIDTH=30%>

<A NAME="top"></A>
<P><FONT SIZE=+2>In this Issue</FONT>
<FONT SIZE=+1>
<UL>
<LI> <A HREF="#article1">Useful New Products</A>
<LI> <A HREF="#article2">Global Products Wins Award</A>
<LI><A HREF="#article3"> Article 3</A>
<LI><A HREF="#article4"> Article 4</A>
<LI> <A HREF="mailto:emailname@domain.name">Contact us</A>
</UL>
</FONT>

<IMG SRC="chair.gif"  WIDTH=151 HEIGHT=246 VALIGN=TOP
ALT="Chair Photo" BORDER=0>
```

FIGURE 3.27 Newsletter HTML code.

```
</TD>
<TD WIDTH=70% VALIGN=TOP>

<A NAME="article1"></A>
<BR><FONT SIZE=+2>Lead Story: New Executive Chairs</FONT>

<P>
Global Products Co. has introduced two new executive chair
models that will increase your employee and customer comfort.
<UL>

<LI><A HREF="../pricelst/pricelst.htm"> Ergo-Executive
Chair</A>: Offers a wide variety of ergonomic adjustments.
<LI> A new model of the <A HREF="../pricelst/pricelst.htm">
Executive Chair</A>, offering new color and fabric selections
for the same price.
</UL>

<P><FONT SIZE=+1>Availability</FONT>

<P>Both models are available now. Contact your local Global
Products retail store or distributor for ordering informa-
tion.

</TD>
</TR>
</TABLE>

<P><A HREF="#top">Back to contents
</A>
<HR SIZE=3>
<A NAME="article2"></A>

<TABLE BORDER=0 CELLPADDING=10 CELLSPACING=10 ALIGN=CENTER
WIDTH=100%>
<TR>
<TD VALIGN=TOP WIDTH=30%>

<IMG SRC="music.gif"  WIDTH=184 HEIGHT=194 VALIGN=TOP
ALT="Music Gala!" BORDER=0>

</TD>
<TD VALIGN=TOP WIDTH=70%
<BR><FONT SIZE=+2>Global Products Wins Sponsorship
Award</FONT>
```

FIGURE 3.27 Continued

```
<P>The Fun Events Association has named Global Products as
the recipient of its annual Corporate Sponsor award, recog-
nizing the company's sponsorship of the First Annual<A
HREF="../calendar/calendar.htm#newyears"> New Year's Eve
Concert</A>.

<P><FONT SIZE=+1>Award Cites Global's Community
Involvement</FONT>

<P>"Global Products Co. is a leader among local businesses in
supporting community events," said the President of the Fun
Events Association.

<P><A HREF="#top">Back to contents</A>

</TD>
</TR>
</TABLE>

<P><HR SIZE=3>
<CENTER>
http://www.globalproductsco.com/newsletter.htm
<BR>Copyright &copy; 1997 <A HREF="dummy.htm">Global Products
Co.</A>
<BR>Questions and comments to: <A
HREF="mailto:emailname@domain.name">emailname@domain.name</A>
<P><A HREF="dummy.htm"><IMG SRC="back.gif" WIDTH=80 HEIGHT=40
BORDER=0></A> 
<A HREF="dummy.htm"><IMG SRC="forward.gif" WIDTH=80 HEIGHT=40
BORDER=0></A> 
<A HREF="dummy.htm "> <IMG SRC="home.gif" WIDTH=80 HEIGHT=40
BORDER=0></A> 
<A HREF="../contents/contents.htm"> <IMG SRC="contents.gif"
WIDTH=80 HEIGHT=40 BORDER=0></A> 
<A HREF="mailto:emailname@domain.name"> <IMG SRC="email.gif"
WIDTH=80 HEIGHT=40 BORDER=0></A>
<BR><FONT SIZE=-1><A HREF="dummy.htm">Back</A> ||
<A HREF="dummy.htm">Forward</A> ||
<A HREF="dummy.htm">Home</A> ||
<A HREF="../contents/contents.htm">Contents</A> ||
<A HREF="mailto:emailname@domain.name">E-Mail</A></FONT>
</BODY>
</HTML>
```

FIGURE 3.27 Continued

 Press Release

Press Releases on a Web site are a convenient way to inform visitors about new developments in your company or organization. An online archive of previous releases, backgrounders, and other documents also provides a useful resource for journalists. See Figure 3.28.

Online Promotion Tips

These tips will help you adapt this template for your promotions:

- Link to pages that present more information on any product, people, or organizations mentioned in the

FIGURE 3.28 Press Release template.

press release. These links can be embedded in the text or images.

- Link to a glossary page for any words that may be unfamiliar and to a **FAQ** page as a convenience for visitors.

- Create a "Media Contacts" page listing the name, telephone number(s), and e-mail address (create an e-mail link) for each public relations representative for your organization, grouping the contacts by department, location, or subject expertise.

Presentation Tips

These tips will enhance the presentation of your information in this template (see corresponding callouts in Figure 3.28):

1. One advantage of an online press release is that you can include a photograph, illustration, or audio or video clip related to the subject.

2. This example follows the most commonly used structure for press releases.

Development Tips

Figure 3.29 lists the HTML code for the Press Release template.

Related templates: FAQ Page

Alternative templates: None

Navigation guidelines: Link to a **Contents** page for a News Release archive section, if you maintain this on your site.

Advanced implementation and design guidelines: None

```
<HTML><HEAD><TITLE>Press Release</TITLE></HEAD>

<BODY BGCOLOR="#ffffff">

<TABLE>
<TR>
<TD NOWRAP>
<IMG SRC="pressban.jpg"  WIDTH=350 HEIGHT=50 ALT="Press
Release">
<IMG SRC="fealogo.jpg " ALT="Logo"  WIDTH=154 HEIGHT=122>
</TD>
</TR>
</TABLE>

<BR>
<CENTER>
<FONT SIZE=+3>Fun Events Association</FONT>
</CENTER>
<HR SIZE=3>

<TABLE BORDER=0 CELLPADDING=5 CELLSPACING=5 ALIGN=CENTER>
<TR>
<TD VALIGN=TOP>
<IMG SRC="pressrel.gif"  WIDTH=300 HEIGHT=190 VALIGN=TOP
ALT="Music Gala!" BORDER=0>

<BR>01 December
<BR>FOR IMMEDIATE RELEASE

<P>Media Contact: <BR>
<BR>Event Planner,
<BR>Tel: 00 000 000 0000
<BR><A
HREF="mailto:emailname@domain.name">emailname@domain.name</A>

<FONT SIZE=+1>
<P><A HREF="../calendar/calendar.htm"><IMG SRC="bluearrow.gif"
ALIGN=MIDDLE BORDER=0>Event Calendar</A>
<P><A HREF="../whatsnew/whatsnew.htm"><IMG SRC="bluearrow.gif"
ALIGN=MIDDLE BORDER=0>What's New?</A>
</FONT>

<TD>
<TD VALIGN=TOP >
<P>
<CENTER>
<FONT SIZE=+1>Fun Events Association Announces First Annual
New Year's Eve Concert</FONT>
<BR><I>City Orchestra Joins the Party</I>
```

FIGURE 3.29 Press Release HTML code.

```
</CENTER>

<P>Web City,  01 December  — Fun Events Association today
announced that it will sponsor the first annual New Year's
Eve Concert and Party, to be held 31 December, beginning at
10:00 pm in the Concert Hall. City Orchestra will perform
favorite music for greeting the New Year. A special post-con-
cert party with Champagne toast at midnight is included in
ticket price.

<P><B>Benefits City Orchestra</B>

<P>A portion of the ticket price will go toward the school
performance fund for City Orchestra. This fund subsidizes the
expense of sending Orchestra members to perform free concerts
and lecture programs in local schools.
</TD>
</TR>
</TABLE>
<CENTER>
<P><BR># # #
</CENTER>

<P><HR SIZE=3>
<CENTER>
http://www.funeventsco.com/pressrel.htm
<BR>Copyright &copy; 1997 <A HREF="dummy.htm">Fun Events
Association</A>
<BR>Questions and comments to: <A
HREF="mailto:emailname@domain.name">emailname@domain.name</A>
<P><A HREF="dummy.htm"><IMG SRC="back.gif" WIDTH=80 HEIGHT=40
BORDER=0></A> 
<A HREF="dummy.htm"><IMG SRC="forward.gif" WIDTH=80 HEIGHT=40
BORDER=0></A> 
<A HREF="dummy.htm "> <IMG SRC="home.gif" WIDTH=80 HEIGHT=40
BORDER=0></A> 
<A HREF="dummy.htm"> <IMG SRC="contents.gif" WIDTH=80
HEIGHT=40 BORDER=0></A> 
<A HREF="mailto:emailname@domain.name"> <IMG SRC="email.gif"
WIDTH=80 HEIGHT=40 BORDER=0></A>
<BR><FONT SIZE=-1><A HREF="dummy.htm">Back</A> ||
<A HREF="dummy.htm">Forward</A> ||
<A HREF="dummy.htm">Home</A> ||
<A HREF="dummy.htm">Contents</A> ||
<A HREF="mailto:emailname@domain.name">E-Mail</A></FONT>
</BODY>
</HTML>
```

FIGURE 3.29 Continued

 Price/Parts Lists

The Price/Parts List template (see Figure 3.30) is designed to present pricing and ordering details separately from a brochure or catalog page. In turn, links on the product name allow visitors to navigate to a **Brochure** or **Catalog Page** to view more information on the product.

Online Promotion Tips

These tips will help you adapt this template for your promotions:

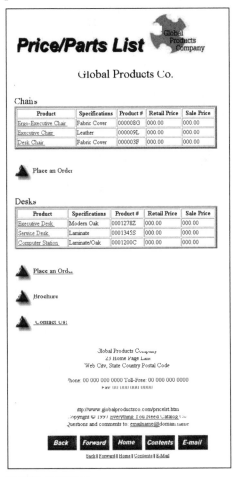

FIGURE 3.30 Price/Parts List template.

- Use this template to give frequent visitors to your site a convenient way to locate product data if they know what they want or know only a product number.

- Specify the currency for all prices.

Presentation Tip

The table can be adapted to present other types of product or pricing information by changing the column headings and table content.

Development Tips

See Figure 3.31 for a listing of the HTML code for the Price/Parts List template.

Use the <TABLE> tag to organize your product information in a readable format. Each table entry can be a link to an individual **Brochure** or **Catalog** page.

Related templates: Brochure, Catalog Page

Alternative templates: None

Navigation guidelines: Link to a **Brochure** page or **Catalog Page** from the product name

Advanced implementation and design guidelines: None

```
<HTML><HEAD><TITLE>Price/Parts List Page</TITLE></HEAD>

<BODY BGCOLOR="#ffffff">

<TABLE>
<TR>
<TD NOWRAP>
<IMG SRC="priceban.jpg" WIDTH=350 HEIGHT=50  ALT="Price/Parts
List">
<IMG SRC="glblogo.jpg " ALT="Logo" WIDTH=154 HEIGHT=122>
</TD>
</TR>
</TABLE>

<CENTER>
<BR>
```

FIGURE 3.31 Price/Parts List HTML code.

```
<FONT SIZE=+3>Global Products Co.</FONT>
</CENTER>

<HR SIZE=3>
<A NAME="chairs"></A>
<P><FONT SIZE=+2>Chairs</FONT>

<TABLE BORDER=5
WIDTH=90%><TR><TH>Product</TH><TH>Specifications</TH><TH>
Product #</TH><TH>Retail Price</TH><TH>Sale Price</TH></TR>
<TR><TD><A HREF="../order/order.htm">Ergo-Executive Chair
</A></TD><TD>Fabric Cover</TD><TD>000008G</TD><TD>000.00</TD>
<TD>000.00</TD> </TR>
<TR><TD><A HREF="../order/order.htm">Executive Chair </A></TD>
<TD>Leather </TD><TD>000009L </TD><TD>000.00 </TD><TD>000.00
</TD></TR>
<TR><TD><A HREF="../order/order.htm">Desk Chair </A></TD>
<TD>Fabric Cover </TD><TD>000003F </TD><TD>000.00
</TD><TD>000.00 </TD></TR>

</TABLE>

<P><BR><FONT SIZE="+1">
<A HREF="../order/order.htm"><IMG SRC="bluearrow.gif"
ALIGN=MIDDLE BORDER=0>Place an Order</A>
</FONT>

<A NAME="desks"></A>
<P><BR><FONT SIZE=+2>Desks</FONT>

<TABLE BORDER=5
WIDTH=90%><TR><TH>Product</TH><TH>Specifications</TH><TH>
Product #</TH><TH>Retail Price</TH><TH>Sale Price</TH></TR>
<TR><TD><A HREF="../order/order.htm">Executive Desk </A></TD>
<TD>Modern Oak </TD><TD>0001278Z </TD><TD>000.00
</TD><TD>000.00 </TD></TR>
<TR><TD><A HREF="../order/order.htm">Service Desk </A></TD>
<TD>Laminate </TD><TD>0001345S </TD><TD>000.00 </TD><TD>000.00
</TD></TR>
<TR><TD><A HREF="../order/order.htm">Computer Station
</A></TD> <TD>Laminate/Oak </TD><TD>0001200C </TD><TD>000.00
</TD><TD>000.00 </TD></TR>
</TABLE>

<P><BR><FONT SIZE="+1">
```

FIGURE 3.31 Continued

```
<A HREF="../order/order.htm"><IMG SRC="bluearrow.gif"
ALIGN=MIDDLE BORDER=0>Place an Order</A>
<P><A HREF="../brochure/brochure.htm"><IMG SRC="bluearrow.gif"
ALIGN=MIDDLE BORDER=0>Brochure</A>
<P><A HREF="mailto:emailname@domain.name"><IMG SRC="bluear-
row.gif" ALIGN=MIDDLE BORDER=0> Contact Us!</A>
</FONT>

<CENTER>

<P><BR>                    Global Products Company
<BR>                       123 Home Page Lane
<BR>                       Web City, State Country Postal Code
<P>                        Phone: 00 000 000 0000
                           Toll-Free: 00 000 000 0000
<BR>                       Fax: 00 000 000 0000

<P><HR SIZE=3>

http://www.globalproductsco.com/pricelst.htm
<BR>Copyright &copy; 1997 <A HREF="dummy.htm">Everything You
Need Catalog Co.</A>
<BR>Questions and comments to: <A
HREF="mailto:emailname@domain.name">emailname@domain.name</A>
<P><A HREF="dummy.htm"><IMG SRC="back.gif" WIDTH=80 HEIGHT=40
BORDER=0></A> 
<A HREF="dummy.htm"><IMG SRC="forward.gif" WIDTH=80 HEIGHT=40
BORDER=0></A> 
<A HREF="dummy.htm "> <IMG SRC="home.gif" WIDTH=80 HEIGHT=40
BORDER=0></A> 
<A HREF="../contents/contents.htm"> <IMG SRC="contents.gif"
WIDTH=80 HEIGHT=40 BORDER=0></A> 
<A HREF="mailto:emailname@domain.name"> <IMG SRC="email.gif"
WIDTH=80 HEIGHT=40 BORDER=0></A>
<BR><FONT SIZE=-1><A HREF="dummy.htm">Back</A> ||
<A HREF="dummy.htm">Forward</A> ||
<A HREF="dummy.htm">Home</A> ||
<A HREF="../contents/contents.htm">Contents</A> ||
<A HREF="mailto:emailname@domain.name">E-Mail</A></FONT>
</BODY>
</HTML>
```

FIGURE 3.31 Continued

 # Product Inquiry Form

Sometimes visitors to your site will not find exactly the product or information they seek. A Product Inquiry Form (see Figure 3.32) gives these visitors an easy way to send you

---

Product Inquiry

Global Products Co.

Complete all items on this form, then click on Send to submit.
Click the Print button on your browser if you want to keep a copy of this form for your records.

Last Name

First Name

Address

Phone

Fax

E-Mail address

I currently use Global products ⊙ Yes ○ No

Product type

Price range

Other specifications

Do you prefer response by ⊙ Email ○ Phone ○ Fax

Would you like to receive e-mail notification
of new products and services? ⊙ Yes ○ No

[Send] [Reset]

Global Products Company
123 Home Page Lane
Web City, State Country Postal Code

Phone: 00 000 000 0000 Toll-Free: 00 000 000 0000
Fax: 00 000 000 0000

emailname@domain name

http://www.globalproductsco.com/inquiry.htm
Copyright © 1997 Global Products Co.
Questions and comments to: emailname@domain.name

[Back] [Forward] [Home] [Contents] [E-mail]
Back ‖ Forward ‖ Home ‖ Contents ‖ E-Mail

FIGURE 3.32 Product Inquiry Form template.

a question, with enough information to help you return a prompt and targeted response.

Online Promotion Tip

Ask all the questions you need in order to return a quality response, but avoid asking too many. It is better to initiate a dialogue with the visitor at this point, one that may involve the exchange of multiple e-mail messages. If you ask too many questions with this initial contact, the visitor may not send the inquiry at all.

Presentation Tips

This form can be adapted to almost any type of product or service. Just add or change the questions.

Development Tips

See Figure 3.33 for a listing of the HTML code for the Product Inquiry Form template.

These tips will help you with additional development:

1. Any of these questions can be adapted to use any of the input formats available on forms: check boxes, radio buttons, pull-down lists, and blanks for text entry.

2. Use the <FORM> construct to capture the visitor's input. When the visitor clicks the Send button, the browser sends the form to the *mailform.cgi* script on your Web server. This script invokes an e-mail program on the server to send this information in an e-mail message to any address(es) you specify in the form's hidden variables. The script then returns a "thank you" page (as specified by the filename entered in the VALUE variable) to the browser as a confirmation for the visitor.

   A general-purpose "thank you" page (THNX.HTM) is included on the CD-ROM. It displays the text "Thanks from Janice King. Thanks for sending your inquiry. We'll be in touch". You can modify this text to fit your needs, then save the file with the same name or

```
<HTML><HEAD><TITLE>Product Inquiry Form</TITLE></HEAD>
<BODY BGCOLOR="#ffffff">

<TABLE>
<TR>
<TD NOWRAP>
<IMG SRC="inqban.jpg" WIDTH=350 HEIGHT=50  ALT="Product
Inquiry">
<IMG SRC="glblogo.jpg " ALT="Logo" WIDTH=154 HEIGHT=122>
</TD>
</TR>
</TABLE>

<CENTER>
<BR><FONT SIZE=+3>Global Products Co.</FONT>
</CENTER>

<HR SIZE=3>
Complete all items on this form, then click on Send to sub-
mit. <BR>Click the Print button on your browser if you want
to keep a copy of this form for your records.
<P>
<FORM ACTION="/cgi-local/mailform.cgi" METHOD="POST">  ←②
 <INPUT TYPE="hidden" NAME="mailformFromEmail" VALUE"Product
Inquiry">
 <INPUT TYPE="hidden" NAME="mailformFromName" VALUE="Potential
Customer">

 <INPUT TYPE="hidden" NAME="mailformToEmail" VALUE="email-
name@domain.name">

 <INPUT TYPE="hidden" NAME="mailformToName" VALUE="Your Name">

 <INPUT TYPE="hidden" NAME="mailformSubject" VALUE="Product
Inquiry">

 <INPUT TYPE="hidden" NAME="mailformURL"
VALUE="http://www.globalproductsco.com/inqthx.htm ">

 <INPUT TYPE="hidden" NAME="mailformBcc" VALUE="">

                    ①
<P>Last Name                 ↙
<BR><INPUT TYPE="text" NAME="1-lastname" SIZE="20">
<BR>First Name
<BR><INPUT TYPE="text" NAME="1a-firstname" SIZE="20">
```

FIGURE 3.33 Product Inquiry Form HTML code.

```
<P> Address
<BR><TEXTAREA NAME="1b-address" ROWS="3" COLS="30"></TEXTAREA>
<P>Phone
<BR><INPUT TYPE="text" NAME="3-phone" SIZE="15">
<BR>Fax
<BR> <INPUT TYPE="text" NAME="4-fax" SIZE="15">
<P>E-Mail address
<BR> <INPUT TYPE="text" NAME="4-email" SIZE="20">

<P>I currently use Global products
<INPUT TYPE=RADIO NAME="5-UseProducts" VALUE="Yes" CHECKED>
Yes
<INPUT TYPE=RADIO NAME="5-UseProducts" VALUE="No"> No

<P>Product type
<BR> <INPUT TYPE="text" NAME="6-ProductType" SIZE="40">
<P>Price range
<BR><INPUT TYPE="text" NAME="7-PriceRange" SIZE="20">
<P>Other specifications
<BR> <TEXTAREA NAME="8-OtherSpecs" ROWS="3"
COLS="30"></TEXTAREA>
<P>Do you prefer response by
<INPUT TYPE=RADIO NAME="9-Response" VALUE="Email"
CHECKED>Email
<INPUT TYPE=RADIO NAME="9-Response" VALUE="Phone">Phone
<INPUT TYPE=RADIO NAME="9-Response" VALUE="Phone">Fax

<P>Would you like to receive e-mail notification <BR>of new
products and services?
<INPUT TYPE=RADIO NAME="a-EmailNotice" VALUE="Yes" CHECKED>
Yes
<INPUT TYPE=RADIO NAME="a-EmailNotice" VALUE="No"> No

<P><INPUT TYPE="SUBMIT" VALUE="Send"> <INPUT TYPE="RESET"
VALUE="Reset">

</FORM>

<CENTER>
<P>                    Global Products Company
<BR>                   123 Home Page Lane
<BR>                   Web City, State Country Postal Code
<P>                    Phone: 00 000 000 0000
                       Toll-Free: 00 000 000 0000
<BR>                   Fax: 00 000 000 0000
<P><A HREF="mailto:emailname@domain.name">emailname@
```

FIGURE 3.33 Continued

```
domain.name</A>
</CENTER>

<P><HR SIZE=3>
<CENTER>
http://www.globalproductsco.com/inquiry.htm
<BR>Copyright &copy; 1997 <A HREF="dummy.htm">Global Products
Co.</A>
<BR>Questions and comments to: <A
HREF="mailto:emailname@domain.name">emailname@domain.name</A>
<P><A HREF="dummy.htm"><IMG SRC="back.gif" WIDTH=80 HEIGHT=40
BORDER=0></A> 
<A HREF="dummy.htm"><IMG SRC="forward.gif" WIDTH=80 HEIGHT=40
BORDER=0></A> 
<A HREF="dummy.htm "> <IMG SRC="home.gif" WIDTH=80 HEIGHT=40
BORDER=0></A> 
<A HREF="../contents/contents.htm"> <IMG SRC="contents.gif"
WIDTH=80 HEIGHT=40 BORDER=0></A> 
<A HREF="mailto:emailname@domain.name"> <IMG SRC="email.gif"
WIDTH=80 HEIGHT=40 BORDER=0></A>
<BR><FONT SIZE=-1><A HREF="dummy.htm">Back</A> ||
<A HREF="dummy.htm">Forward</A> ||
<A HREF="dummy.htm">Home</A> ||
<A HREF="../contents/contents.htm">Contents</A> ||
<A HREF="mailto:emailname@domain.name">E-Mail</A></FONT>
</BODY>
</HTML>
```

FIGURE 3.33 Continued

a different name. Remember to change the file directory and name entered for the VALUE field in the form's HTML file so the script will display the correct "thank you" page. The purpose of the THNX.HTM file is to confirm to your visitor that the form has been processed successfully. If you leave the mailformURL variable blank, the browser will simply return to the form and the visitor may be confused about whether the form was processed.

Related templates: None
Alternative templates: None

Navigation guidelines: You may want to write a different script to return the visitor to a **Brochure**, **Catalog**, or home page after this form has been processed.

Advanced implementation and design guidelines: None

 # Product Order Form

The Order Form template (see Figure 3.34) provides a basic order form that visitors can use to make online purchases from your Web site. The visitor must complete all information, including product data and prices.

Online Promotion Tips

These tips will help you adapt this template for your promotions:

- This form offers the familiarity of printed order forms in catalogs.

- Place shipping information on this form or on a separate page with a link.

- Add a box to the form to allow a visitor to request gift wrapping or a gift card.

Presentation Tip

You can adapt any or all elements on this form as necessary to match your ordering procedures and information requirements or to comply with local commerce laws.

Development Tips

Figure 3.35 lists the HTML code for the Product Order Form template.

Use the <FORM> construct to capture the visitor's input. When the visitor clicks the Send button, the browser sends the form to the *mailform.cgi* script on your Web server. This script invokes an e-mail program on the server to send this information in an e-mail message to any address(es) you specify in the form's hidden variables. The script then returns a "thank you" page (as specified by the filename entered in the VALUE variable) to the browser as a confirmation for the visitor.

A general-purpose "thank you" page (THNX.HTM) is included on the CD-ROM. It displays the text "Thanks from

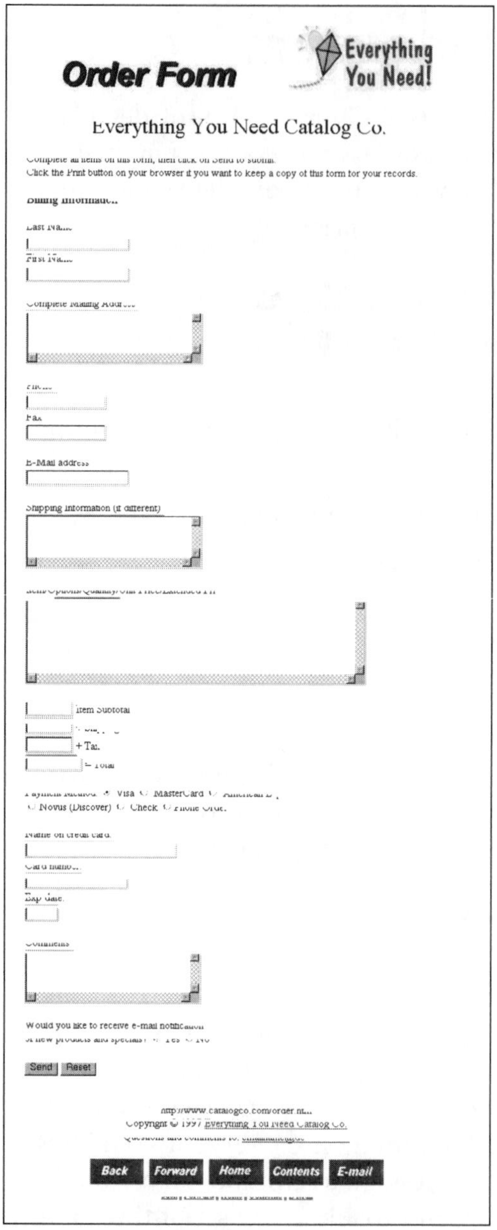

FIGURE 3.34 Product Order Form template.

```
<HTML><HEAD><TITLE>Order Form</TITLE></HEAD>
<BODY BGCOLOR="#ffffff">

<CENTER>

<TABLE>
<TR>
<TD NOWRAP>
<IMG SRC="orderban.jpg"  WIDTH=350 HEIGHT=50 ALT="Order Form">
<IMG SRC="catlogo1.jpg " WIDTH=210 HEIGHT=100 ALT="Logo" >
</TD>
</TR>
</TABLE>

<BR><FONT SIZE=+3>Everything You Need Catalog Co.</FONT>
</CENTER>
<HR SIZE=3>
Complete all items on this form, then click on Send to sub-
mit. <BR>Click the Print button on your browser if you want
to keep a copy of this form for your records.
<P>
<FORM ACTION="/cgi-local/mailform.cgi" METHOD="POST">
 <INPUT TYPE="hidden" NAME="mailformFromEmail" VALUE"Product
Order">
 <INPUT TYPE="hidden" NAME="mailformFromName"
VALUE="Customer">

 <INPUT TYPE="hidden" NAME="mailformToEmail" VALUE="email-
name@domain.name">

 <INPUT TYPE="hidden" NAME="mailformToName" VALUE="Your Name">

 <INPUT TYPE="hidden" NAME="mailformSubject" VALUE="Product
Order">

 <INPUT TYPE="hidden" NAME="mailformURL"
VALUE="http://www.globalproductsco.com/orderthx.htm ">

 <INPUT TYPE="hidden" NAME="mailformBcc" VALUE="">

<P><FONT SIZE=+1>Billing Information</FONT>
<P>Last Name
<BR> <INPUT TYPE="text" NAME="1-lastname" SIZE="20">
 <BR>First Name
<BR><INPUT TYPE="text" NAME="1a-firstname" SIZE="20">
```

FIGURE 3.35 Product Order Form HTML code.

```
<P>Complete Mailing Address<BR><TEXTAREA NAME="2-address"
ROWS="3" COLS="30"></TEXTAREA>
<P>Phone
<BR><INPUT TYPE="text" NAME="3-phone" SIZE="15">
<BR>Fax
<BR><INPUT TYPE="text" NAME="4-fax" SIZE="15">
 <P>E-Mail address
<BR><INPUT TYPE="text" NAME="4-email" SIZE="20">

<P>Shipping Information (if different)
<BR><TEXTAREA NAME="5-shippinginfo" ROWS="3"
COLS="30"></TEXTAREA>

<P>Item/Options/Quantity/Unit Price/Extended Price<BR>
<TEXTAREA NAME="5-items" ROWS="6" COLS="60"></TEXTAREA>
<P><INPUT TYPE="text" NAME="6-subtotal" SIZE="8"> Item
Subtotal
<BR><INPUT TYPE="text" NAME="7-shipping" SIZE="8"> + Shipping
<BR><INPUT TYPE="text" NAME="8-tax" SIZE="8"> + Tax
<BR> <INPUT TYPE="text" NAME="9-total" SIZE="10"> = Total
<P>Payment Method:
<INPUT TYPE=RADIO NAME="c-CardType" VALUE="Visa" CHECKED>
VISA
<INPUT TYPE=RADIO NAME="c-CardType" VALUE="Mastercard">
MasterCard
<INPUT TYPE=RADIO NAME="c-CardType" VALUE="Amex">  American
Express
<BR><INPUT TYPE=RADIO NAME="c-CardType" VALUE="JCB" >JCB
<INPUT TYPE=RADIO NAME="c-CardType" VALUE="Check" > Check
<INPUT TYPE=RADIO NAME="c-CardType" VALUE="PhoneOrder">Phone
Order

<P>Name on credit card:
<BR><INPUT TYPE="text" NAME="d-NameOnCard" SIZE="30">

<BR>Card number:
<BR><INPUT TYPE="text" NAME="e-CardNumber" SIZE="20">

 <BR>Exp date:
<BR> <INPUT TYPE="text" NAME="f-CardDate" SIZE="10">

<P>Comments<BR><TEXTAREA NAME="g-comments" ROWS="3"
COLS="30"></TEXTAREA>
<P>Would you like to receive e-mail notification <BR>of new
products and specials?
```

FIGURE 3.35 Continued

```
<INPUT TYPE=RADIO NAME="h-MailingList" VALUE="yes" CHECKED
>Yes
 <INPUT TYPE=RADIO NAME="h-MailingList" VALUE="no"  >No

<P><INPUT TYPE="SUBMIT" VALUE="Send"> <INPUT TYPE="RESET"
VALUE="Reset">

 </FORM>

<P><HR SIZE=3>
<CENTER>
http://www.catalogco.com/order.htm
<BR>Copyright &copy; 1997 <A HREF="dummy.htm">Everything You
Need Catalog Co.</A>
<BR>Questions and comments to: <A
HREF="mailto:emailname@domain.name">emailname@domain.name</A>
<P><A HREF="dummy.htm"><IMG SRC="back.gif" WIDTH=80 HEIGHT=40
BORDER=0></A> 
<A HREF="dummy.htm"><IMG SRC="forward.gif" WIDTH=80 HEIGHT=40
BORDER=0></A> 
<A HREF="dummy.htm "> <IMG SRC="home.gif" WIDTH=80 HEIGHT=40
BORDER=0></A> 
<A HREF="dummy.htm"> <IMG SRC="contents.gif" WIDTH=80
HEIGHT=40 BORDER=0></A> 
<A HREF="mailto:emailname@domain.name"> <IMG SRC="email.gif"
WIDTH=80 HEIGHT=40 BORDER=0></A>
<BR><FONT SIZE=-1><A HREF="dummy.htm">Back</A> ||
<A HREF="dummy.htm">Forward</A> ||
<A HREF="dummy.htm">Home</A> ||
<A HREF="dummy.htm">Contents</A> ||
<A HREF="mailto:emailname@domain.name">E-Mail</A></FONT>
</BODY>
</HTML>
```

FIGURE 3.35 Continued

Janice King. Thanks for sending your inquiry. We'll be in touch". You can modify this text to fit your needs, then save the file with the same name or a different name. Remember to change the file directory and name entered for the VALUE field in the form's HTML file so the script will display the correct "thank you" page.

The purpose of the THNX.HTM file is to confirm to your visitor that the form has been processed successfully. If you leave the mailformURL variable blank, the browser will simply return to the form and the visitor may be confused about whether the form was processed.

Related templates: Brochure, Catalog Page, Price/Parts List

Alternative templates: None

Navigation guidelines: None

Advanced implementation and design guidelines: You can automate many aspects of this form by implementing a "shopping cart" program on your site (see Chapter 4).

 Profile

A Profile (see Figure 3.36) features an executive or employee of your organization. This template is also useful for consultants and service providers who want to promote their expertise.

Online Promotion Tip

Adapt the categories of information on this template to better reflect your profession and the interests of your target markets.

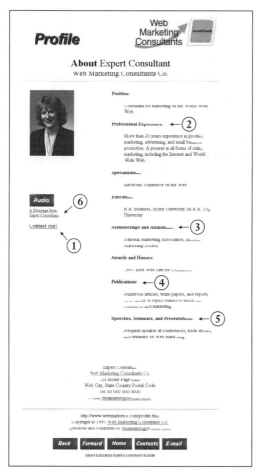

FIGURE 3.36 Profile Template.

Presentation Tips

You can adapt this template to include any information about a person. The example here is designed to present the expertise of a consultant. These tips will enhance the presentation of your information in this template (see corresponding callouts in Figure 3.36):

1. Link to an e-mail form the visitor can use to send a message to the person profiled.

2. Describe any specialized knowledge, experience, or services offered by this person; link to pages that provide additional detail if appropriate.

3. List relevant professional groups and link to their Web sites if appropriate.

4. List any books, articles, or other published works; link to pages that present more information or the works themselves.

5. List recent events or a summary of public-speaking experience; include a video or audio clip if available. Link to a **Seminar Description** page or the site for an external conference or other event.

6. Record a personal message in an audio file (a sample is on the CD-ROM).

Development Tips

See Figure 3.37 for the HTML code for the Profile template.

Related templates: Brochure, Services List

Alternative templates: None

Navigation guidelines: Create a link to a **Brochure** page, **Services** page, or other document to encourage the visitor to obtain more information if you are promoting consulting or other personal and professional services.

Advanced implementation and design guidelines: Add an audio or video clip with a personal greeting or an excerpt from a speech given by the person profiled (examples are included on the CD-ROM).

```
<HTML><HEAD><TITLE>Company Executive Profile
Page</TITLE></HEAD>

<BODY BGCOLOR="#ffffff">

<CENTER>


<TABLE>
<TR>
<TD NOWRAP>
<IMG SRC="execban.jpg"  WIDTH=350 HEIGHT=50 ALT="Executive
Profile">
<IMG SRC="wmclogo.jpg " ALT="Logo" WIDTH=261 HEIGHT=100>
</TD>
</TR>
</TABLE>


<P>
<FONT SIZE=+3><B>About </B>Expert Consultant</FONT>
<BR><FONT SIZE=+2>Web Marketing Consultants Co.</FONT>
<HR SIZE=3>

<TABLE BORDER=0 CELLPADDING=10 CELLSPACING=10 ALIGN=CENTER>

<TR>
<TD VALIGN=TOP WIDTH=30%>
<P><IMG SRC="king.jpg"  WIDTH=144 HEIGHT=206 VALIGN=TOP
ALT="Consultant Photo" BORDER=0></A>
<PRE>


</PRE>
<A HREF="audio.wav"> <IMG SRC="audio.gif" WIDTH=80 HEIGHT=40
BORDER=0 ALT="Audio Clip" BORDER=0></A>
<BR><A HREF="audio.wav"><FONT SIZE=-1>A Message from<BR>
Expert Consultant</A></FONT></P>
<P><A HREF="mailto:emailname@domain.name"><FONT
SIZE=+1>Contact Me!</A></FONT>
</TD>
<TD  VALIGN=TOP WIDTH=70%>

<B>Position: </B><UL>Consultant for marketing on the World
Wide Web.</UL>
```

FIGURE 3.37 Profile HTML code.

```
<P><B>Professional Experience:</B> <UL>More than 20 years
experience in product marketing, advertising, and small busi-
ness promotion. A pioneer in all forms of online marketing,
including the Internet and World Wide Web.</UL>

<P><B>Specialization:</B> <UL>Electronic commerce on the
Web.</UL>

<P><B>Education: </B> <UL>B.A. Business, Home University;
M.B.A. Top University</UL>

<P><B>Memberships and Affiliations: </B> <UL>National
Marketing Association, Internet Marketing Society</UL>

<P><B>Awards and Honors: </B> <UL>1997: Best Web Site for
Commerce</UL>

<P><B>Publications:</B>  <UL>Numerous articles, white papers,
and reports on a variety of topics related to electronic com-
merce and marketing.</UL>

<P><B>Speeches, Seminars, and Presentations: </B> <UL>Frequent
speaker at conferences, trade shows, and seminars on Web mar-
keting. </UL>

</TD>
</TR>
</TABLE>

<P><BR>Expert Consultant
<BR><A HREF="dummy.htm">Web Marketing Consultants Co.</A>
<BR>123 Home Page Lane
<BR>Web City, State  Country  Postal Code
<BR>Tel: 00 000 000 0000
<BR>e-mail:<A HREF="mailto: emailname@domain.name"> email-
name@domain.name</A>

<P><HR SIZE=3>
<CENTER>
http://www.webmarketco.com/profile.htm
<BR>Copyright &copy; 1997 <A HREF="dummy.htm">Web Marketing
Consultants Co.</A>
<BR>Questions and comments to: <A
HREF="mailto:emailname@domain.name">emailname@domain.name</A>
<P><A HREF="dummy.htm"><IMG SRC="back.gif" WIDTH=80 HEIGHT=40
```

FIGURE 3.37 Continued

```
BORDER=0></A> 
<A HREF="dummy.htm"><IMG SRC="forward.gif" WIDTH=80 HEIGHT=40
BORDER=0></A> 
<A HREF="dummy.htm "> <IMG SRC="home.gif" WIDTH=80 HEIGHT=40
BORDER=0></A> 
<A HREF="dummy.htm"> <IMG SRC="contents.gif" WIDTH=80
HEIGHT=40 BORDER=0></A> 
<A HREF="mailto:emailname@domain.name"> <IMG SRC="email.gif"
WIDTH=80 HEIGHT=40 BORDER=0></A>
<BR><FONT SIZE=-1><A HREF="dummy.htm">Back</A> ||
<A HREF="dummy.htm">Forward</A> ||
<A HREF="dummy.htm">Home</A> ||
<A HREF="dummy.htm">Contents</A> ||
<A HREF="mailto:emailname@domain.name">E-Mail</A></FONT>
</BODY>
</HTML>
```

FIGURE 3.37 Continued

 Selection Guide

The Selection Guide template (see Figure 3.38) enables visitors to find products, events, or other items of interest on your site based on their responses to a series of questions or choices.

Online Promotion Tip

Adapt this form to the types of products, events, or services you are promoting on the site.

FIGURE 3.38 Selection Guide template.

Presentation Tip

Organize choices into logical categories based on the structure of content on the site or the types of inquiries typically made by prospects.

Development Tips

See the HTML code for the Selection Guide template in Figure 3.39.

Use the <FORM> construct to capture the visitor's input. When the visitor clicks the Send button, the browser sends the form to the *mailform.cgi* script on your Web server. This script invokes an e-mail program on the server to send this information in an e-mail message to any address(es) you specify in the form's hidden variables. The script then returns a "thank you" page (as specified by the filename entered in the VALUE variable) to the browser as a confirmation for the visitor.

A general-purpose "thank you" page (THNX.HTM) is included on the CD-ROM. It displays the text "Thanks from Janice King. Thanks for sending your inquiry. We'll be in touch". You can modify this text to fit your needs, then save the file with the same name or a different name. Remember to change the file directory and name entered for the VALUE field in the form's HTML file so the script will display the correct "thank you" page.

The purpose of the THNX.HTM file is to confirm to your visitor that the form has been processed successfully. If you leave the mailformURL variable blank, the browser will simply return to the form and the visitor may be confused about whether the form was processed.

Related templates: Brochure, Catalog Page, Event Calendar, Services List

Alternative templates: None

Navigation guidelines: Link to this page from any page on your site where a visitor may need guidance in selecting the item of interest.

Advanced implementation and design guidelines: You may want to write a different script to return the visitor to a **Brochure**, **Catalog**, or home page after this form has been processed.

```
<HTML><HEAD><TITLE>Selection Guide</TITLE></HEAD>

<BODY BGCOLOR="#ffffff">

<TABLE>
<TR>
<TD NOWRAP>
<IMG SRC="guideban.jpg"  WIDTH=350 HEIGHT=50  ALT="Guide">
<IMG SRC="fealogo.jpg " ALT="Logo"  WIDTH=154 HEIGHT=122>
</TD>
</TR>
</TABLE>


<BR>
<CENTER>
<FONT SIZE=+3>Fun Events Association</FONT>
</CENTER>
<HR SIZE=3>
<P>
Use this form to search for events of specific interest.
Enter your choices for each category, then click Send to sub-
mit the form.

<FORM ACTION="/cgi-local/mailform.cgi" METHOD="POST">
 <INPUT TYPE="hidden" NAME="mailformFromEmail" VALUE="Website
Visitor">
 <INPUT TYPE="hidden" NAME="mailformFromName" VALUE="Selection
Guide">

 <INPUT TYPE="hidden" NAME="mailformToEmail" VALUE="email-
name@domain.name">

 <INPUT TYPE="hidden" NAME="mailformToName" VALUE="Your Name">

 <INPUT TYPE="hidden" NAME="mailformSubject" VALUE="Selection
Guide">

 <INPUT TYPE="hidden" NAME="mailformURL"
VALUE="http://www.globalproductsco.com/guidethx.htm ">

 <INPUT TYPE="hidden" NAME="mailformBcc" VALUE="">
<P><FONT SIZE=+1>Month:</FONT>
<BR><INPUT TYPE=CHECKBOX VALUE="1" NAME="January" >  January
 <INPUT TYPE=CHECKBOX VALUE="1" NAME="February">February
 <INPUT TYPE=CHECKBOX VALUE="1" NAME="March">March
```

FIGURE 3.39 Selection Guide HTML code.

```
<BR><INPUT TYPE=CHECKBOX VALUE="1" NAME="April">April
<INPUT TYPE=CHECKBOX VALUE="1" NAME="May">May
<INPUT TYPE=CHECKBOX VALUE="1" NAME="June">June
<BR><INPUT TYPE=CHECKBOX VALUE="1" NAME="July">July
<INPUT TYPE=CHECKBOX VALUE="1" NAME="August">August
<INPUT TYPE=CHECKBOX VALUE="1" NAME="September">September
<BR><INPUT TYPE=CHECKBOX VALUE="1" NAME="October">October
<INPUT TYPE=CHECKBOX VALUE="1" NAME="November">November
<INPUT TYPE=CHECKBOX VALUE="1" NAME="December">December

<P><FONT SIZE=+1>Type of Event:</FONT>
<BR><INPUT TYPE=CHECKBOX VALUE="1" NAME="Concerts">Concerts
<INPUT TYPE=CHECKBOX VALUE="1" NAME="Sports">Sports
<BR><INPUT TYPE=CHECKBOX VALUE="1" NAME="Art Tours">Art Tours
<INPUT TYPE=CHECKBOX VALUE="1" NAME="Outdoors">Outdoors
<BR><INPUT TYPE=CHECKBOX VALUE="1" NAME="Theatre">Theatre
<INPUT TYPE=CHECKBOX VALUE="1" NAME="Family">Family
<BR><INPUT TYPE=CHECKBOX VALUE="1" NAME="Dance">Dance

<P><FONT SIZE=+1>Location:</FONT>
<BR><INPUT TYPE=CHECKBOX VALUE="1" NAME="CityCenter">
CityCenter
 <INPUT TYPE=CHECKBOX VALUE="1" NAME="Suburbs">Suburbs
<P><FONT SIZE=+1>Time of Day:</FONT>
<BR><INPUT TYPE=CHECKBOX VALUE="1" NAME=
<INPUT TYPE=CHECKBOX VALUE="1" NAME="Morning">Morning
<INPUT TYPE=CHECKBOX VALUE="1" NAME="Afternoon">Afternoon
<INPUT TYPE=CHECKBOX VALUE="1" NAME="Evening">Evening
<INPUT TYPE=CHECKBOX VALUE="1" NAME="Weekend">Weekend

<P>
<INPUT TYPE="SUBMIT" VALUE="Send"> <INPUT TYPE="RESET"
VALUE="Reset">

 </FORM>

<CENTER>
<P>Fun Events Association
<BR>123 Home Page Lane
<BR>Web City, State  Country  Postal Code

<P>Phone: 00 000 000 0000 Toll-Free: 00 000 000 0000
<BR>Fax: 00 000 000 0000
</CENTER>

<P><HR SIZE=3>
```

FIGURE 3.39 Continued

```
<CENTER>
http://www.funeventsco.com/guide.htm
<BR>Copyright &copy; 1997 <A HREF="dummy.htm">Fun Events
Association</A>
<BR>Questions and comments to: <A
HREF="mailto:emailname@domain.name">emailname@domain.name</A>
<P><A HREF="dummy.htm"><IMG SRC="back.gif" WIDTH=80 HEIGHT=40
BORDER=0></A> 
<A HREF="dummy.htm"><IMG SRC="forward.gif" WIDTH=80 HEIGHT=40
BORDER=0></A> 
<A HREF="dummy.htm "> <IMG SRC="home.gif" WIDTH=80 HEIGHT=40
BORDER=0></A> 
<A HREF="dummy.htm"> <IMG SRC="contents.gif" WIDTH=80
HEIGHT=40 BORDER=0></A> 
<A HREF="mailto:emailname@domain.name"> <IMG SRC="email.gif"
WIDTH=80 HEIGHT=40 BORDER=0></A>
<BR><FONT SIZE=-1><A HREF="dummy.htm">Back</A> ||
<A HREF="dummy.htm">Forward</A> ||
<A HREF="dummy.htm">Home</A> ||
<A HREF="dummy.htm">Contents</A> ||
<A HREF="mailto:emailname@domain.name">E-Mail</A></FONT>
</BODY>
</HTML>
```

FIGURE 3.39 Continued

Seminar Description

Any educational event (class, workshop, seminar), whether sponsored by an organization or individual, requires a description page to attract enrollment; see Figure 3.40. The Seminar Description template is designed to present the most commonly requested information about a course or event and encourage visitor response via links to an **Event Registration Form** and e-mail inquiry.

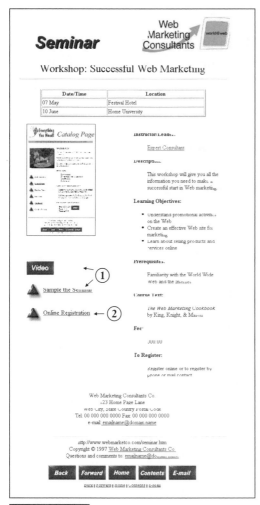

FIGURE 3.40 Seminar Description template.

Online Promotion Tips

These tips will help you adapt this template for your promotions:

- Include complete information on this page to allow visitors to make an immediate decision about enrollment.

- Specify the currency for all fees; list fees for seminar options or group discounts if applicable.

- Link to an **Event Calendar** page to present a complete schedule or listing of available seminars.

Presentation Tips

These tips will enhance the presentation of your information in this template (see corresponding callouts in Figure 3.40):

1. Link to a video clip of the actual seminar (a sample is on the CD-ROM).

2. Link to an **Event Registration Form** if you permit online registration. Otherwise, include all information necessary for the visitor to register via phone, fax, or postal mail.

Development Tips

Figure 3.41 shows the HTML code for the Seminar Description template. For seminars offered on multiple dates, use the <TABLE> tag to present the seminar schedule and locations at the top of the page.

Related templates: Event Calendar, Event Registration Form

Alternative templates: Brochure

Navigation guidelines: Consider creating cross-links between this page and related courses as well as an **Event Calendar** page.

Advanced implementation and design guidelines: Include a video or audio clip from an actual session as a way for visitors to preview the course.

```
<HTML><HEAD><TITLE>Seminar Description Page</TITLE></HEAD>

<BODY BGCOLOR="#ffffff">

<CENTER>

<TABLE>
<TR>
<TD NOWRAP>
<IMG SRC="semban.jpg"  WIDTH=350 HEIGHT=50 ALT="Seminar">
<IMG SRC="wmclogo.jpg " ALT="Logo" WIDTH=261 HEIGHT=100>
</TD>
</TR>
</TABLE>


<BR>
<FONT SIZE=+3>Workshop: Successful Web Marketing</FONT>

<HR SIZE=3>
<P>
<TABLE BORDER=2 WIDTH=80%>
<TR><TH>Date/Time</TH><TH>Location</TH></TR>
<TR><TD>07 May</TD><TD>Festival Hotel</TD></TR>
<TR><TD>10 June</TD><TD>Home University</TD></TR>
</TABLE>

<TABLE BORDER=0 CELLPADDING=10 CELLSPACING=10 ALIGN=CENTER>

<TR>
<TD VALIGN=TOP WIDTH=40%>
<IMG SRC="catitm1.gif"  WIDTH=200 HEIGHT=316 VALIGN=TOP
ALT="Catalog Page Screen Shot" BORDER=1></A>
<PRE>


</PRE>
<P><A HREF="jim.avi"> <IMG SRC="video.gif" WIDTH=80 HEIGHT=40
BORDER=0 ALT="Video Clip" BORDER=0></A>
<FONT SIZE=+1>
<P><A HREF="jim.avi"><IMG SRC="bluearrow.gif" ALIGN=MIDDLE
BORDER=0>Sample the Seminar</A>
<P><A HREF="../event/eventfrm.htm"><IMG SRC="bluearrow.gif"
ALIGN=MIDDLE BORDER=0>Online Registration</A>
</FONT>
</TD>
```

FIGURE 3.41 Seminar Description HTML code.

```
<TD  VALIGN=TOP WIDTH=60%>


<P><BR><B>Instructor/Leader:<UL></B> <A
HREF="../exprof/exprof.htm">Expert Consultant</A></UL>

<P><B>Description: </B><UL>This workshop will give you all
the information you need to make a successful start in Web
marketing.</UL>

<P><B>Learning Objectives:</B>
<UL>
<LI> Understand promotional activities on the Web
<LI> Create an effective Web site for marketing
<LI> Learn about selling products and services online
</UL>

<P><B>Prerequisites: </B><UL>Familiarity with the World Wide
Web and the Internet</UL>

<P><B>Course Text:</B><UL> <I>The Web Marketing Cookbook</I>
by King, Knight, & Mason</UL>

<P><B>Fee:</B><UL> 000.00</UL>

<P><B>To Register: </B><UL>Register online or to register by
phone or mail contact:</UL>

</TD>
</TR>
</TABLE>


Web Marketing Consultants Co.
<BR>123 Home Page Lane
<BR>Web City, State  Country  Postal Code
<BR>Tel: 00 000 000 0000  Fax: 00 000 000 0000
<BR>e-mail:<A HREF="mailto: emailname@domain.name"> email-
name@domain.name</A>


</CENTER>

<P><HR SIZE=3>
<CENTER>
http://www.webmarketco.com/seminar.htm
```

FIGURE 3.41 Continued

```
<BR>Copyright &copy; 1997 <A HREF="dummy.htm">Web Marketing
Consultants Co.</A>
<BR>Questions and comments to: <A
HREF="mailto:emailname@domain.name">emailname@domain.name</A>
<P><A HREF="dummy.htm"><IMG SRC="back.gif" WIDTH=80 HEIGHT=40
BORDER=0></A> 
<A HREF="dummy.htm"><IMG SRC="forward.gif" WIDTH=80 HEIGHT=40
BORDER=0></A> 
<A HREF="dummy.htm "> <IMG SRC="home.gif" WIDTH=80 HEIGHT=40
BORDER=0></A> 
<A HREF="dummy.htm"> <IMG SRC="contents.gif" WIDTH=80
HEIGHT=40 BORDER=0></A> 
<A HREF="mailto:emailname@domain.name"> <IMG SRC="email.gif"
WIDTH=80 HEIGHT=40 BORDER=0></A>
<BR><FONT SIZE=-1><A HREF="dummy.htm">Back</A> ||
<A HREF="dummy.htm">Forward</A> ||
<A HREF="dummy.htm">Home</A> ||
<A HREF="dummy.htm">Contents</A> ||
<A HREF="mailto:emailname@domain.name">E-Mail</A></FONT>
</BODY>
</HTML>
```

FIGURE 3.41 Continued

↳ Services List

A Services List (see Figure 3.42) is useful for consultants or organizations that promote services instead of tangible products.

Online Promotion Tips

These tips will help you adapt this template for your promotions:

- Write your service descriptions with benefits statements.
- Link to pages that provide more information or an online **Brochure** for each service.
- Include information on service packages.

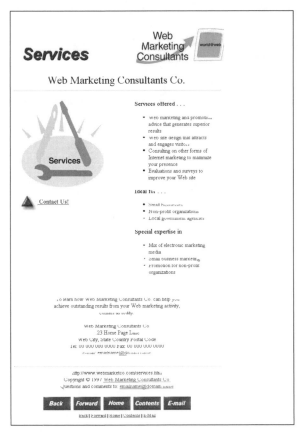

FIGURE 3.42 Services List template.

Presentation Tip

Use bullet lists and groupings to make information quick and easy for visitors to read.

Development Tips

See Figure 3.43 for the HTML code for the Services List template.

Related templates: Brochure

Alternative templates: None

Navigation guidelines: Add a link to the next page in the navigation path you have defined for the site, such as a **Brochure** page.

Advanced implementation and design guidelines: An alternative approach is to implement this list as a table, with each column listing services by category, person, or other grouping criteria.

```
<HTML><HEAD><TITLE>Services List Page</TITLE></HEAD>

<BODY BGCOLOR="#ffffff">

<CENTER>

<TABLE>
<TR>
<TD NOWRAP>
<IMG SRC="serban.jpg"  WIDTH=350 HEIGHT=50 ALT="Services
List">
<IMG SRC="wmclogo.jpg " ALT="Logo" WIDTH=261 HEIGHT=100>
</TD>
</TR>
</TABLE>

<BR>
<FONT SIZE=+3> Web Marketing Consultants Co.</FONT>

<HR SIZE=3>

<TABLE BORDER=0 CELLPADDING=10 CELLSPACING=10 ALIGN=CENTER>

<TR>
<TD VALIGN=TOP WIDTH=30%>
```

FIGURE 3.43 Services List HTML code.

```
<P><IMG SRC="servs.gif"  WIDTH=300 HEIGHT=247 VALIGN=TOP
ALT="Services " BORDER=0></A>


<P><FONT SIZE="+1"><A HREF="mailto:emailname@domain.name"><IMG
SRC="bluearrow.gif" ALIGN=MIDDLE BORDER=0> Contact Us!</A>
</FONT>

</TD>
<TD VALIGN=TOP  WIDTH=70%</TD>
<P><FONT SIZE=+1>Services offered . . .</FONT>
<UL>
<LI> Web marketing and promotion advice that generates supe-
rior results
<LI> Web site design that attracts and engages visitors
<LI> Consulting on other forms of Internet marketing to maxi-
mize your presence
<LI> Evaluations and surveys to improve your Web site
</UL>
<P><FONT SIZE=+1>Ideal for . . .</FONT>
<UL>
<LI> Small businesses
<LI> Non-profit organizations
<LI> Local government agencies
</UL>
<P><FONT SIZE=+1>Special expertise in . . .</FONT>
<UL>
<LI> Mix of electronic marketing media
<LI> Small business marketing
<LI> Promotion for non-profit organizations
</UL>

</TD>
</TR>
</TABLE>

<P>To learn how Web Marketing Consultants Co. can help
you<BR> achieve outstanding results from your Web marketing
activity, <BR>contact us today:


<P>
Web Marketing Consultants Co.
<BR>123 Home Page Lane
<BR>Web City, State  Country  Postal Code
```

FIGURE 3.43 Continued

```
<BR>Tel: 00 000 000 0000   Fax: 00 000 000 0000
<BR>e-mail:<A HREF="mailto: emailname@domain.name"> email-
name@domain.name</A>
</CENTER>

<P><HR SIZE=3>
<CENTER>
http://www.webmarketco.com/services.htm
<BR>Copyright &copy; 1997 <A HREF="dummy.htm">Web Marketing
Consultants Co.</A>
<BR>Questions and comments to: <A
HREF="mailto:emailname@domain.name">emailname@domain.name</A>
<P><A HREF="dummy.htm"><IMG SRC="back.gif" WIDTH=80 HEIGHT=40
BORDER=0></A> 
<A HREF="dummy.htm"><IMG SRC="forward.gif" WIDTH=80 HEIGHT=40
BORDER=0></A> 
<A HREF="dummy.htm "> <IMG SRC="home.gif" WIDTH=80 HEIGHT=40
BORDER=0></A> 
<A HREF="dummy.htm"> <IMG SRC="contents.gif" WIDTH=80
HEIGHT=40 BORDER=0></A> 
<A HREF="mailto:emailname@domain.name"> <IMG SRC="email.gif"
WIDTH=80 HEIGHT=40 BORDER=0></A>
<BR><FONT SIZE=-1><A HREF="dummy.htm">Back</A> ||
<A HREF="dummy.htm">Forward</A> ||
<A HREF="dummy.htm">Home</A> ||
<A HREF="dummy.htm">Contents</A> ||
<A HREF="mailto:emailname@domain.name">E-Mail</A></FONT>
</BODY>
</HTML>
```

FIGURE 3.43 Continued

 # Starter Page

The Starter template (see Figure 3.44) is useful if you are uncertain about the type of page you want to produce or if any of the other templates don't serve your purpose. It offers all the elements you need to create a Web page; you can use only the elements you want when adapting it for your content. For example, delete the placeholders for audio and video clips if you do not want to include them on your page.

Online Promotion Tip

Look again at the other templates because they are designed specifically for promotional communication.

FIGURE 3.44 Starter Page template.

Presentation Tip

Remember to delete any elements that you do not want to use on the page when you are adapting this template.

Development Tips

Figure 3.45 lists the HTML code for the Starter Page template.

Related templates: None

Alternative templates: None

Navigation guidelines: Add links to specific pages on your site based on the content of the new page you create from this template.

Advanced implementation and design guidelines: You can use tables to control the layout of the page and to avoid using frames. For example, by using tables you can create an index to your page in small type that appears unobtrusively down the left side of each page. See the discussion of tables and multicolumn layouts in Chapters 6 and 7 for more information; frames are discussed in Chapter 11.

```
<HTML><HEAD><TITLE>All-Purpose Page</TITLE></HEAD>

<BODY BGCOLOR="#ffffff">

<TABLE>
<TR>
<TD NOWRAP>
<IMG SRC="startban.jpg" WIDTH=350 HEIGHT=50  ALT="Starter
Page">
<IMG SRC="glblogo.jpg " ALT="Logo" WIDTH=154 HEIGHT=122>
</TD>
</TR>
</TABLE>

<CENTER>
<P>
<FONT SIZE=+3>Starter Page</FONT>
<HR SIZE=3>
```

FIGURE 3.45 Starter Page HTML code.

```
<P>
</CENTER>

<TABLE BORDER=0 CELLPADDING=10 CELLSPACING=10>
<TR>
<TD VALIGN=TOP WIDTH=30%>
<BR>
<IMG SRC="catitml.jpg"  WIDTH=252 HEIGHT=202 VALIGN=TOP
ALT="Product Image" BORDER=0>

<P><IMG SRC="bluearrow.gif" WIDTH=49 HEIGHT=46>
<P><A HREF="dummy.htm"><IMG SRC="blank.gif" WIDTH=80 HEIGHT=40
BORDER=0><P><A HREF="audio.au"><IMG SRC="soundbtn.gif"
WIDTH=40 HEIGHT=40 BORDER=0 ALT="Audio Clip"></A>
<P><A HREF="video.avi"><IMG SRC="filmbtn.gif" WIDTH=40
HEIGHT=40 BORDER=0 ALT="Video Clip"></A>



</TD>
<TD VALIGN=TOP WIDTH=70%>
<FONT SIZE=+2>How to Use This Template</FONT>
<P>
This template is a good place to start if you are uncertain
about the type of page you want to produce or if any of the
other templates don't serve your purposes.
<P>
It has all the elements you need to create a Web page; you
can use only the elements you want for each page. For exam-
ple, delete the placeholders for audio and video clips if you
do not want to include them on your page.

<BR>
<BR><FONT SIZE=+1>Ideas for Use</FONT>
<UL>
<LI>Title page for a page group (examples: catalog, newspa-
per, or brochure)
<LI>Pages that require a unique or flexible layout
<LI>Pages that need a mix of text, images, audio, and video
elements
</UL>

</TD>
</TR>
</TABLE>
```

FIGURE 3.45 Continued

```
<TABLE BORDER=5><TR><TH>Column Header 1</TH><TH>Column Header
2</TH><TH>Column Header 3</TH><TH>Column Header 4</TH></TR>
<TR><TD>  </TD><TD>  </TD><TD>  </TD><TD> 
</TD>
<TR><TD>  </TD><TD>  </TD><TD>  </TD><TD> 
</TD>
<P>
</TABLE>

<P><HR SIZE=3>
<CENTER>
http://www.globalproductsco.com/starter.htm
<BR>Copyright &copy; 1997 <A HREF="dummy.htm">Global Products
Co.</A>
<BR>Questions and comments to: <A
HREF="mailto:emailname@domain.name">emailname@domain.name</A>
<P><A HREF="dummy.htm"><IMG SRC="back.gif" WIDTH=80 HEIGHT=40
BORDER=0></A> 
<A HREF="dummy.htm"><IMG SRC="forward.gif" WIDTH=80 HEIGHT=40
BORDER=0></A> 
<A HREF="dummy.htm "> <IMG SRC="home.gif" WIDTH=80 HEIGHT=40
BORDER=0></A> 
<A HREF="../contents/contents.htm"> <IMG SRC="contents.gif"
WIDTH=80 HEIGHT=40 BORDER=0></A> 
<A HREF="mailto:emailname@domain.name"> <IMG SRC="email.gif"
WIDTH=80 HEIGHT=40 BORDER=0></A>
<BR><FONT SIZE=-1><A HREF="dummy.htm">Back</A> ||
<A HREF="dummy.htm">Forward</A> ||
<A HREF="dummy.htm">Home</A> ||
<A HREF="../contents/contents.htm">Contents</A> ||
<A HREF="mailto:emailname@domain.name">E-Mail</A></FONT>
</BODY>
</HTML>
```

FIGURE 3.45 Continued

↳ Visitor Registration/Survey Form

Inviting feedback from visitors is one of the best ways to obtain successful results from your Web site. The Visitor Registration/Survey Form template (see Figure 3.46) allows you to gather this feedback as well as register visitors for future contact via e-mail or to access any restricted areas you may establish on your site.

Online Promotion Tips

These tips will help you adapt this template for your promotions:

- Be careful about the number and nature of questions you include on this form. If you ask too many or too personal questions on this form, the visitor may not submit it.

- Don't display this form as the first page a visitor sees on your site, and don't force visitors to complete this form before you give them access to the content. Visitors are likely to leave your site because they perceive such an action as unwelcoming and intrusive. Instead, allow visitors to access this form from the home page or other appropriate page as an optional action.

Presentation Tip

Adapt questions to the interests of visitors and your need for market research. Always include at least one question that allows a free-form, essay-type response.

Development Tips

See Figure 3.47 for the HTML code for the Visitor Registration/Survey template.

1. Use the <FORM> construct to capture the visitor's input. When the visitor clicks the Send button, the

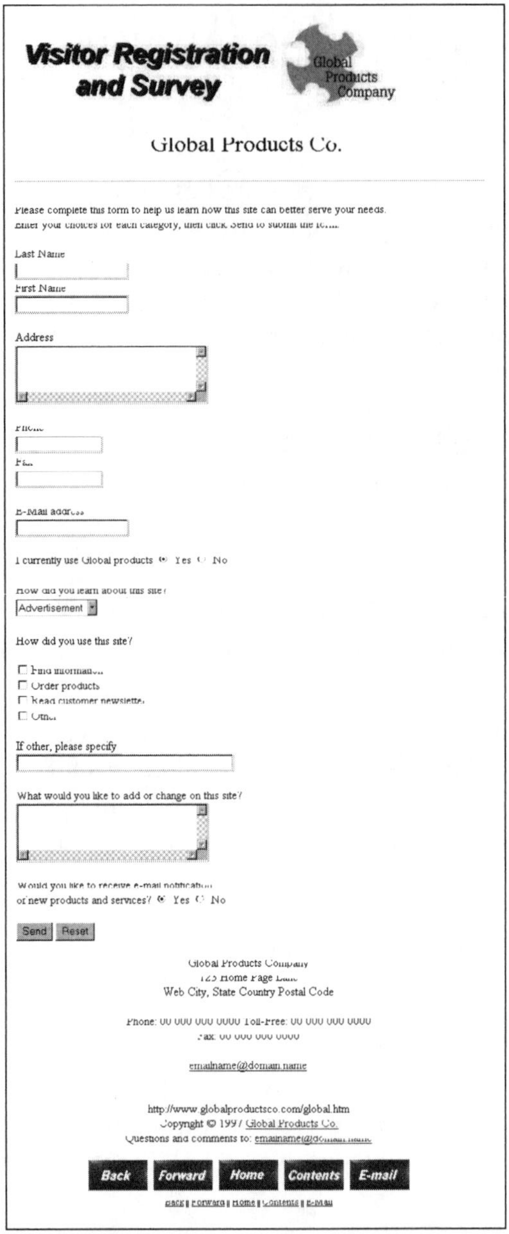

FIGURE 3.46 Visitor Registration/Survey Form template.

browser sends the form to the *mailform.cgi* script on your Web server. This script invokes an e-mail program on the server to send this information in an

```
<HTML><HEAD><TITLE>Visitor Registration/Survey
Page</TITLE></HEAD>

<BODY BGCOLOR="#ffffff">

<TABLE>
<TR>
<TD NOWRAP>
<IMG SRC="survban.jpg" WIDTH=350 HEIGHT=100  ALT="Survey">
<IMG SRC="glblogo.jpg " ALT="Logo" WIDTH=154 HEIGHT=122>
</TD>
</TR>
</TABLE>

<CENTER>
<BR>
<FONT SIZE=+3>Global Products Co.</FONT>
<P>
</CENTER>
<HR SIZE=3>
<P>Please complete this form to help us learn how this site
can better serve your needs.
<BR> Enter your choices for each category, then click Send to
submit the form.

<FORM ACTION="/cgi-local/mailform.cgi" METHOD="POST">   ← ①
 <INPUT TYPE="hidden" NAME="mailformFromEmail" VALUE="Website
Visitor">
 <INPUT TYPE="hidden" NAME="mailformFromName" VALUE="Website
Visitor">

 <INPUT TYPE="hidden" NAME="mailformToEmail" VALUE="email-
name@domain.name">

 <INPUT TYPE="hidden" NAME="mailformToName" VALUE="Your Name">

 <INPUT TYPE="hidden" NAME="mailformSubject" VALUE="Visitor
Survey">

 <INPUT TYPE="hidden" NAME="mailformURL"
VALUE="http://www.globalproductsco.com/survthx.htm ">

 <INPUT TYPE="hidden" NAME="mailformBcc" VALUE="">

<P>Last Name     ← ②
<BR><INPUT TYPE="text" NAME="1-lastname" SIZE="20">
```

FIGURE 3.47 Visitor Registration/Survey Form HTML code.

Web Marketing Templates

```
<BR>First Name
<BR><INPUT TYPE="text" NAME="1a-firstname" SIZE="20">
<P> Address
<BR><TEXTAREA NAME="2-address" ROWS="3" COLS="30"></TEXTAREA>
<P>Phone
<BR><INPUT TYPE="text" NAME="3-phone" SIZE="15">
<BR>Fax
<BR><INPUT TYPE="text" NAME="4-fax" SIZE="15">
<P>E-Mail address
<BR><INPUT TYPE="text" NAME="5-email" SIZE="20">

<P>I currently use Global products
<INPUT TYPE=RADIO NAME="6-UseProducts" VALUE="Yes" CHECKED>
Yes
<INPUT TYPE=RADIO NAME="6-UseProducts" VALUE="No"> No
<P>How did you learn about this site?<BR>
<SELECT NAME="7-FoundUs">
<OPTION VALUE="Advertisement">Advertisement
<OPTION VALUE="Newsletter">Newsletter
<OPTION VALUE="SearchTool">Search Tool
<OPTION VALUE="Salesperson">Salesperson
<OPTION VALUE="AnotherUser">Another User
</SELECT>
<P>How did you use this site?<BR>
<BR><INPUT TYPE=CHECKBOX NAME="8-FindInfo" VALUE="1">Find
information
<BR><INPUT TYPE=CHECKBOX NAME="8-OrderProducts"
VALUE="1">Order products
<BR><INPUT TYPE=CHECKBOX NAME="8-ReadNewsletter"
VALUE="1">Read customer newsletter
<BR><INPUT TYPE=CHECKBOX NAME="8-Other"  VALUE="1">Other
<P>If other, please specify
<BR><INPUT TYPE="text" NAME="8-OtherUse" SIZE="40">

<P>What would you like to add or change on this site?
<BR><TEXTAREA NAME="9-AddChange" ROWS="3"
COLS="30"></TEXTAREA>
<P>Would you like to receive e-mail notification<BR> of new
products and services?
<INPUT TYPE=RADIO NAME="a-EmailNotice" VALUE="Yes" CHECKED>
Yes
<INPUT TYPE=RADIO NAME="a-EmailNotice" VALUE="No"> No

<P>
<INPUT TYPE="SUBMIT" VALUE="Send"> <INPUT TYPE="RESET"
```

FIGURE 3.47 Continued

```
VALUE="Reset">

 </FORM>

<CENTER>
<P>                     Global Products Company
<BR>                    123 Home Page Lane
<BR>                    Web City, State Country Postal Code
<P>                     Phone: 00 000 000 0000
                        Toll-Free: 00 000 000 0000
<BR>                    Fax: 00 000 000 0000
<P><A HREF="mailto:emailname@domain.name">emailname@domain.
name</A>
</CENTER>


<P><HR SIZE=3>
<CENTER>
http://www.globalproductsco.com/global.htm
<BR>Copyright &copy; 1997 <A HREF="dummy.htm">Global Products
Co.</A>
<BR>Questions and comments to: <A
HREF="mailto:emailname@domain.name">emailname@domain.name</A>
<P><A HREF="dummy.htm"><IMG SRC="back.gif" WIDTH=80 HEIGHT=40
BORDER=0></A> 
<A HREF="dummy.htm"><IMG SRC="forward.gif" WIDTH=80 HEIGHT=40
BORDER=0></A> 
<A HREF="dummy.htm "> <IMG SRC="home.gif" WIDTH=80 HEIGHT=40
BORDER=0></A> 
<A HREF="../contents/contents.htm"> <IMG SRC="contents.gif"
WIDTH=80 HEIGHT=40 BORDER=0></A> 
<A HREF="mailto:emailname@domain.name"> <IMG SRC="email.gif"
WIDTH=80 HEIGHT=40 BORDER=0></A>
<BR><FONT SIZE=-1><A HREF="dummy.htm">Back</A> ||
<A HREF="dummy.htm">Forward</A> ||
<A HREF="dummy.htm">Home</A> ||
<A HREF="../contents/contents.htm">Contents</A> ||
<A HREF="mailto:emailname@domain.name">E-Mail</A></FONT>
</BODY>
</HTML>
```

FIGURE 3.47 Continued

e-mail message to any address(es) you specify in the form's hidden variables. The script then returns a "thank you" page to the browser as a confirmation for the visitor.

A general-purpose "thank you" page (THNX.HTM) is included on the CD-ROM. It displays the text "Thanks from Janice King. Thanks for sending your inquiry. We'll be in touch". You can modify this text to fit your needs, then save the file with the same name or a different name. Remember to change the file directory and name entered for the VALUE field in the form's HTML file so the script will display the correct "thank you" page.

The purpose of the THNX.HTM file is to confirm to your visitor that the form has been processed successfully. If you leave the mailformURL variable blank, the browser will simply return to the form and the visitor may be confused about whether the form was processed.

2. Any of these questions can be adapted to use any of the input formats available on forms: check boxes, radio buttons, pull-down lists, and blanks for text entry.

Related templates: None
Alternative templates: None
Navigation guidelines: Link to this page from your home page, online **Brochure**, or other page that presents information for which you would like visitor feedback.
Advanced implementation and design guidelines: None

↳ What's New Page

The What's New template creates a page for attracting visitors to the latest promotion from your site or business. Consider what visitors will expect when they click on the link to a What's New page (see Figure 3.49). You may want to create separate links and pages for the following items:

- <u>New from XYZ:</u> This type of What's New page lists new products, services, events, or promotions from your organization. Information is presented in a bullet list or a text paragraph with links to additional pages on the site for detailed information. This page also could include links to recent press releases.

- <u>New on this site:</u> This type of What's New page describes new features (such as a keyword search capability) and content available on the site, again in the form of a bullet list or short text paragraphs. Provide a link to each feature or page listed.

The What's New template can be adapted easily to serve both of these approaches; the example shown here combines the two.

Online Promotion Tips

These tips will help you adapt this template for your promotions:

- Highlight online promotions and information on new products or services available from your organization, whether available online or not.

- Place a link to this page on the home and **Contents** pages for your site and on other related pages.

Presentation Tips

These tips will enhance the presentation of your information in this template (see corresponding callouts in Figure 3.48):

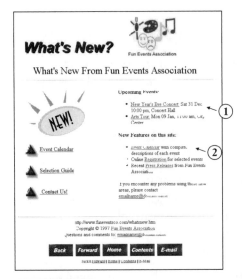

FIGURE 3.48 What's New Page template.

1. Create links to the pages that present more information on each product or topic listed here.

2. Use this area to announce new pages, forms, or capabilities such as a search tool or online selection guide. Link to these capabilities directly from this list.

Development Tips

Figure 3.49 lists the HTML code for the What's New template.

Related templates: None

Alternative templates: None

Navigation guidelines: Verify that all links from this page continue to work each time you change the organization of the site.

Advanced implementation and design guidelines: None

```
<HTML><HEAD><TITLE>What's New</TITLE></HEAD>

<BODY BGCOLOR="#ffffff">

<TABLE>
<TR>
<TD NOWRAP>
<IMG SRC="whatban.jpg"  WIDTH=350 HEIGHT=50  ALT="Whats New">
<IMG SRC="fealogo.jpg " ALT="Logo"  WIDTH=154 HEIGHT=122>
</TD>
</TR>
</TABLE>

<BR>
<CENTER>
<FONT SIZE=+3>What's New From Fun Events Association</FONT>
</CENTER>
<HR SIZE=3>

<TABLE BORDER=0 CELLPADDING=10 CELLSPACING=10 ALIGN=CENTER>

<TR>
<TD VALIGN=TOP>
<IMG SRC="new.gif"  WIDTH=199 HEIGHT=147 VALIGN=TOP
ALT="What's New!" BORDER=0></A>
<FONT SIZE=+1>
<P><A HREF="../calendar/calendar.htm"><IMG SRC="bluearrow.gif"
ALIGN=MIDDLE BORDER=0>Event Calendar</A>
<P><A HREF="../guide/guide.htm"><IMG SRC="bluearrow.gif"
ALIGN=MIDDLE BORDER=0>Selection Guide</A>
<P><A HREF="mailto:emailname@domain.name"><IMG SRC="bluear-
row.gif" ALIGN=MIDDLE BORDER=0> Contact Us!</A>

</TD>
<TD VALIGN=TOP WIDTH=60%>
<P>
<FONT SIZE=+1>Upcoming Events:</FONT>
<UL>
<LI><A HREF="../calendar/calendar.htm#newyears">New Year's Eve
Concert:</A> Sat 31 Dec, 10:00 pm, Concert Hall
<LI><A HREF="../calendar/calendar.htm#artstour">Arts Tour:</A>
Mon 09 Jan, 11:00 am, City Center
</UL>

<P><FONT SIZE=+1>New Features on this site:</FONT>
```

FIGURE 3.49 What's New Page HTML code.

```
<UL>
<LI> <A HREF="../calendar/calendar.htm">Event Calendar</A>
with complete descriptions of each event
<LI>Online <A HREF="../event/eventfrm.htm"> Registration</A>
for selected events
<LI> Recent <A HREF="../pressrel/pressrel.htm">Press
Releases</A> from Fun Events Association
</UL>
<P>If you encounter any problems using these new areas,
please contact
<A
HREF="mailto:emailname@domain.name">emailname@domain.name</A>

</TD>
</TR>
</TABLE>

<P><HR SIZE=3>
<CENTER>
http://www.funeventsco.com/whatsnew.htm
<BR>Copyright &copy; 1997 <A HREF="dummy.htm">Fun Events
Association</A>
<BR>Questions and comments to: <A
HREF="mailto:emailname@domain.name">emailname@domain.name</A>
<P><A HREF="dummy.htm"><IMG SRC="back.gif" WIDTH=80 HEIGHT=40
BORDER=0></A> 
<A HREF="dummy.htm"><IMG SRC="forward.gif" WIDTH=80 HEIGHT=40
BORDER=0></A> 
<A HREF="dummy.htm "> <IMG SRC="home.gif" WIDTH=80 HEIGHT=40
BORDER=0></A> 
<A HREF="dummy.htm"> <IMG SRC="contents.gif" WIDTH=80
HEIGHT=40 BORDER=0></A> 
<A HREF="mailto:emailname@domain.name"> <IMG SRC="email.gif"
WIDTH=80 HEIGHT=40 BORDER=0></A>
<BR><FONT SIZE=-1><A HREF="dummy.htm">Back</A> ||
<A HREF="dummy.htm">Forward</A> ||
<A HREF="dummy.htm">Home</A> ||
<A HREF="dummy.htm">Contents</A> ||
<A HREF="mailto:emailname@domain.name">E-Mail</A></FONT>
</BODY>
</HTML>
```

FIGURE 3.49 Continued

CHAPTER FOUR

COOKING UP RICHES WITH WEB COMMERCE

Whether yours is a business selling products, a consultancy selling services, or a nonprofit organization selling memberships or events, it is possible to conduct the complete sales transaction on the Web. This chapter describes techniques and activities for electronic commerce and offers tips for motivating visitors to make purchases or donations on your site.

The tools and methods for Web commerce continue to evolve. We encourage you to discuss the topics in this chapter with your Internet Service Provider, research them on the Web, talk to other marketers who are experienced in Web marketing, and refer to the resources listed in Appendix C.

↳ Successful Selling on the Web

Selling online requires a somewhat different process than the one you may follow for sales via telephone, a personal visit to a prospect, or in a retail store. However, the steps for accepting orders online are easy to learn and implement, and they can integrate well with your other selling methods.

Suitable Products for Online Sales

Any product, service, or event ticket that can be sold via mail or telephone orders can be suitable for sales via a Web page (see Figure 4.1). Specialized products and services can be sold to visitors who find your site through matching keywords in one of the Web search sites. Software products, research reports, books, and other information or materials that can be delivered immediately through a download from the Web page are ideal for online sales.

You cannot realistically expect to sell anything and everything on a Web page. Items that may not generate the online sales volumes you expect include the following:

- Expensive products or services that require a long time and a large amount of information before the visitor will make the decision to purchase.

Business Type	Online Sales Activities
Manufacturer or Distributor (Global Products Co.)	Distribute product information, help visitors find a dealer or store, accept orders from established customers.
Catalog company or retail store (Everything You Need Catalog Co.)	Sell products from an online catalog.
Non-Profit Organization (Fun Events Association)	Sell memberships, courses, merchandise, and event tickets; solicit contributions.
Consultant or Service Provider (Expert Consultant)	Sell books, tapes and seminar registrations; distribute information on services.

FIGURE 4.1 Examples of Web commerce.

- Very complex products that require detailed information or a personal demonstration to understand.

- Products and services that have not been tested in your target market.

In these cases, your Web site can add value to your marketing efforts by helping you to identify interested

Electronic Commerce for Nonprofit Organizations

Many nonprofit organizations generate income through memberships, fees for programs and events, and the sale of merchandise. All of these revenue sources can be promoted online, using the principles and techniques of electronic commerce described in this chapter. Many of the activities and issues will be the same as those for a profit-oriented business.

prospects. For prospects themselves, the Web site offers immediate access to basic product information before they visit a retail store or send you an online inquiry for detailed materials.

Motivating Visitors to Buy

As a result of your planning process (see Chapter 5), you should be confident that selling your product or service on the Web is feasible and that members of your target audience will be interested in making purchases online. Beyond these two essential prerequisites, you can implement any of several techniques to increase the likelihood that your Web-based sales efforts will be successful. These techniques include the following:

- Place a strong call to action on every page that is intended to lead to an online sale (see detailed discussion of a call-to-action statement later in this chapter).

- Develop special promotions that are available only online, such as packages or special pricing.

- Verify that all product and pricing information remains complete and current, especially as you market products over time.

- Look for opportunities to cross-sell and up-sell your products and services, which can increase a visitor's interest in buying and increase the average sale amount. For example, create links among catalog pages to show accessories or related items, or link a services page to a brochure page for selling a complete product package.

- Respond promptly to all orders and inquiries you receive from visitors. A successful shopping experience on your site will encourage visitors to return for future purchases and to recommend your site to other prospects.

- Establish a program for automatically notifying visitors of new products or promotions via e-mail. Each time you remind customers of what's available on your site, you encourage repeat visits and increase the chance for repeat purchases. However, be careful that you do not send e-mail notifications repeatedly or too often, as this may annoy customers. The Order Form, Product Inquiry Form, and Visitor Registration/Survey templates are designed to help you start this program.

Security and Authentication Issues

The security of a customer's credit-card information has been a primary concern of Web marketers. However, one of the greatest demonstrations of secure electronic commerce was made with ticket sales for the 1996 Summer Olympic Games. According to a source from IBM Corporation, which handled the Web sales, more than 10,000 tickets were sold online using secure credit-card transactions, with no cases of fraud.[7]

Security methods have been in place for some time to protect a customer's confidential information when it is transmitted over the Internet. These methods provide two essential functions: encryption and authentication. *Encryption* is a technique to encode text and data transmitted over computer networks by using complex mathematical algorithms. Although no encryption algorithm is foolproof, many of them are so complex they can be considered unbreakable. Even though many complicated issues such as governmental regulation are yet to be resolved, it is certain that encryption technology will continue to evolve and that it will provide a standard of security that businesses and consumers will accept.

Authentication is a function that verifies the identity of the person submitting an order on your Web site. This technology is emerging in the public Internet market and will continue to evolve over the next few years.

Talk with your Internet Service Provider about the security methods available for your site. As an additional safeguard, confirm all online sales via a return e-mail message or telephone call to the customer before processing or shipping the order.[8]

⤵ Integrating Web and Offline Sales

Most businesses conduct their sales activities in a variety of ways: through retail stores, dealers, or sales representatives, and through catalogs and other forms of direct marketing. A Web site can enhance these activities not only by attracting new customers, but also by motivating them to explore all your sales outlets.

Generating In-Person Traffic from a Web Site

In addition to making sales online, your goal may be to motivate prospects to visit your retail store, dealer location, event, program office, or other location. These ideas can help you prompt visitors to take the next step after viewing your Web page:

- Include a link to a Locator page that lists all stores, dealers, offices, or other sites. The Locator template is designed for this purpose; see Chapter 3 for ideas on how it can be implemented with advanced scripting and presentation capabilities.

- Describe the types of products, services, or activities that are available in your physical location but not on your Web site. For example, a bookstore that attracts traffic through events such as book signings, author readings, children's storytellers, and seasonal attractions can use the rich information available on its Web site to entice customers to visit the store. In this way, the Web site becomes a sampler for the interesting activities in the store.

- Announce events or price reductions on short notice, without prior publicity or advertising in other media. If you have built a database of customers who want to receive notices about new promotions on your site, you can send them a brief e-mail message and encourage them to visit your site again for details.

Local-Area Marketing

Locally focused businesses and organizations can benefit from Web marketing in several ways. You can sell products to customers outside your area easily and inexpensively, creating a new line of revenue at a lower cost than traditional direct-mail methods. You can also use the Web to promote special events, programs, or other marketing activities that would be too expensive to advertise in other media.

Your Web site also can attract travelers, newcomers, and even longtime residents in the area who find it via an online search. It may seem that potential customers, members, and others should be able to find you easily through local telephone directories or other print resources. But it is difficult to do so when a prospect doesn't know the name of your business or group or the categories in which it might be listed.

Using the search tools on the Web removes these limitations. The prospect can enter a product or topic and city as keywords and—if you have designed your content to facilitate keyword searches—find your Web site.

> **TIP**
>
> This promotional capability is especially beneficial for nonprofit organizations and groups that do not maintain an office, instead using volunteers to handle memberships and other inquiries.

Selling Internationally

Selling to international customers via the Web involves many of the same issues as selling to them via other methods, especially direct mail. Product availability, trade laws, import/export regulations, tariffs, shipments, and currency exchange are among the issues you will need to consider. An attorney and export agent experienced in both international sales and electronic marketing can guide your efforts. Also talk with your banker about options for accepting international credit cards such as JCB or Eurocard.

Chapter 10 presents additional discussion of the issues and techniques for marketing to an international audience via a Web site.

↳ Conducting Web-Based Commerce

Completing a sales transaction on your Web site encompasses several processes and activities. First, of course, you must attract visitors to your site. Then you must motivate them to make a purchase and guide them through all the necessary steps. And throughout the transaction, you must give visitors easy access to standard ordering information such as payment terms, shipping schedules, and return policies.

Helping Visitors Find Your Site

The first requirement for Web commerce is to ensure that prospects and customers in your target markets will find your site. You can take several steps to encourage visits to your Web site:

- Register with Web search sites such as Yahoo!, AltaVista, Lycos, and Excite. Check these sites (URLs are listed in Appendix C) for instructions on submitting a registration for your site.

- Print the URL for your site on all brochures, newsletters, and other promotional materials—even your business cards and stationery. This action will not only encourage prospects to visit your site, but it may prompt them to save your material for future reference if they do not plan an immediate product search or purchase.

- Announce your site to current customers, members, donors, prospects, dealers, and business partners—anyone who may be interested in visiting your site themselves or who could recommend it to others.

- Continually promote the site. Standard marketing wisdom states that prospects must receive multiple exposures to an advertisement before they will recognize or remember it. This wisdom also applies to a Web site, where visitors may need several reminders that your site even exists before they will visit it.

TIP

Proofread your URL listings in all media to make sure they are spelled correctly and include all needed punctuation; if possible, print the URL on a single, unbroken line to avoid hyphenation.

The Call to Action

Every Web page you create for a promotional purpose should present a call to action—a phrase or paragraph that encourages the visitor to make a purchase or contact you for detailed product information, an appointment, or other sales activity. Without a clear and specific call to action, the visitor may not be motivated to take the next step or, worse yet, not know how to do so.

State the call to action on every page that leads to the online sale, event registration, or other action you want the visitor to take. Place an Order Now! or Register Now! button or link on every page for the promotion, allowing the visitor to reach the Order Form or Registration Form directly. Don't make visitors scroll through multiple pages of additional information before they can make a purchase—they may lose their enthusiasm for buying.

All too many call-to-action statements read like this: *For more information Click here or call (800) 555-DULL.* To be effective, your call to action should give your visitors something specific to do, and a good reason for doing it. A call to action also becomes more powerful if you use it to reinforce your key benefit or message. For example, this call to action reinforces a key benefit: *Buy Wonder Product and gain more time for fun! Order Now!*

A call-to-action statement can contain links to any of the following:

- An Order Form from every page that describes a product or service the visitor can purchase online

- An Event Registration Form from every page that describes a course, performance, or other event

- A Product Inquiry Form, Visitor Registration/Survey Form, or e-mail message that enables the visitor to send you a specific question or request

A call to action can be presented in a single sentence or a brief paragraph. Give specific instructions on all the ways a visitor can take the action or obtain more information, including offline methods. In addition to an online order form, inquiry form, or e-mail link, include text on the Web page that presents all the ways a visitor can reach you: toll-free, direct-dial, and fax telephone numbers, as well as postal addresses for sales offices, dealers, retail stores, or other sources.

Internet telephone may be another option for visitors to contact you. This technology allows a visitor to click on a link in your Web page and initiate a voice call to your sales or information contact directly over the Internet. Voice calls from a Web page will give visitors the satisfaction of real-time, personal service although with poorer voice quality.

Ordering Methods

Developing a Web site with electronic commerce capabilities will require more time, effort, and expense on your part than a site that simply presents promotional information. However, we believe your investment will be rewarded by better results and higher sales.

While a Web site can direct visitors to offline purchasing methods, we recommend developing a secure, online ordering capability for several reasons. The most important is that online ordering gives visitors an easy and immediate way to make a purchase, which increases their motivation to complete the transaction.

In addition, because customers and prospects can access your Web site 24 hours a day, from any location in the world, they will want to make purchases or contact you at any time. These visits represent incremental sales opportunities that your business can realize during nonworking hours or other times when sales staff may not be available.

Even with a full online ordering capability, you can give customers a choice of methods for making a purchase from a Web site. The visitor can print an online Order Form, then fax it to your sales representative or use it as a reference when placing an order by telephone. An e-mail message can be a simple way to submit orders that do not contain confidential information, such as when a customer has established an account with your company. Or, you can place the telephone number for your sales center in a prominent place on each page, encouraging visitors to call when they are ready to order.

The capabilities you offer for online ordering also can encourage visitor purchases. The Order Form template is designed for a simple online transaction, where the visitor completes all information before submitting the form (see Chapter 3 for details). This approach will be adequate if you sell a small number of products or services online.

As your site grows or if you sell a large number of products, you should consider a "shopping cart" program for conducting the online sales transaction. This program saves a visitor's selections as he or she navigates among different catalog pages on your site, then automatically enters the information for those items on the Order Form.

When the visitor is ready to finalize the order, the program displays the selections, requests confirmation, and allows the visitor to make changes. When the selections are complete, the program prompts the visitor for any remaining information, such as shipping address, that is required to process the order.

A shopping cart capability greatly simplifies the sales process for visitors, which can encourage them to make additional purchases in the future. Because it requires custom programming based on your site design and product offerings, providing an example is beyond the scope of this book. You can obtain more information from your Internet Service Provider or by searching the Web with the keywords **shopping + cart + program**.

Completing the Transaction

Use the Brochure, FAQ, Catalog Page, Order Form, or other template to provide all the information a visitor will need to complete the sales transaction. Examples include the following:

- Purchasing, refund, and cancellation terms
- Shipping costs, methods, and schedules
- Credit and payment terms
- How visitors can contact you about a problem, return, exchange, or cancellation
- How a visitor can obtain offline assistance with an order, problem, or request

Local commerce laws may specify the types and wording of information you must give to purchasers for an online sale; consult your attorney for guidance. In addition, check the template descriptions in Chapter 3 for additional ideas on using them for Web commerce.

Trends in Web Marketing and Electronic Commerce

Once you have established your information and procedures for Web-based commerce, your work isn't done. New technologies that facilitate electronic commerce on the Web will continue to emerge at a rapid pace over the coming years.

The list below presents what we believe will be the developments with the greatest impact on Web marketing, but other issues may emerge as well. You will need to monitor information from both online sources and Web-focused magazines in order to keep pace with these capabilities and others that will enhance your online commerce.

- Security methods that are standardized across different browsers and credit-card companies.

- Internet telephone, the ability for a visitor to click a link on your Web page and make a live telephone call to your sales representative without terminating the Internet session.

- Digital cash and other forms of electronic payment.

- Intelligent agents that will help more visitors find your site based on automatic searches of pages across the entire Web.

- Market penetration of Web access and changing demographics of Web visitors.

- Internet kiosks in public areas such as airports and government buildings.

PART II

COOKING

TECHNIQUES

FOR WEB

COMMUNICATION

CHAPTER FIVE

PLANNING YOUR MENU

In your eagerness to create a Web site, you may want to jump immediately to work with the templates in Chapter 3. But your Web marketing efforts will be more successful if you begin with a solid plan. This chapter describes all the factors to consider when planning and discusses how to identify the members of your Web marketing team.

What Is Your Goal?

As with any promotional activity, you should have clear and well-considered goals for developing and maintaining a Web site. These goals will not only give you a means to measure results, but they also will guide your choices about the amount and type of content and interaction you implement on the site. The most common goals for creating a promotional Web site are to do the following:

- Generate revenue directly from the site by selling a product or service, accepting registrations for events or classes, or soliciting memberships and contributions. In this case, a visitor's activity on your Web site will encompass the complete sales cycle for your product or service. You will need to plan for all information and interaction that will be necessary to yield profitable results.

- Capture the names and contact information of qualified leads for follow-up by a salesperson, dealer, or telemarketer. Plan how the Web will integrate with your existing methods and systems for tracking and responding to prospects' information requests.

- Build a relationship and distribute information in support of a visit by a salesperson or dealer, or entice the prospect to visit a store or attend an event. Plan how the Web will integrate with your other advertising and promotional efforts.

- Sustain customer, participant, donor, or member loyalty by providing easily accessible newsletters and other materials online. Plan how you can use the Web to create opportunities to promote additional or new products, events, services, or programs to these visitors.

Your Web site may reflect only one or any combination of these goals. And you may have both short-term and long-term goals—corresponding to your overall promotional activity or the sales cycle for your products or services—that will be reflected in the content on your site.

Who Are Your Guests?

Every form of promotional communication is directed to a defined target audience, even if it is seen by a much broader set of people. The definition of your target audience may remain the same when you bring your promotion to the Web, or you may want to take advantage of the Web's coverage to reach new audiences. For example, a business or consultant with primarily local customers can use a Web site to communicate with prospects across the globe just as easily as with those across town.

Include an audience description in your site plan, style guide, and other planning documents (see discussion later in this chapter). This description will help the different people involved in the development of your Web site maintain a common focus. It also helps you avoid being distracted by the perceived characteristics of Web users, which are

---

Marketing to Children

If children are a targeted audience, you must be sensitive to legal and ethical factors about the techniques and messages you present on your site. There is considerable controversy around marketing to children within North America, and there may be significant differences in viewpoints and restrictions on this activity in other countries. Monitor the development of laws and guidelines on this topic to ensure that your site remains in compliance. Search keywords: **advertising + children**.

---

changing and becoming more like broader demographics as more businesses and consumers obtain Web access.

When defining the target audience(s) for your site, consider people in these groups:

- *Prospects and customers.* Consider companies or people who are buyers, contributors, members, or clients. You may further segment "explorers" from prospects who are ready to buy immediately if they can find what they want. You also may categorize prospects and customers by factors such as industry, geographic location, demographic profile, and previous purchases or contributions.

- *Journalists and analysts.* Reporters and editors at magazines and newspapers, as well as industry or academic researchers may visit your site.

- *Salespeople and dealers.* Don't be surprised to find that the people who sell your product will also want to find useful information on the Web site. Companies with extensive dealer, retail, or franchise networks often maintain a distinct area of the Web site specifically for communication with this audience.

- *Additional audiences.* Business partners and affiliated organizations, investors and financial partners, and employees also may have an interest in your site.

You may want to organize areas of the site with content targeted specifically to each audience. For example, create separate customer and dealer areas or areas that are organized according to audience interests, location, or other factors.

Finally, consider the Web literacy of audience members, especially if you want to implement advanced capabilities such as Java applets for navigation or interaction. Given their slow speed, the fact that visitors may disable them in their browsers, and that not all browsers support them, advanced capabilities will be significantly more frustrating for visitors if they are novice users of the Web or computers in general.

↳ What Will Visitors Want?

Identify the types of information visitors will want to access, and the types of activity they will want to conduct on your site. Examples include the following:

- Retrieving information about a specific product, service, or event

- Purchasing a product or registering for an activity online

- Reviewing background information on a consultant, company, or organization

- Researching information on a specific topic or interest

- Finding the location of the nearest store or dealer

- Contacting you via e-mail to discuss a need or ask a question

Analyzing visitors' needs and expectations will help you choose the best way to implement information and interactivity for the Web site. For example, you can determine whether to offer complete documents, such as brochures or articles, or instead place a "quick-read" summary on the Web. Just remember—you don't necessarily need to make all of these items available on the day you open the site. Identify which items match our advice of starting simple, then add more information and capabilities as you gain experience with Web marketing.

↳ What Will You Serve?

You have identified your goals and audience; now you're ready to identify the types of content you will place on the site. As a start, you can just pick up all of your current promotion materials, adapt them to the templates in this book, or give them to a Web developer for programming into Web pages.

However, you can improve the quality of your site by carefully evaluating several topics related to online promotion, including the following:

- General promotional or competitive factors that are driving content on your site

- How Web promotion will support your product, company, or organization brand

- The depth of content and level of sophistication for the interactivity you want to implement on the site

- Whether you will implement links to external sites or make sensitive information available on the site

What Factors Are Driving Content on Your Site?

Any of the factors below—and many others as well—can influence your choices for content:

- Ongoing promotion of specific products, services, programs, and activities as well as general promotion and branding of your company or organization

- Introduction of new products and services

- Events such as trade shows, seminars and classes, performances, athletic activities, community festivals, holidays, and others

- Competitor actions or trends in the market, community, or political climate that affect your company or organization

Assess these factors before you implement a Web site to help you prioritize the development of content, whether it is based on your current print materials or new content you create specifically for the Web. Then review your assessment periodically to determine whether you need to add new content or restructure the Web site.

You won't necessarily need to publish all of your print materials on the Web site. Certain products, activities, or topics simply may be too complex to present effectively on the Web. In this case, you can create a Web page that presents an overview and links to an order form where the visitor can request the print document. The guidelines in Chapter 6 will help you restructure your existing print material for presentation on Web pages.

CAUTION

Don't rush to publish incomplete information. Just as you would not print a brochure with information that might soon change, avoid the temptation to place information on a Web page before it is complete and ready for public consumption.

Supporting Your Brand

Even though you may think that branding is a concern only for large consumer-goods companies, it is also a consideration for small businesses—and even nonprofit organizations. In a simple definition, a *brand* is created by the perceptions and associations you want to leave in a prospect's mind for your product or service, company or organization.

For example, a brand can convey impressions such as high quality, safety, emotional appeal, or advocacy. In print materials, branding is conveyed through techniques such as logos, color and design, style, paper type and size, as well as the tone, style, and content of the words and images. Branding also can be conveyed on your Web site, through the types of content you present and its tone, style, and visual design.

Although it is tempting to use a very different visual and writing style for your Web content, consider what impact this will make on your brand. In most cases, it is better to maintain a congruency in the way you present a brand in print materials and on a Web page. Visitors who are already familiar with the brand will recognize it immediately and transfer their associations (positive ones, we hope) to your site. And for visitors who discover your product, company, or organization for the first time by visiting the site, you can begin creating a positive brand in their minds.

Text versus Graphics

Many Web sites make extensive use of graphical and multi-media elements to create pages that are visually attractive. But remember that some or even many visitors will access your site over slow, dial-up connections and may be using their browser with the image-display feature turned off. You need to take this type of access into account and provide navigation aids in the form of text as well as graphics.

We recommend that you minimize the use of graphics, at least initially (see Chapter 7 for a detailed discussion). However, there may be situations when creating a graphics-intense page or site is appropriate. Consider that different people process information differently; some are better able to understand text, while others need to see a photograph, diagram, or other visual in order to fully understand the topic of your page. And product images are essential for making an online sale—most prospects need to see a photo or sketch before they will purchase a tangible product.

The most tempting place to use a lot of images is on the home page for the site. But how many times have you accessed a Web site with the image-display feature in your browser turned off, only to be greeted by one or more image boxes—but no text—when the page loads? The only way to determine where you are and where you may want to go next is to scroll down the page, hoping to find text links or, more likely, to load the images and find the site map.

Always structure your site so visitors can navigate and access information through text links as well as site-map images if you use them. This guideline does not necessarily mean you need to develop and maintain a complete, text-only version of your site. Instead, you can simply make the associated text links visible in or adjacent to every graphical link or map on a page. We have implemented this approach in the templates for this book, using <ALT=> tags for images and placing a text link with each graphical navigation button that appears on a page.

Utility versus "Cool"

Related to the decision about creating a text-oriented or graphics-oriented site is whether you want to emphasize utility or entertainment in your site. Much of what has been written about marketing on the Web has focused on the need to entertain visitors in order to interest them in exploring your site and returning in the future. A high entertainment quotient is appropriate for some sites, especially those that emphasize mass-market consumer products or leisure activities. However, we believe pages or site areas with a focus on entertainment will not necessarily serve you well if visitors come to your site expecting to find useful information or make a purchase. In this case, they will value the quality of your content over the visual appeal of its presentation.

It is also easy to get sidetracked by the temptation to add many graphics, Java applets, video clips, and other flashy elements to your site. Instead, we recommend starting simple—emphasizing the completeness and accuracy of your text and basic images—then adding the more complex elements to your site over time. This approach offers several advantages:

- You can implement new sections or the entire site quickly because less programming is required.

- Simpler pages load more quickly, a feature that many visitors appreciate more than seeing "pretty pictures."

- You can take the time to carefully evaluate the need for additional content, graphics, and other complex elements after you gain an understanding of how visitors are interacting with the site and after you have collected visitor feedback.

- You can avoid the costs of the extensive design and programming work for advanced capabilities, which becomes even more expensive if you must make changes later.

Certain types of complex programming can be beneficial to your Web site. One example is CGI scripts, which are the basis for creating interactive forms. An *interactive form* is a Web page that looks like a printed form, with labels and blanks for entering specific information. The visitor uses the mouse to move around the form, types text entries, then clicks on a Submit or Send button when finished. All information the visitor enters is sent to the CGI script on your Web server for processing.

For our purposes, the most common function a script performs is to format the visitor information into an e-mail message, then send it to you or your company for action. The CD-ROM includes a general-purpose, form-processing script, called *mailform.cgi*, that creates an e-mail message from a visitor's inputs on a web form. It is the most important script for marketing on the Web and the only script required for many Web sites.

Other examples of useful scripts involve validating credit-card numbers, building guest-book entries, posting to a bulletin board, searching for keywords within a Web site, and adding data to an online database. All of these scripts work basically the same way: The user fills out a form, then submits it to the script on the Web server for processing and action.

If you want to write your own CGI scripts, remember the following points:

- Writing the code for a script is more challenging than writing HTML code.

- This programming requires knowledge of your Web server, for example, how it structures files and processes data.

- Different servers support CGI in different ways.

In addition to scripts, complex graphics or multimedia elements may enhance your message or presentation in certain situations. Examples include the following:

- If your site is targeted to or attracts a large number of international visitors, images and video or audio clips may be more effective for presenting your message in a universally understandable form.

- If you are confident that members of your target audience can access your site over a high-speed network link.

- If the subject of your promotion involves images, multimedia, or related products and services.

You will need to consider the trade-off between loading speed and the impact of your presentation when choosing how to use multimedia and graphical elements on a page (see Chapter 7 for details).

Links to Other Sites

As part of your planning, consider whether you will offer links to external sites. Think of links as another way to build a complete promotional environment for your product, service, event, or organization. Choose links that will support and enhance your business image, rather than just provide entertainment or a reflection of your own interests and tastes. Examples to consider include the following:

- Local-language versions of your site
- Sites for dealers, retail stores, business partners, affiliated organizations, local groups, and customers
- Sites for related industry, trade, and professional organizations
- Research and reference sites
- Event calendar sites

More ideas on creating promotional links to other sites are presented in Chapter 8 and by industry in Chapter 2.

Controlling Access
to Selected Content

If appropriate, implement a password scheme to protect access to pages that contain pricing, shipment details, credit or dealer terms, and other confidential information. This method enables you to maintain sensitive information on the same server as other Web pages without making it easily available to your competitors.

A password scheme also can be used to control access to digitized merchandise such as software that is available for downloading from your Web site. After the visitor pays for the purchase online using a credit card, he or she could be given the password to a Web page that controls the software download. While not absolutely guaranteeing privacy, a password scheme will be adequate for most commercial uses. Details of implementing password controls are discussed in Chapter 11. Other Web security issues you will want to consider are discussed in Chapter 4.

Who Are the Cooks?

Web development tools and templates such as those provided in this book can make it relatively easy for you to create a simple and attractive Web site. But if you want to place a large amount of content on the site or implement capabilities that require extensive design or programming, you will probably turn to experts for assistance.

More complex Web development projects involve a variety of roles, which may be handled by many different individuals or by only a few. You may handle all of these roles yourself, some may be handled in-house by employees, or you may use outside consultants, programmers, and Web development firms.

Project Manager

The project manager is responsible for overall project planning and management, especially for initial site development.

This person coordinates internal and external resources—both people and content. A project manager may continue these responsibilities after the initial development is complete, focusing on maintaining and enhancing the content and performance of the site.

Web Site Developers

The person serving in the developer role is often called the Webmaster for the site. A developer must be able to create the HTML files, scripts, and specialized programs that will actually implement the content and interactivity of your site. The developer also must be able to load and maintain the HTML and program files on your Web server. If you implement advanced capabilities such as Java applets or VRML, you may need to find additional developers who offer this specialized expertise.

As a Webmaster, this person is responsible for decisions about implementation details and technology choices and will be involved in ongoing maintenance of the site.

Content Experts

The content experts are usually members of your marketing, public relations, outreach, or fund-raising staff. Content experts determine what type of information, materials, and messages should be presented on the Web site. They also may provide the information required by writers and graphic designers to create page content that will meet the interests and needs of the targeted audience(s).

Writers and Editors

Working with the graphic designer, project manager, and developers, the writers and editors structure text for effective presentation online. They ensure the content matches the storyboards, site plan, templates, and style guide. They write new text or adapt existing materials for Web presentation and design the navigation paths within the site.

It is important that these individuals understand the very fundamental differences between writing for online communications and writing for print materials. Writers who have experience with other types of online projects, such as online documentation for software products or writing for a multimedia CD-ROM, will find that their techniques and knowledge are directly applicable to effective content presentation on the Web.

Graphic Designers

A graphic designer can give your Web site superior visual appeal by creating the overall page design as well as individual images, other graphical elements, and multimedia elements. The designer must understand different file formats for images and know how to obtain the best trade-off of image quality and loading speed. Like writers, a graphic designer must understand the differences and limitations of presenting information on a Web page in comparison to print materials.

Multimedia Developers

Incorporating animation, audio, or video elements in your Web pages may mean engaging the services of specialists in each of these media. These developers can offer knowledge of effective techniques as well as skills in the production tools necessary to create high-quality multimedia elements.

Attorney

An attorney can help you address several important issues for the content and activity on your Web site, including the following:

- Compliance with laws and regulations for commerce, advertising, and promotional activities

- Protection of your copyrights, trademarks, and proprietary information

- Licenses for content, images, multimedia elements, and programs created by others

Review your plans with an attorney before you begin development and whenever you add significant new capabilities to your site.

Selecting and Working with a Web Designer

While proven techniques and tools in this book make it possible for almost anyone to create professional-quality Web sites, many companies and organizations will contract with external vendors to build sites.

The advantages of having a professional Web site developer construct the site are usually related to time savings and the valuable experience that full-time programmers bring to the project.

If you choose to work with an external developer, we recommend reviewing the criteria listed below before entering into this important business relationship:

- What direct experience does the company have in developing commercial Web sites?

- Who are the principals of the company, and what is their individual experience in the industry?

- Are work samples and references easily available for review? Ask for the URLs of active Web sites and review them as part of your evaluation.

- What kinds of services are offered beyond basic HTML programming (for example, CGI scripting, Java programming, animated GIFs, audio files, database development, Shockwave, Quicktime VR, and others)?

- Does the developer offer only programming and design services, or is Web hosting included in the project?

- Does the developer run its own network server, or does it contract with another vendor?

- Is the server equipment reliable and secure with multiple redundancies? Ask for details on the specific configurations and capacities of both server equipment and network links.

- How much time will the developer require to complete your project?

- Is there a printed price sheet for services? What are the payment terms?

- What additional fees may be required to maintain the site in the future? Are there ongoing maintenance fees? What are the charges for making changes?

- Will the developer facilitate nonprogramming activities such as domain registration?

- Does the developer offer graphic design or copywriting services?

- Do you feel comfortable working with the developer and sharing operational and marketing information about your company or organization?

- Does the developer have a business license, and is it affiliated with any professional associations?

- Is the developer willing to give you control of the site when development is complete? Will the developer be available for additional support in the future (at an hourly consulting fee)?

Because the Web communications industry is relatively new and evolving, many standards are yet to be established. A wide range of skill levels are available, and business practices vary dramatically from one Web site developer to another. As with any business purchase, place a strong emphasis on obtaining and reviewing references and work samples. Additionally, we suggest signing a written agreement on the pertinent issues in the form of a contract or letter of agreement.

Create a Planning Framework

Four types of planning documents—a site plan, storyboards, navigation flowchart, and style guide—will help you define a clear framework for organizing the different types of content on your site. This framework will assist you in selecting the best content and ensuring consistency across different areas of the site, to reduce development time and effort. A planning framework also will help you define the visitor's interaction with your site and avoid navigation problems. The first three documents are described here; style guides are discussed in Chapters 6 and 7.

Site Plan

A *site plan* document presents your information and decisions about the planning factors covered in this chapter. It can be brief or lengthy, depending on the scope of your site. However, a site plan should provide sufficient detail so that all of the people who develop or implement site content gain the following:

- A common understanding of your goals for the site and a profile of the target audience(s).

- Information on existing print materials to be adapted to the Web, including whether electronic (computer) files are available that contain the text, images, and other graphical elements. In addition, list any multimedia elements you plan to use on the site and note whether these are already available in a digitized file, must be converted from an existing recording, or require a new recording or programming (for animation).

- A set of development principles for content, presentation, and navigation on the site.

- Policies about acceptable content and information on the review process for content on the site. This policy is especially important if multiple people can create or update content on your site (see additional discussion in the "Review Process" section later in this chapter).

Figure 5.1 contains a worksheet that you will find useful for creating a site plan.

Storyboards

Storyboarding is a technique used in film and multimedia production to plan the visuals and flow of the story or interaction. For a Web site, storyboards can help you plan the content and appearance of each page and chart the navigation paths a visitor can take through your site.

Site Plan Worksheet
Goal:
Description of Target Audience:
Visitor Expectations for Site:
Site Content and Activity:
Design Principles:
Security or Access Considerations:
Roles and Resources:
Completed by: _____Date: _____

FIGURE 5.1 Worksheet for creating a site plan.

You can print the template pages from the CD-ROM included with this book to use as instant storyboards, or you can create sketches on paper (see Figure 5.2).

Creating storyboards can help you identify standard pages that will serve multiple purposes in your site.[9] For example, a single Company Profile page could serve the link <u>Learn More About XYZ Company</u> that appears on several different pages. Using a standard page not only simplifies site maintenance when standard information about your company changes (such as a telephone number), but it also ensures consistency. Other ideas for standard, multipurpose pages include a list of trademark acknowledgments, list of store or office locations, and a Frequently Asked Questions (FAQ) page.

Storyboards also help you identify forms and other pages that require scripts or special programming to operate correctly or create interactivity with visitors. Chapter 11 presents a complete discussion of advanced options for Web programming.

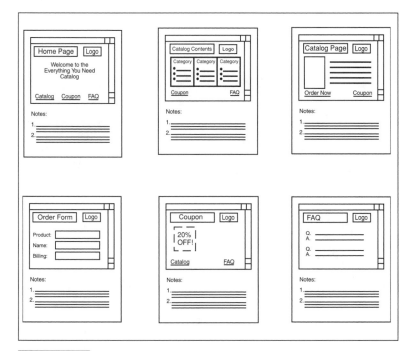

FIGURE 5.2 Web page storyboards.

Navigation Flowchart

After you have created storyboards for each page or area in your site, create a navigation flowchart to show how individual pages will link to each other (see Figure 5.3). A navigation flowchart helps you to verify that you are guiding visitors logically through the content or areas on your site.

The flowchart also can help you identify multiple paths through your site that may be appropriate for visitors to take, based on their information needs or the interaction you want to create. See Chapter 8 for a detailed discussion of creating interaction with visitors on a site.

Plan for Different Browsers

We have designed the templates on the CD-ROM included with this book to be compatible with most graphical browsers (comparable to Netscape version 1.2 or higher) running on Microsoft Windows, Apple Macintosh, and UNIX computers.

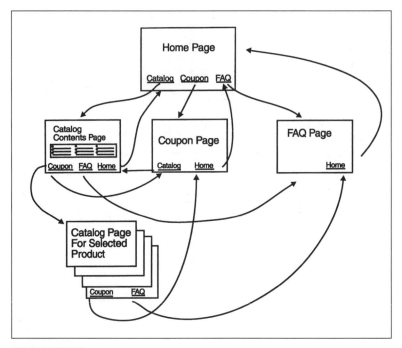

FIGURE 5.3 Navigation flowchart.

However, different browsers offer different capabilities for displaying Web pages and supporting visitor interactivity. In addition, browser vendors are continually improving and expanding these capabilities, and new tools will continue to be offered for designing and publishing Web pages.

Make an initial assessment of the specific browsers you want to support when you plan the presentation format and interactivity for your site. Then periodically evaluate new browser capabilities to determine whether you want to use them to enhance your site.

Think carefully about the level of browser sophistication among members of your target audience before implementing advanced features on your site. Carefully consider these questions:

- If only 5 percent of your audience is using browsers that support Java applets, do you really want to go to the effort and expense to develop them?

- Are there other, more low-tech ways to accomplish the same marketing goal?

- If you decide to use an advanced feature, will you want to give your visitors two ways to navigate your site: one low-tech and one high-tech?

New and emerging technologies will always be implemented on Web sites to take advantage of the Web's communications power. But be careful to consider how expensive and difficult the feature is to implement and maintain, the proportion of your target audience that will be able to enjoy the feature, and whether there are alternative methods to accomplish the same thing for a broader audience. And whatever you do, always plan on presenting the most important information on each page with plain, clearly formatted text.

For a lengthy document or one with numerous images, offer options for downloading an individual page or a complete document. The most common formats are Postscript file, a Portable Document Format (PDF) file, or text file. PDF is an on-screen formatting technology that enables a high degree of fidelity to a printed page with different typefaces and embedded graphical elements. PDF allows you to deliver documents with great visual appeal, but at a cost: PDF files result in greatly increased file size and download time.

All of these file formats give the visitor other choices for printing the document, in addition to the print function in the visitor's browser. Options for printing may be a good way to overcome the limitations of browsers and a visitor's impatience with reading a lengthy document online. However, you will still need to consider whether visitors will be inclined to wait for a lengthy download instead.

Review and Testing Process

If you have defined a review and approval process for print materials, you can adapt this for the content on your Web site. This process can help you ensure consistency between print and online materials and avoid embarrassing errors such as misspellings, missing text, and reversed photos. In addition, you will need to test your Web pages once they are loaded onto your server to ensure that their appearance and operation are correct.

Conduct this review both before and after the actual Web pages are developed:

- Before: Verify the accuracy and completeness of all text and the quality of images.

- After: Verify the correct placement and appearance of all content on each page, acceptable presentation in different browsers, and correct operation of all links.

Remember to repeat this review and testing process each time you change the page content, alter navigation, or add new pages to the site. Don't make the mistake of assuming that because links on your pages work correctly on your PC they will continue to work correctly after you load those pages onto your Web server. Always test *every* change you make *on the server*; see Appendix B for detailed instructions.

CHAPTER SIX

TEXT INGREDIENTS

Content in the form of text and graphical information is key to the success of your site. This challenge is true whether you are adapting print materials or creating completely new content for the Web site. You will need to determine how to best present that content across the site as a whole and whether to present it on a single page or multiple, linked Web pages.

This chapter covers guidelines for organizing and presenting text content on Web pages, as well as considerations for writing style and tone. In addition, this chapter describes how to convert print materials into appealing and useful Web documents.

Web Documents

Before you begin adapting or creating content for your Web site, it is important to understand the concept of a Web document and the choices it offers for structuring information. As we define it, a *Web document* is a set of related content that is stored on a single Web page or multiple, linked pages.

A Web document may be the equivalent of a print document, as when you load the pictures and text from a print brochure onto a Web page. Or it may be something you create fresh, taking advantage of the Web's linking and multimedia capabilities to present your product, promotion, or topic in the most dynamic way possible. The content for a Web document may be segmented across multiple pages to match the print document, but you should consider the guidelines presented in the section "Content Across Multiple Web Pages" later in this chapter for more effective ways to structure multipage documents.

Converting Print Materials to Web Documents

At first, you will want to convert your existing brochures and other print materials to Web documents as quickly and easily as possible. After you gain experience, you may want to create Web documents that do not have corresponding print materials.

Of course, the easiest way to transfer your print materials to a Web document is to use the templates included on the CD-ROM with this book. We have designed the templates to replicate the promotional materials most commonly used by small businesses and nonprofit organizations. To adapt them to your needs, simply load the template files into your word processor or HTML editor and follow the instructions presented in Appendix A.

You may have print materials that don't fit any of the templates or content that you want to present in a particular way. The guidelines in this chapter will help you determine the best structure for translating these materials to Web pages. Once you have defined this structure, you can take it to a Web developer for programming the content or use it when creating your own HTML files.

Defining a General Structure for Site Content

Before beginning work with the templates in this book or creating your own HTML files, you will need to define guidelines for consistently structuring and presenting all content across your Web site. These guidelines will make your content more understandable for visitors as they navigate, and easier for you to expand and maintain. Develop guidelines to present content consistently through the following:

- The way content is organized across the site and within similar pages

- The writing and presentation style for content on all pages

- Use and style of headlines, subheads, bullet lists, and other elements that structure the text for easier reading

- Placement of content on pages that present similar types of information (using the templates in this book will give you a great start for this consistency)

- The content and format of the standard footer for each page

- Color, size, font, and other formatting standards applied to the text

You may have identified many of these guidelines in your planning process (see Chapter 5) or in a style guide (see discussion later in this chapter and in Chapter 7).

Content on a Single Web Page

The first decision you will need to make when adapting a particular printed document is whether its content should be presented completely on a single Web page or split across multiple pages. In general, the text and images in printed documents of fewer than four pages (8.5" x 11" or A4) can usually appear on a single Web page without requiring too much time to load or becoming too cumbersome for the visitor to read online. All of the templates in this book are designed to create single-page Web documents.

If the document or text is longer than four printed pages, you will need to make different choices based on its complexity and length. Your options are to do one of the following:

- Place the entire document on a single Web page, using the segmenting techniques described in the next section

- Break the document across multiple pages, following the guidelines presented later in this chapter

When converting print materials of any length you must consider the number of images, other graphical elements, and multimedia elements that will appear on the Web page. These elements can increase the loading time for the page beyond an acceptable length. In this case, you may want to split the text and graphical content across several Web pages in order to speed loading times.

To assure reasonable loading times, we recommend that you create pages with a file size no larger than 30 kilobytes, including in-line graphics. Chapter 7 presents additional guidelines on maximum file sizes for the different elements on a Web page.

However, file size isn't the only factor to consider when choosing whether to segment a particular set of content over multiple, short pages or place it on a single, long page. Figure 6.1 describes additional factors to consider.

Segmenting Content on a Single Web Page

Content on a single Web page will be more appealing to visitors if you do not present it in a long, unbroken block of text. Any combination of the techniques that follow will create a more attractive layout for long text, as well as make it easier for visitors to read:

- *Subheads*. Use the subheads already written in the text or write new subheads specifically for the document's appearance on the Web page. As a guideline, use a subhead for every three or four paragraphs of text (usually the equivalent of a single screen of information). You can use the heading definitions in HTML to define different levels of subheads, which will appear in different sizes to show the hierarchy of content in the document. The <H1> tag is the largest and is typically used for a page title; the <H2> tag for major subheads; the <H3> tag for minor subheads or section titles, and so on.

- *Bullet lists*. Look for sentences or paragraphs containing information that can be rewritten into bullet-list form (like this).

- *Divider lines*. Divider lines can be created in several ways to divide sections of the document. The easiest divider line to use is the <HR> tag, which causes the browser to insert a "horizontal rule." You can even control its thickness (for example, SIZE=3) and width (for example,

Multiple Short Pages	Single Long Page
Advantages: • Quick loading time. • Focus the visitor's attention on a single topic or product.	**Advantages:** • Complete information about a product or topic in one place. • Eliminates or minimizes links to other pages, saving time and avoiding confusion for the visitor. • If the page is built correctly, the text at the top of the page is readable immediately as the page loads.
Drawbacks: • Visitor may need to load multiple pages, with the associated server delays, in order to find complete information on a product or topic. • Content may become too "choppy," making it difficult for a visitor to follow the flow of a concept or related set of information.	**Drawbacks:** • Long loading time, especially if the document contains many images and graphical elements. • Visitors may not be willing to read long content online. • Requires effective use of an index, intra-page links, divider lines, and other layout techniques to guide the visitor to specific content within the page.

FIGURE 6.1 Considerations for Web page length.

WIDTH=50%) across the page. You can also create text lines with the hyphen (-), underscore (_), or other symbol key by typing it directly into the document text. Graphical lines are usually created as images in GIF files that, like any other in-line image, must be loaded separately on the page. However, because these image files are usually small, they will not significantly lengthen loading times for the page. The advantage of using graphical lines is that they can incorporate color and texture.

- *Multicolumn tables.* You can use a borderless, two-column table to handle content that typically appears in a sidebar or "pull quote" (see Appendix D for a definition) in a brochure or article. Load the main portion of the text into the widest column of the table, then use the other column for the sidebar text. This is an effective method for presenting the key points in the content, highlighting a quote, or presenting a list of features and benefits. (See the discussion on tables in the section "Content Elements for a Web Page" later in this chapter for considerations on presenting data tables effectively on a Web page.)

In addition to these techniques, creating white space around individual paragraphs or blocks of text also improves its readability on a single page; see Chapter 7 for guidelines.

Content on Multiple Web Pages

Consider the guidelines below when you choose to split long documents across multiple Web pages.

- Keep closely related information on a single page. For example, place all information about a specific product or topic on a "main" page, but place information on optional accessories or service programs on separate pages, with links from the main page. Figure 6.2 shows a variety of possible ways to segment content across pages based on the document type. Additional ideas for each template are presented in Chapter 3.

- Repeat and reinforce important information. Don't assume visitors see information or messages presented on another page. Repeat and reinforce this information or your key promotional messages on each page where they are relevant.

- Determine whether you want to segment the content based strictly on length or by topic or document ele-

Template	Content on Main Page	Content on Linked Pages
Article	Main text of the article.	Sidebar text, references or footnotes, glossary, author's biography.
Brochure	Product, service, event, or company description. Key promotional messages, feature/benefit list, and call to action.	Detailed specifications for a product or service, supplemental information about specific features or aspects of your promotion.
Catalog Page	Basic product, course, event, or program description; price information and call to action.	Supplemental information about the purchase, shipping information, order terms, return policy, guarantee statement.
Event Calendar	Table of events, courses, or programs.	Detailed descriptions and information on registration procedure or ticket purchase.
Newsletter	Index of the issue's contents and a brief synopsis of each article.	Article text, subscription information.

FIGURE 6.2 Choices for segmenting content across multiple Web pages.

ment. Segmenting a long document after a certain amount of text is an adaptation of the "Continued on p. xx" technique used in magazines. If segmenting a document according to this "next" or "more" concept, write the link text that appears on the main page to describe what will be presented on the "next" page, for example,

More Web Marketing Wisdom.[10] Segmenting by topic or element means placing supplemental information such as sidebars or footnotes on separate Web pages that are linked to the main page (see Figure 6.2).

- For very long documents or those with multiple images on the Web page, you may want to display a "preview" page—such as an abstract of an article—allowing visitors to determine their interest before spending the time required to load the entire document. Provide a title page for multipart documents, with direct links to each page in the set.[10] An example of this approach is provided by the Newsletter template, which can be used as a "Front Page" of links to articles that are stored on individual Web pages.

- You can place only selected sections of a printed document onto separate Web pages. Make this choice by determining the best way to maintain a good flow of information or based on how the content is structured in the print document.[11] For example, sidebars, footnotes, appendices, glossaries, and other types of content that often appear in a special area of printed materials are often good candidates for placement on a separate Web page.

- Convert the document to Web pages while maintaining a one-to-one match with the print pages. For example, page 1 of a multipage brochure on a Web page would present exactly the same content as its printed counterpart, continuing this match for all pages in the brochure.

CAUTION

If you are reproducing a lengthy document from another source, copyright and presentation issues may determine how you can segment the content. See Chapter 10 for details.

Examples of Print Material Conversions

Figures 6.3, 6.4, and 6.5 illustrate the transformation in layout and structure that can occur when you convert print materials to Web pages. These examples show just a few of the possibilities; your presentation choices may be different—and just as effective.

Brochure

Figure 6.3 shows how two common brochure formats could be converted to Web pages. In the top example, a single-sheet, trifold brochure is replicated on a single Web page. All text and images from the print brochure are included, in a sequence that matches how a reader would see the print version. This type of conversion is very easy to perform using the Brochure template.

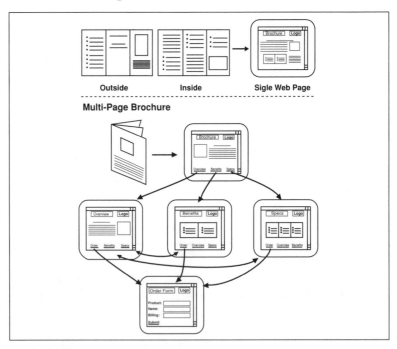

FIGURE 6.3 Converting a brochure to a Web page.

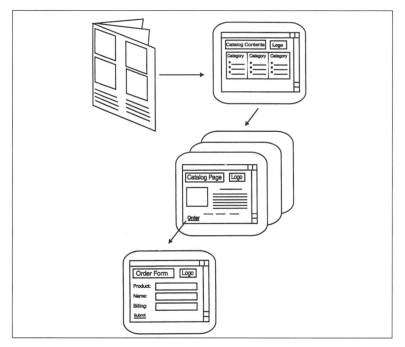

FIGURE 6.4 Converting a catalog to a Web page.

The second brochure example, in the lower portion of the figure, shows an eight-page, booklet-style brochure with lengthy text and numerous photographs, diagrams, or other illustrations. This example shows a conversion to multiple Web pages, using the Brochure template for each page. The guidelines presented for the Brochure template in Chapter 3 offer additional ideas for adapting a printed brochure to a Web page.

Catalog

Figure 6.4 shows how a printed catalog can be converted for online sales via Web pages. This conversion uses three templates:

- The Catalog Contents Page, which gives the visitor a fast method for finding specific links to product pages.

- A Catalog Page for each product. While our examples show one product per Web page, you may want to place multiple, related items on a single catalog page.

- The Order Form, placed on its own Web page that can be reached from any of the individual catalog pages.

Additional guidelines for structuring content in these templates are presented in Chapter 3.

Newsletter

Figure 6.5 shows one method for converting a newsletter to Web pages. In this method, the Newsletter template is used as a "Front Page" that presents an index of links to individual articles. The articles themselves are stored on separate Web pages and use the Article template. A link connects each article back to the Front Page of the newsletter, as a way to help the visitor reorient before viewing another article.

For short newsletters (fewer than four printed pages), an alternative method is to place all of the newsletter content on a single Web page. You may also want to review the guidelines presented for the Article and Newsletter templates in Chapter 3.

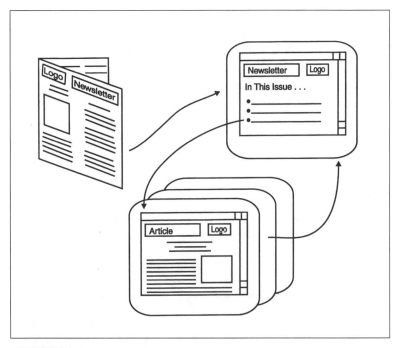

FIGURE 6.5 Converting a newsletter to a Web page.

Structuring Web Pages for Printing

The discussion in this chapter assumes that visitors will read all content on a page while it is displayed in their browsers. However, in many instances visitors will want to print the page—for the greater ease of reading the text offline or to keep the document for future reference.

The simplest way to offer a printed document is to rely on the print capability in the visitor's browser. In this case, you place the entire document into a single HTML file, allowing the visitor's browser to break it automatically into pages while printing. If the Web document is segmented across multiple pages, the visitor will need to load and print each page individually—a process that is time-consuming, inconvenient, and open to error. Another consideration is that the visitor's printer may not support all aspects of your document, such as graphics.

As an alternative, you can create a non-HTML file that contains a separate print version of the complete document in text, Postscript, or PDF format. Some Web sites offer two versions of very long documents. One version is structured into small segments on multiple Web pages for online viewing; the other version contains the complete document in a single file for printing, often in compressed form for faster transfer.

When defining a print file, specify margins of at least one-half inch on the page format to accommodate printing on both 8 1/2" x 11" and A4 (21 cm x 30 cm) printers.[12]

Writing Techniques for Web Documents

In some ways, writing text specifically for a Web document will be much the same as for any other type of promotional material. You will write catchy headlines, use action verbs, address the visitor directly, and choose language that conveys a sense of enthusiasm about your product or topic. However, when creating a Web document, you may want to write with a length and structure for both paragraphs and sentences that is best suited to Web presentation.

CAUTION

If you are adapting an existing print document for the Web, you may not want to change the text as recommended here. There are several reasons for preserving the text as written:

- To avoid confusing visitors who may see both the print and Web version of the material

- To avoid deleting information inadvertently or introducing errors

- To comply with copyright or other restrictions on how the content may be presented, especially if you obtain it from an external source

Think Short

The text for Web pages is more effective if it is shorter and crisper than what you may be accustomed to writing for print materials. Short, declarative, or imperative sentences are easier to understand both for international visitors and when visitors read text on the screen. Write shorter paragraphs— even single-sentence paragraphs. For complex information, use bullet lists and tables instead of paragraphs.

Shorten the line length of displayed text. An ideal line length is between eight and ten words; this can be created by any of these methods:

- Placing specific line breaks into the text using the <BREAK> tag in HTML.

- Creating indents by using the <PRE> tags to surround text that contains tab settings.

- Our favorite technique is to use multiple, successive <UL> tags with no <LI> tags. This is a simple way to indent or provide wider left margins.

- Placing the text into a borderless table with two or three columns. This method has the advantage of creating white space on one or both sides of the text. You can use the side columns for callouts or links.

- Be careful that you don't shorten the line length too much, especially when placing text into a table. Layouts that allow fewer than five words per line make it difficult for visitors to read and understand the text. Finally, remember that visitors can change the fonts used by their browsers, which can have a significant impact on how your text appears (see Chapter 7).

Writing Guidelines

Here are additional guidelines to keep in mind when adapting print materials for Web pages or when creating a new Web document:

- Don't reference other blocks of text or images—even if they are located on the same page—with words alone such as "as described above" or "as shown in Figure 1." Create a link to these items instead, whether they are located on the same page or other pages on your site.

- Write in an inverted-pyramid structure, with the most important information at the top of the page. This is the same style that journalists use when writing a newspaper article. By placing your key information, message, or call to action at the top of the page, you catch a visitor's attention and encourage further reading to learn about the details. This approach also ensures that you present the essential information to visitors who do not scroll down to view the complete page.

- Don't rely on punctuation to convey meaning, as it can be nearly impossible to see on screen.[13]

- Avoid using acronyms, or show the component words on each page where the acronym appears. If content on your site includes numerous acronyms or other specialized terms, create a glossary page of definitions, and link to that page from the first appearance of each acronym or term on each Web page.

- For more than five to seven items in a bullet list, group the items into separate lists according to category or topic. Bullet lists can contain items that are all links, all text, or a mix.

- Some writers use underlining to add emphasis to individual words, sentences, or paragraphs. However, on the Web underlining usually indicates the text is an active link. Remove the underline from any text that will not be a link and use bold or italic format instead.

- Check your text for writing techniques that may not be applicable or understandable to an international audience. Techniques such as humor, emotion, slang, and cultural references do not translate well and may be offensive to international visitors.

- It is easy for errors of fact or omission to find their way onto a Web page, causing you embarrassment and perhaps legal problems. Fortunately, correcting errors on a Web page is as simple as uploading a new HTML file onto your Web server—much faster and simpler than correcting errors in a printed document. Check each page carefully for misspelled words, improper grammar or word usage, incorrect punctuation, reversed images, and missing text.

Content Elements for a Web Page

Web pages can reproduce many of the elements used in print materials to organize text, as shown in Figure 6.6. But Web pages also can include several types of content elements that are not used in print materials. You can use any or all of the elements described in this section on a Web page, whether it is based on a converted print document or new content.

Content Element in Print Material	Content Element on a Web Page
Headlines and subheads	Headlines and subheads, although with limited capabilities for size and formatting.
Overlines (a line of text that appears above and provides a lead-in to the main headline)	Can be created by placing a subhead above the main headline.
Body copy	Content of the Web page.
Bullet and numbered lists	Bullet and numbered lists.
Sidebars	Create a multi-column layout using a borderless table, and place the sidebar text into one of the columns.
Captions and callouts	Captions can appear underneath or wrapped around images using the <ALIGN=> tag.
Pull quotes	Place the quote text in a box using simple one-row, one-column table surrounded by a border.

FIGURE 6.6 Differences in treatment of content elements.

Location Indicator

In a large Web site, a location indicator gives the visitor important clues about the hierarchical organization of the site and the relationship of the current page to others; for example,

```
Home Page:Level 1:Level 2:Current Page
```

The location indicator also identifies pages that a visitor may want to bookmark in his or her browser. It typically appears at the top of the page. As shown here, creating a link for each level shown in the location indicator gives visitors an easy way to navigate within the hierarchy.

Page Banner

A page banner can serve as a location identifier, page-type identifier, or headline. It can appear as an image or text block. The templates included with this book use an image banner to identify the type of content on the page. A banner is an optional element for a Web page, used in addition to or in place of a headline.

The words that appear at the top of each page—whether in a headline or page banner—must entice the visitor to explore further. State clearly what type of content is presented on the page, present a benefit statement, or ask a question to engage the visitor's interest. Also remember that the first 10-50 words in the page title, headlines, and text are displayed by the search sites when they find your site as the result of a search. Most of the search sites also index any <META> tags that you include on a Web page. <META> tags provide descriptive information about your site with text that the browser does not display.

Tables

Tables can be used in two ways on Web pages: as a content element to present data or as a layout technique. Several templates on the CD-ROM use tables for layout; see the discussion of this technique earlier in this chapter and in Chapter 7.

When presenting data tables on a Web page, you may need to restructure them to fit within the limited space of a screen display. For example, you may need to split large amounts of data across several tables. Or, you may find it more effective to summarize the data or present it in a graph instead.

Links

Links are a significant content element on most Web pages, helping visitors find additional information on your site or connect to other sites. See Chapter 8 for a detailed discussion on structuring navigation with links and writing the link text.

Footer Elements

The bottom area of a Web page typically presents a standard set of information that helps both the visitor and the developer track the page's content and location. Examples of this standard information include the page revision date, URL notation, copyright notice, visitor counter, links to other pages on the site, and a link for sending an e-mail message to the marketing contact or Webmaster for the site. We have included several of these standard elements in the footer for all templates on the CD-ROM.

Revision Date

There is some debate among marketers about whether to include a revision date notation on a Web page. If it has been a long time since the date shown on a page, visitors may think the information is no longer valid. Or, they may think you don't update your site very often and they will lose interest in visiting it again.

However, if the information has limited time value or a specific date association, you may want to include a notation such as one of these:

- "Last Updated (date)"
- "Current as of (date)"
- "Valid through (date)"

Even though this notation appears most often at the bottom of a page, you should place it in a location that reflects its importance for visitor knowledge. As an example, for a limited-time online promotion, place the expiration date near the top of the page so visitors see it immediately.

URL Notation

Show the complete URL (address) a visitor would need to type to reach this specific page or the home page for the site.

Contact Information

While you can expect that most visitors will contact you via an e-mail link or inquiry form from your Web site, you should also include a complete set of contact information. This can appear in the footer or content area of each page. Complete contact information includes postal address and voice, fax, and toll-free telephone numbers. If your site targets an international audience, remember to include the country name and dialing codes.

Create a Content Style Guide

A content style guide specifies your decisions and standards for the content that appears on your Web site. It reflects many of the decisions you made in your planning process (see Chapter 5), and it is a companion document to a presentation style guide (see Chapter 7). The content style guide should cover the following:

- The type of content that can be placed on the site and choices for maintaining congruency with print materials

- Guidelines for structuring content on a single Web page and segmenting it across multiple pages

- Writing style and tone; your choices for handling acronyms and other issues of word usage

- International considerations for subject matter, writing style, promotional messages, and cultural references

A content style guide is especially useful if numerous writers and content experts contribute to your site. You will also find it helpful for maintaining consistency of content on the site over time.

Style and Tone in Web Text

Style is your choice of words, the way you structure a sentence, how you organize information, and how the text creates an impression in the visitor's mind about your site, company, or organization. Some marketers use a very formal style in the text; others use a very informal style that is closer to spoken conversation. Your writing style should reflect the target audience's use of language and preferred degree of formality (especially for variations among international markets).

The tone of the text that appears on a Web page is also important for creating the desired impression in the visitor's mind. Tone can be described by words such as *upbeat, empathetic, knowledgeable,* or *conservative*. It is achieved cumulatively through the combined effect of the content itself, how it is presented on the Web page, and your specific word choices.

The tone of your writing must match the visual style you present on the site. For example, a very formal tone in the text would dampen the impact of a visual style that was intended to convey excitement and energy.

Some Web marketers—consciously or not—apply a very different style and tone to the content of a Web site than they use in print materials. When writing or adapting content for your Web site, ask these questions to determine the style and tone you want to use:

- "What are the expectations and sensitivities of our target audiences?"

- "What sense of our product, program, or organization do we want to create in the visitor's mind?"

- "Is this the same sense that we create with our print materials?"

- "Do we want to carry-over the same style and tone from our print materials to our Web pages, or create a different sense on the Web?"

No matter which writing style and tone you use, apply them consistently throughout the site because inconsistencies in text and visual styles are very disconcerting for the visitor. For example, don't use a very formal and subdued style on one page, then switch to a very vivid and "hip" style on another. Specify your preferences for writing style and tone as part of the style guide for the site, which will help to avoid the discontinuity that can occur when multiple writers contribute to your content.

CHAPTER SEVEN

VISUAL AND MULTIMEDIA INGREDIENTS

An advantage of the World Wide Web is its ability to present visually appealing documents that combine text with images and multimedia elements—audio, video, and animation. By using the basic layout capabilities of HTML and the advanced capabilities in certain browsers, you can create attractive and well-organized Web pages. But just as easily, you can create pages that require long load times or are difficult for visitors to read because of poor layout or overuse of graphical and multimedia elements.

It is also important to remember that you will not be able to reproduce exactly the layout of print materials on a Web page. Indeed, the appearance of text and visuals will sometimes be dramatically different on a Web page than in a print document. This difference is the result of the inherent limitations of Web presentation (such as smaller screen space and fewer formatting capabilities), as well as the requirements for presenting online information effectively.

This chapter covers the design aspects of Web pages and offers guidelines for using images and multimedia elements.

General Guidelines for Web Presentation

The following guidelines will help you establish the key design principles for pages on your site.

- Create a standard page layout for placement of text and images, applying that design consistently to all pages in the site.

- Implement images and multimedia elements carefully, minimizing the number on each page to reduce loading time. Use graphical and multimedia elements only when they will support your objective for the page and add clarity or important supplemental information to the text. Don't implement an element just because you think all Web pages need flashy images and multimedia or because you think they are necessary to attract visitors.

- Whenever possible, use the same images on multiple pages. This will speed-up the page loading time because the browser will need to load the image from the Web server only once.

- Link to large images instead of loading them in-line on the page.

- Don't create images that are larger than the typical display window in a browser.

- Keep in mind that images or symbols may convey different meanings in different cultures, so make your choices carefully (see Chapter 10 for guidelines).

- Remember that the speed of the connection you use to build and test your site may be much faster than the average connection speed of your visitors.

- Look at other sites for ideas: sites for competitors or similar organizations certainly, but also other sites that are targeted to your audience or have a similar goal. Identify and understand what you like and don't like about the organization and presentation of content on each site. Are the pages visually appealing? Easy to read? Do they load quickly? What is the balance of text and graphical images in the page?

TIP

Look at sites for organizations that are similar in size or market coverage to yours. This will give you ideas that are more realistic to implement on your site.

↳ Use a Standard Page Layout

For most print materials, graphic designers create a standard page layout or design to ensure consistent sizing and placement of text and images in multipage documents. You can apply the principles of a standard layout to your Web pages with dual benefits:

- Making pages easier for you to design, create, and maintain

- Making it easier for visitors to understand the organization of your site and find information quickly

Among the factors you should consider when creating a standard layout for your Web pages are the following:

- Consistent placement of banners, icons, navigation buttons and bars, footers, location indicators, and other text or graphical elements that appear on all or most pages

- Consistent appearance of text in headlines, narrative paragraphs, bullet lists, tables, and links

- Single-column or multicolumn layout presentation of text with consistent margins and use of white space

- Consistent sizing and placement of graphics on like pages, such as product photos on catalog pages

The templates in this book are based on a standard layout design and give you a great start for creating a well-designed site.

Frames and Page Layout

Some browsers support the appearance of multiple, independent frames on a Web page. Frames are similar to separate windows in a graphical user interface such as the Macintosh or Microsoft Windows. Frames offer many possibilities for creative layout, but they also have significant drawbacks; see Chapter 11 for more information.

Create White Space

An important design consideration for both print materials and Web documents is the amount and placement of white space on the page. White space helps visitors identify different parts of a Web document quickly and read it easily. Remember, more white space must appear around and between text paragraphs and other elements on Web pages because it is more difficult for visitors to read large amounts of text online.

You can create white space on a page with any of these methods:

- Using a borderless table to create a multi-column layout, leaving one column empty and placing the text in the other column(s)

- Using the <BREAK> or <PRE> tags for the text

- Inserting an extra blank line between paragraphs

- Using multiple successive <UL> tags without the usual accompanying <LI> tags

- Using a graphic image that is as wide as your desired indentation but only one pixel high

The <PRE> tag in HTML will present text in the exact format you defined in your word processing program, including fonts, line length and spacing, indents, and paragraph spacing. In comparison, HTML offers fewer choices and control for these formatting capabilities. Although using the <PRE> tag may seem to be the best way to control the layout of a Web page, this technique also has limitations:

- Unless you format a short line length, browsers cannot adjust (wrap) the text to fit the size of the visitor's display window. This may mean that some text will be cut off from the right side of the display window.

- The <PRE> tag also causes the browser to use a different font than the default, which is not always desirable for clarity or attractiveness.

Select a Color Scheme

Ensure that your Web pages are readable by carefully choosing the combination of colors used for the text and background. The most easily readable color combination is this one:

Text: Black

Background: White
Available Links: Blue
Visited Links: Magenta or red
Bullets and Divider Lines: Gray, blue, or red

The legibility of your text is diminished by these factors:

- A patterned background

- A combination of colors that do not have adequate contrast, such as red text on a blue background or different shades of the same color, such as light gray on dark gray

- A black background with white, yellow, or red text (in printed materials this is called reversed text)

No matter which color combination you choose, test its appearance in different browsers and in a printout of the Web page to ensure the text is legible. If you choose a color scheme that is different from our recommendation, consider these guidelines:

- Differences in meaning are associated with certain colors by people in other cultures. If you market extensively to an international audience, be especially careful in choosing colors for icons, bullets, and other nonphotographic images.

- Remember that visitors may set a different color scheme in the browser that overrides your color assignments for all or selected elements of the page. Consider what impact these changes may have on the subtle meaning or information you are trying to convey with a specific color choice.

- Choose colors that will create positive associations for the brand you want to build or maintain on the Web site. For example, if you use certain shades of red in your print materials, use closely matching colors in logos and other graphical elements on the Web pages. As an alternative, you may want to implement a color scheme that reflects the unique style and tone of the site's content, especially if it is different from that in your print materials.

- Not all visitors will be viewing your site on a high-resolution VGA monitor, so your site's background color may not look the same on their monitors as it does on yours. It is advisable to stick with one of the 256 (8-bit) VGA display colors so that a lower-resolution monitor will not need to display a dithered rendition of your otherwise magnificent, 24-bit custom background color.

Guidelines for Images

As used in this book, the term images encompasses the following:

- Photographs of products, buildings, people, scenery, or objects

- Diagrams of processes, configurations, or relationships

- Illustrations for concepts or when a realistic representation of something is not required

- Charts and tables that present data

- Screen captures of software programs or online displays

- Icons for symbolic representation of an object, place, event, or activity

- Logos and decorative elements

Web pages can present images in either of two formats:

- JPEG (Joint Photographic Experts Group), used for photographs and complex images that require a large number of colors or high resolution. This format, also known as JPG, is preferred for portraits.

- GIF (Graphics Interchange Format), typically used for icons, decorative elements, diagrams, and other non-photograph images. You can animate a GIF image or set its background color to be transparent, making the image appear to "float" on the page.

The templates on the CD-ROM support both JPEG and GIF formats.

Logos and Other Company Identity Elements

Present your company logo, product symbols, and other images that make up your organizational identity in a way that is consistent with their use and appearance on print materials. Verify that logos meet any standards you have defined for size, appearance, and color; this consistency can be important for protecting the trademark registration of your logo symbol.

You also may want to create a separate logo for the Web site. At a minimum, the company and site logo should appear on the home page and any other pages that are lead-ins to the major areas of content on your site. All templates on the CD-ROM include a placeholder for your organization or site logo, loaded in-line as a GIF file.

Decorative Elements

Bullet symbols, divider lines and boxed areas, colored or textured backgrounds, and icons are all examples of decorative elements that can enhance the visual appeal of a Web page. For example, instead of a simple round bullet symbol, you can use a graphical bullet to draw the visitor's eye to a new promotion, product, link, or topic on the page.

You can create your own decorative elements or images, purchase collections designed specifically for the Web, or download images from the Web itself. However, be certain you are not violating copyright or licensing restrictions when you reuse a downloaded image on your site. To find image collections on the Web, search with the keywords: **Web + page + graphics**.

Images and Loading Times

Remember that each image or graphical element that you specify as in-line will add to the loading time for the Web page. This loading time is additive: The more images you use, the longer the loading time. Figure 7.1 shows recommended file sizes for the different types of images and graphical elements.

Presentation Tips for All Images

The following tips will improve the presentation speed and quality of images on a Web page:

- Verify that a scanned photograph has sufficient sharpness and contrast to be easily recognizable on a Web page. Clarity is especially important for product photos that must highlight physical details. Remember that the low resolution of most computer monitors automatically lessens the quality of photos.

- Specify *width* and *height* attributes for all images to allow the browser to display the surrounding text on the Web page immediately while the images continue to load. Verify that images are no wider than 480 pixels to ensure they will fit into the default browser window. We have implemented these standards for the templates that include images.

- To speed loading time, minimize the color palette of images and allow the visitor to link to large images as a separate file instead of loading them in-line on the page.

Graphical Element	Maximum File Size
JPEG or GIF Image	30 kb
Background Image (JPEG or GIF)	5 kb
Page Banner	10 kb
Logo	10 kb
Decorative Elements	5 kb
Navigation Bar	10 kb
Navigation Buttons	5 kb

FIGURE 7.1 Recommended file sizes for images.

- Specify an <ALT> text tag in the HTML code for each large or linked image on the page. The <ALT> tag appears in the image placeholder box when the visitor has disabled image display in the browser. The text for an <ALT> tag can describe the image or show a text link if the visitor can navigate to another page by clicking on the image. Make the <ALT> text as descriptive as possible, allowing visitors to determine what the image presents or where it will lead. This guideline is especially important if the image is a site map or navigation bar, which the visitor may want to view separately from other images on the page.

TIP

Place a regular text caption underneath or adjacent to images such as diagrams, concept illustrations, or photographs of products, people, places, or activities. A caption can reinforce or explain what is presented in the image, which is useful information even for the visitor who has turned off image display.

Image Clarity

A common phenomenon with images—and colors in general and photos in particular—is that visitors complain the photo is dark. In many cases, this is a result of a poorly adjusted contrast or brightness setting on the visitor's monitor. Most people don't realize they can control these settings. Sometimes poor representation of the image is related to the limitations of the monitor itself. While this may not be relevant to the initial programming, it is relevant to testing your Web pages for viewability.

Guidelines for Multimedia Elements

As stated in Chapter 5, we recommend that you minimize the use of multimedia elements because of the long loading times and complexity they add to Web pages. However, some products or promotions will be well served by multimedia, or you may be ready to add these elements to selected pages. The guidelines in this section will help you present multimedia with a high-quality impact and a minimum of development pain.

Audio

An effective use of audio on a Web page is to create a link to an audio file that presents a sample of music, a performance, or a speech. No matter how you decide to use audio clips on a Web page, always capture them from a high-quality recording. Sample audio is included on the CD-ROM.

Many of the same constraints described in the next section for video elements also apply to audio: large file sizes for certain formats, download requirements, separate player tools for the browser, and poor sound quality.

TIP

To overcome some of the limitations described here we recommend using MIDI (Musical Instrument Digital Interface) format when recording original music. This format provides excellent compression and good sound quality on almost any sound card.

CAUTION

Make sure you have the rights or a license to use any audio or video element that is produced by someone else or is not owned by your company. This means you cannot include a clip from your favorite music recording without obtaining permission or a license (see Chapter 10 for details).

Video

Placing video clips on a Web page can be effective for promoting films, videos, or performances as well as to present product demonstrations, excerpts from speeches and events, and customer testimonials. A sample is included on the CD-ROM.

However, realize that current Web technology places several constraints on the visitor's experience with video elements, including the following:

- *Poor playback quality for both picture and sound, even on high-end personal computers.* For visitors accustomed to the high resolution of film projectors and televisions, Web videos will seem very grainy and difficult to view. This poor impression may negatively influence the visitor's perception of your site or organization ("Can't they show anything better than that?").

- *Large files and long download times.* Video clips are typically stored in huge files (AVI or MPEG format) that the visitor must download before viewing. In addition, most browsers do not support video directly, meaning the visitor must use a separate tool to view the video file after download—a tool the visitor may not have. Even though many of these tools are available for download from their developers' Web sites, you should not count on the visitor's patience and willingness to do so. However, you can encourage visitors to add the necessary video capabilities to their browsers by providing links to these developer sites from your pages that contain video clips.

- *"Jerky" playback.* Computers with older, slow processors cannot support the speed required for smooth video playback.

T I P

Indicate the file type and size next to the link for a video or audio clip, using a standard notation such as this: (.AU audio, 350 kb).

Animation

Most Web browsers support display of animated graphical objects on a page. Examples of animated objects include the following:

- Blinking bullets, text, or other images.

- A logo or image that spins or emerges gradually, or animation that is applied to a selected part of the image (see examples on the CD-ROM).

- Marquees, a line of text that scrolls horizontally across the visitor's display (usually at the bottom of the browser window). Companies use marquees to announce a special promotion or a new area on the site, or to present a welcome message on the home page. Not all browsers support marquees; they can be created with an HTML tag or Java, Javascript, or CGI programming.

While animated objects can attract a visitor's attention, they also can distract from the text and other images that appear on the page. Even if the visitor tries to focus on the text, it is more difficult to read and comprehend because of the peripheral distraction caused by an animated object. The visitor's distraction is only increased when multiple animated objects appear on the page. And animation that runs continuously can annoy visitors, prompting them to leave because they may believe (falsely) that more of the same animation is programmed into all areas of your site.

A more effective use of animation is to simulate an action, process, or activity. For example, you can animate a graph to show changes in data over time, or simulate a demonstration by creating an animation from several sequential images.

TIP

Placeholders for audio and video elements are included on the Starter template.

↳ Guidelines for Forms

Web pages that include forms should follow the same presentation guidelines you have defined for your site. In addition, consider these guidelines:

- Always state directions for completing the form at the top of the page; see the form templates on the CD-ROM for ideas.

- Display a Send or Submit button at the bottom of the page. If you place this button at the top of the page, the visitor may click on it before completing all entries on the form.

- Present input areas and text labels consistently.

- Size the input areas to give the visitor sufficient space for entering the requested information. For example, allow a minimum of 12 characters for a person's last name.

- Consider responses from international visitors when designing forms. For example, add a field for country, or create a blank, multiline block for all address information, as we have done with the Order Form and Visitor Registration/Survey templates.

- If you have collected information from the visitor's earlier interaction with your site, you can write a script to enter that information automatically into the appropriate fields on the form. For example, if the visitor has linked to an Order Form from the catalog page for an individual product, the script could fill-in the fields that request information such as product number, name, and price. (See Chapter 3 for a discussion of how the individual forms templates are processed with scripts.)

Create a Presentation Style Guide

In Chapter 6 we discussed the value of creating a content style guide for your Web site. A similar style guide that focuses on presentation also can be useful, especially if multiple designers and developers create your pages. A presentation style guide should cover the following:

- A list of graphical elements and information (for example, organization logo, page banner, and standard navigation buttons) that must appear on every page.[9]

- Guidelines for presenting text and graphical elements consistently, including choices for formatting, size, and white space.

- A description and illustration of your standard page layout.

- How to maintain a consistent style and tone with both graphics and text on all Web pages. Also, identify whether you want this style and tone to be the same or different from that of your print materials.

- Implementation of multimedia elements, if used.

- International considerations for the use of colors, images, icons, and multimedia elements.

No matter what your choices for these issues, you want to maintain a consistent presentation across all Web pages. Develop a common "look and feel" for visuals, text, and multimedia that can be applied consistently to different pages and types of content, as well as over time. We have implemented this consistency with the templates included in this book through elements such as the overall layout, standard elements at the top and bottom of the page, and consistent text formats.

CHAPTER EIGHT

NAVIGATION: GUIDING VISITORS THROUGH YOUR BUFFET

For visitors, the ease with which they can explore and interact with your Web site can be just as important as its content. This chapter offers techniques for encouraging visitor exploration and interaction, creating beneficial navigation paths, and presenting links on Web pages.

↳ Encouraging Visitor Exploration

You have an idea for how visitors should explore your site: first looking at the home page, then a brochure page, then a services page, and so on. However, given the flexible navigation that is inherent to the Web, visitors can explore your site by following almost any path. They can enter your site on a specific page other than your home page, explore other pages seemingly at random, even skip pages that you think are important to view. As a result, almost any element or portion of the site must be able to stand on its own.

You must consider this free-form exploration when preparing content and planning navigation for your site. You will need to plan for providing context clues, matching visitor expectations for links, and guiding a visitor's exploration.

Context Clues for Web Navigation

With print materials we assume that people read sequentially, or if not, they have enough clues to know where they are within the physical and logical flow of the document. For example, in a printed catalog the reader can easily see the index of products at the beginning, the pages for individual products in the middle, and the order form at the end.

On the Web, visitors can enter your site almost anywhere by typing a specific page URL, saving it as a bookmark, or clicking on it in the list created by a Web search site. This type of access enables visitors to link directly to the information they want, but they then view the page without a sense of context for your site. This means you must provide these contextual clues on each page through location indicators, page links to related information, and standard navigation elements. For example, you can guide visitors through an online catalog by creating links among the Catalog Contents Page, Catalog Page, and Order Form templates, as shown in Figure 8.1.

To give visitors context clues, every Web page should have a page banner or title that identifies its contents, as well as a link to your home page. The templates in this book provide context clues through the page banner, company or site logo, and footer elements. Additional clues can be provided by a location identifier (see Chapter 6) and the specific links available on each page.

Visitor Expectations for Links

Visitors understand that any link that appears on a Web page is an invitation to explore. But does your content and

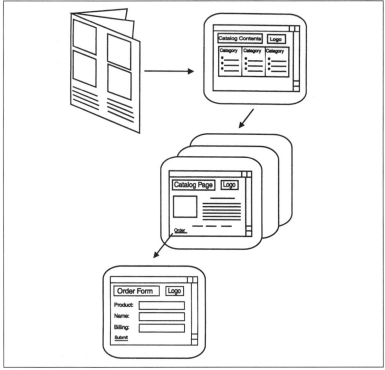

FIGURE 8.1 Providing context clues for Web navigation.

navigation deliver what visitors want to see? Figure 8.2 shows visitor expectations when they follow certain types of links.

Apply this information as you define the navigation paths through your site or create links on specific pages. Matching visitor expectations will not only give them a positive experience with your site, but it will encourage them to stay longer and explore further.

Guiding Visitors with Navigation Information

Two types of navigation information can be very helpful to visitors, whether are exploring your site for the first time or

Type of Link	What the Visitor Expects to See
Word or phrase.	More information on that topic or a glossary definition.
Names: product, person, company, course, event.	Brochure, catalog page, profile, seminar description, event calendar, or e-mail form that provides more information or a way to communicate with the subject.
Call to action.	Order form, e-mail form, or other page for taking the specified action.
Help or Questions link.	FAQ document, inquiry form, or page with relevant instructions or detailed information.
Image or multimedia placeholder.	Download of the full image or multimedia element.
URL of a page within your site or an external site.	Navigation to that page.

FIGURE 8.2 Visitor expectations for links.

visit it frequently. A Read Me First section on the home page for your site is a valuable feature for first-time visitors. You may also place it on a separate Web page with a link from the home page. This information should give new visitors an orientation to the content and navigation for your site. Guidance is especially important if your site is directed to an audience with many inexperienced Web users.

A What's New page can be very helpful for guiding both new and repeat visitors in exploring your site. You can direct visitors to new pages, products, promotions, or features on the site. The link to a What's New page usually appears on the home page and any other major entry pages for your site. For more ideas, see the What's New Page template in Chapter 3.

Navigation Elements

Web pages can include any mix of standard navigation elements: buttons, bars, links, and site maps.

Buttons

Buttons are small, individual icons that represent distinct navigation commands. The templates on the CD-ROM use a standard set of navigation buttons for the actions Back, Forward, Home, Contents, and e-mail to the site contact.

Directional Buttons

Remember that any directional buttons (for example, Back and Forward) on a Web page refer to navigation within your site. Usually this means moving from one page or document to another that is closely related, such as from one catalog page to the next, in a sequence you have defined. This navigation is different from the Back and Forward buttons on the visitor's browser, which may lead to other pages on your site, or even to other sites, based on what the visitor has previously viewed.

Bars

Multiple navigation commands can be placed together on a single graphical bar, with each command operating in the same manner as a button. A navigation bar offers the advantage of faster loading times than multiple button images that, although smaller, must be loaded individually.

You can create a navigation bar as an image map, using a graphics program such as *Paintshop Pro* in combination with an image-map creation tool such as *Mapedit*. See Chapter 11 for details on this technique; information about the programs is available in Appendix C.

Links

Text links to other pages within your site or on external sites can appear in a variety of ways. They may be embedded in the document text, appear on a list, or be displayed in a line across the top or bottom of the Web page. Text links also can appear in a site-map image.

If you use a graphical site map, navigation bar, or buttons, always include text links for navigating on the site. Embed these links within the image using an <ALT> tag (as we have done on the templates), place them next to the graphic, or group the text links at the bottom of the Web page.

TIP

If you group text links at the bottom of each page, you can aid a visitor's navigation by "delinking" the name of the current page, making it appear as plain text instead of a link.

Site Maps

A graphical image can depict the organization of major areas on your site, with navigation via embedded links or buttons. A site map typically appears at the top of the home page and can be a very effective way to encourage visitor exploration of your site.

Site maps are images and often large files that may require a long time to load. Because visitors who have turned off image loading in their browsers may not even see your site map, remember to apply these tips:

- Use a descriptive phrase with the <ALT> tag to indicate the image is a site map.

- Make text links visible within the image, or place them adjacent to the image. This will allow visitors who do not load the image to still benefit from its navigation function.

- Size the image smaller than the typical display window. This will allow visitors to see the text that follows the image. Otherwise, they may not realize the page offers more content.

General Guidelines for Links

Apply the guidelines here to give visitors an understandable and consistent experience when they navigate around your site:

- Place links to the items of most interest to repeat visitors, such as the What's New Page, at the top of the home page.

- To avoid losing visitors who don't scroll down a long page, place the key navigation links at the top and bottom of the page. For example, place the <u>Order Now</u> link next to the image or description for each item on a catalog page that displays multiple products.

- Place standard navigation links such as <u>Back</u> and <u>Forward</u> at the bottom of the page. The appearance of these links at the top of the page may seem like you're encouraging visitors to leave immediately, even before they view the content of that page.

- Place administrative links such as "send us your comments on this site" at the bottom of the page.

- Don't show links that are not yet operational. If you want to include a nonoperational link for competitive or other promotional factors, display the link text in a different color to show it as inactive. You may also want to place the text "Coming Soon" next to the link.

- For links within a page, present a bullet list index of all items or topics at the top of the page, then place a Top or Return to Contents link at the end of each section. These intrapage links help visitors regain their orientation and move to a new area on the page without scrolling. Look at the Newsletter template for an example of this technique.

- Always display the standard navigation links, bars, or buttons for your site in the same position on the page (usually at the bottom) and in the same format on every page. If certain navigation options are not available for a specific page, show them in a different color to indicate they are not active; gray is the color most commonly used for this purpose.[14] In this book, the standard navigation buttons appear in the footer on all templates.

- When linking to a glossary definition for a word, phrase, or acronym, create an active link only for the first occurrence.[10] Making every occurrence an active link will distract visitors, not help them.

And the most important guideline of all: Test every link you create on a page! Verify that the link will go to your intended destination and that the link text matches the visitor's expectation for content or interaction.

Navigation Within the Site

Because you want visitors to explore your site fully, planning effective navigation among its pages is crucial. You may have created a navigation flowchart as part of the planning process for your site (see Chapter 5). This flowchart is a great way to define how you want visitors to explore your site. Together with the paths defined by the navigation flowchart, apply the guidelines in this section when testing navigation or making additions or changes to your site.

Probably the most important guideline is to minimize the number of links a visitor must make to reach any specific destination in your site—especially for interactions that lead to a sale or an inquiry. For example, include an <u>Order Now</u> link on each page that describes a product or service offered for sale on your Web site. Or, include a <u>Contact Us</u> link on each page. Figure 8.3 recommends specific navigation paths for common types of promotional activities conducted on a Web site.

If you want to make a sale online, set up the link sequence to ensure that the visitor keeps moving toward the sale. Each page should present a call to action and link to the Order Form page. Don't force visitors to view multiple layers of pages, going through the complete sales or communication steps you've defined, until they reach the information or action they want. They may lose their way, lose their patience, or forget what they wanted before they reach your intended destination.[8]

These guidelines also will help you create effective intra-site navigation:

- Verify that all pages are reachable by at least one link and that no links dead-end, that is, point to a nonexisting page.

- If your site is large and complex, create a Table of Contents (see the Contents template), a site map, or a search capability (see Chapter 11). Visitors will appreciate the ability to find specific information quickly.

Navigation to Other Sites

As discussed in Chapters 2 and 5, you may want to create links from your pages to other sites maintained by sponsors,

Promotional Activity	Navigation Path
Selling a product online through a Catalog or Brochure.	Link to an Order Form from the Brochure or Catalog Page.
Announcing a new product or service.	Link to a Brochure from the Press Release page.
Promoting a course, workshop, or event.	Link to a Registration Form and Seminar Page from an Event Calendar.
Attracting clients for a consulting or service business.	Cross-link Brochure, Profile, and Services List pages.
Encouraging visits to a dealer or retail store.	Cross-link Brochure, Coupon, and Locator pages.
Recruiting members or donors.	Link to an Order Form from a Brochure page; to an Event Calendar from a Newsletter page.
Providing general company or organization information.	Link to a FAQ and a Newsletter from a Company Profile page.
Gathering feedback from visitors.	Link to a Visitor Survey from any page.

FIGURE 8.3 Defining navigation to match promotional goals.

business partners, or dealers as well as to industry or topic sites. Visitors usually consider these links valuable because they lead to additional information. However, you want to consider carefully the number and type of external links you create. These guidelines will help you make appropriate choices:

- Minimize the number of links to external sites. When you send visitors to other sites, they may not recognize the change and may not remember to come back.

- Place a phrase next to the link to indicate it is an external site.

- Select only links that are relevant and create a positive association for your business or organization. For example, if you are trying to promote the expertise of your business, link to sites such as professional associations or business partners. Avoid the temptation to link to "favorite cool" sites that reflect your personality more than your business.

- Make sure the links work and test them regularly. Even though you have no control over what someone else does with his or her site, a link that does not work will reflect poorly on you.

> **TIP**
>
> An alternative to linking to other sites is to place some of that content (text or images) on your pages—but obtain permission from the source before doing so. (See Chapter 10 for additional discussion.)

- You can place links to external sites in the text, in a bullet list, or on a separate Web page created just for this purpose (that is, a "Links" page). Write an explanatory sentence or paragraph adjacent to the link text that describes the content on the site and why you think it is worth a visit. Placing the links on a separate page makes them less convenient for visitors to find, but it has the advantage of minimizing the temptation for visitors to leave your site.

↳ Writing the Link Text

What if this entire sentence was a link on your Web page? Would you be able to guess where it might lead, or why you would want to go there? This example illustrates the importance of writing the link text in a way that encourages the visitor to explore.

Don't write long sentences as links; these make it too difficult for visitors to determine where the link will lead or what type of interaction it will activate. Instead, make the link from a keyword or short phrase (for a topic link) or a verb-object pair (for taking an action). Here are a few examples:

- <u>Order this item</u> (emphasis is on the action).

- Check the <u>Locator</u> for a store near you (emphasis is on the page content).

- <u>Arts Tour</u> (emphasis is on the topic).

You can always place descriptive text around the link to indicate where it leads or present the benefit of activating that link.

Other guidelines to remember when writing link text include the following:

- Don't make the link text too short and cryptic or visitors won't be motivated to follow it.

- Place the most important links at the top of a bullet list or at the left on a horizontal line.

- In bullet lists, use a parallel structure for the link text as much as possible. For example, in a list of catalog pages, start each link with the product name.

- Alert visitors to a link that leads to a large image or multimedia file that may take a long time to load. Simply state the file size and format next to the link text, for example: Product photo (.JPG, 150k).

- If the link leads to an external site, indicate this in the descriptive text for the link.

- Assume that visitors know they must click on the link text in order to navigate. Do not use phrases such as "click here" or "select this link" unless they are part of specific instructions for a visitor to take action.

About URLs

In the HTML code for a Web page, links point to a specific URL for a Web page or file. If you show the URL as the link text or in the descriptor, remember these facts:

- Not all URLs start with the "www" notation.

- Some Web servers require a case-sensitive URL; the visitor must match any uppercase letters exactly when typing the URL.

- Some URLs contain special symbols such as ~ (tilde) or : (colon).

- The filenames for some Web pages do not include an extension; others use .html, .shtml, or .htm.

- Some servers require a link to a specific page, not just the domain name. For example, a link to a specific page on the Web server for the domain *xyz.com* would be: *www.xyz.com/home.htm*.

If a filename is not indicated in a URL, the Web server for that domain will assume that you want a file named *index.html* in the specified directory, for example: *www.xyz.com/main/index.html*. Note also that if a visitor omits the trailing slash in the URL *www.xyz.com/main*, the server will assume this is a reference to a directory named *main* and not to a file named *main.html*.

For your own pages, work with your service provider to create URLs that will be easy for visitors to type directly into their browsers. Use short names, all lowercase letters, and no special characters.[15]

Interacting with Visitors

Direct-response marketers have long understood the value of engaging a prospect in a mail package or advertisement—the more time a prospect spends with the material, the more likely he or she will place an order or make a donation.

You can replicate this engagement on a Web site through the interaction it offers to visitors. Creating interaction goes beyond ensuring the ease of a visitor's navigation and exploration. It also means giving visitors opportunities and incentives to enter a dialogue with you, a dialogue that helps build relationships—and sales.

These templates can help you initiate and sustain successful interaction with visitors:

- *Visitor Registration/Survey*. Gathers a range of information about visitor interests, needs, and demographics.

- *Product Inquiry*. Helps the visitor send you a detailed request for information about a product or service offered by your company or organization.

- *Selection Guide*. Enables the visitor to see specific information about your products, or link to specific pages on your site, according to the responses entered on this template.

See Chapter 3 for ideas on specific promotional techniques for these templates. At a minimum, include a simple e-mail link to the contact person for your site to encourage visitor interaction.

Feedback for Forms

Interaction is especially important when visitors complete forms on your site. Program a response action in the script you create for handling online forms submitted by visitors.

Usually you want the completed form to be sent to your company in an e-mail message. But what happens after the form is submitted and the e-mail massage is sent to you? The universal form-handling script *mailform.cgi*, which we provide on the CD-ROM, allows you to specify the URL of the page you want to display for the visitor as a way to acknowledge receipt of the form. This can be a Thank You page, or you may want to return the visitor to the catalog page. Choose an action that will help the visitor avoid confusion about whether the form was successfully processed.

The script running on the server can create a new page on the fly and send it back to the browser, or it can load another page such as the Thank You page (THNX.HTM) included on the CD-ROM. The script we include on the CD-ROM, *mailform.cgi*, handles this task. You can modify THNX.HTM to include your information or specify the URL of the page you want the script to display when it is done sending the e-mail from the form.

When creating your own forms, don't assume that visitors will want or be able to receive a response via e-mail. Even if you ask visitors to enter an e-mail address on a form, they may make a mistake. And, unfortunately, there is currently no way for a form to capture the visitor's correct e-mail address automatically. Due to privacy considerations, this information is not currently provided by browsers. Always ask for a telephone or fax number or a postal address, and ask the visitor to check the preferred response method on the form.

CHAPTER NINE

GUIDELINES AND MAKEOVERS

This chapter summarizes our top guidelines and ideas for creating both Web pages and a complete site that will help you realize your Web marketing goals. Before you go online with your Web site, you will also want to check our list of common mistakes presented here. And if you want ideas for improving current Web pages, check the "Makeovers" section.

↳ Top Keys for a Successful Web Site

These guidelines will help you develop a Web site that is appealing to visitors and effective as a promotional tool for your company or organization.

1. The content is well organized and presented clearly and consistently, both within pages and across the site as a whole. Visitors can easily find the information they want, which is reliably up-to-date and in compliance with all applicable laws and regulations.

2. Visitors are able at any point to communicate with you through a form or e-mail link. An inquiry form and visitor survey are available on the site to encourage feedback from visitors. All forms submitted by visitors are acknowledged with a response page created by a script, or an e-mail message.

3. If the site will be used for electronic commerce, it is structured with content and functions that will simplify and ensure security for the visitor's ordering process. Offline options for making a purchase or visiting a store are also presented.

4. The interests and concerns of international visitors are accommodated through presentation of international purchasing options, country-specific information, or local-language text.

5. Navigation is clear and fully operational, and it encourages visitor exploration of your site. Aids such as a contents page or search capability are available for large sites.

6. Links to external sites add value to the visitor's experience with your site and create cross-promotion opportunities with other Web marketers.

7. The Web site is promoted through all other marketing materials and activities to encourage visits and referrals from customers and prospects.

8. A planning process is in place for developing and maintaining content and navigation on the site. Audience interests and site results are evaluated regularly to identify any needed changes or additions to the site.

↳ Top Keys for Effective Web Pages

1. Pages load quickly, especially the text content. Large images and multimedia elements are stored in separate files instead of loaded in-line with the page.

2. A strong and clear call to action appears on all pages that lead to an online sale, motivating visitors to make a purchase or inquiry. Pages that lead to an online sale are linked together in a logical sequence, with the option to navigate directly to an order or inquiry form at any point.

3. Pages reflect a standard layout and color scheme. The techniques for creating white space are used appropriately to create an appealing and easy-to-read layout on each page.

4. For content that is split across multiple Web pages, the segmentation is logical and clearly presented to visitors. Techniques for segmenting content on single Web pages are used effectively.

5. Text is written in an inverted-pyramid structure, with short sentences and paragraphs to convey key messages to visitors quickly and understandably. The style and

tone of text, images, and multimedia elements are congruent and consistent on all pages.

6. Link text emphasizes the most important words or phrases and clearly identifies where the link will lead or the type of interaction it will activate.

7. Multimedia elements are used selectively, and with consideration for the capabilities and speed of visitors' access.

↰ Common Mistakes on Web Sites

In your explorations of the Web, you have probably found sites that are ugly, confusing, or frustrating to visit. The reasons for this are probably a combination of the common mistakes listed here.

1. A poorly organized site, with no contents page, map, or other navigation aids.

2. Large pages that take a long time to load and require repeat scrolling to view completely because they contain lengthy text and large images or multimedia objects.

3. Animation effects that distract the visitor's attention from the primary information and objective on the page.

4. No opportunity for visitors to provide feedback or initiate interaction with the site owner.

5. Out-of-date, incomplete, or inaccurate content; poor-quality photographs or other images.

6. Ignoring international visitors or showing a lack of consideration for cultural and message differences.

7. A bland or missing call to action on pages that lead to a sale or inquiry.

8. Errors of fact or omission. These errors are an embarrassment and may cause legal problems. Fortunately, correcting errors on a Web page is as simple as uploading a new HTML file—much faster and simpler than correcting errors in a printed document. Check each page carefully for misspelled words, improper grammar or word usage, incorrect punctuation, reversed images, and missing text.

↳ Web Page Makeovers

In their rush to place content onto a Web site, many marketers and developers have made poor choices for structure and presentation. This section shows some of the most common problems on Web pages and demonstrates how they can be corrected by using the templates on the CD-ROM.

Insufficient White Space

Figure 9.1 shows the result of using an inadequate amount of white space between paragraphs and subheads. In addition, limited white space between text and images creates Web pages that are cluttered and difficult for visitors to read.

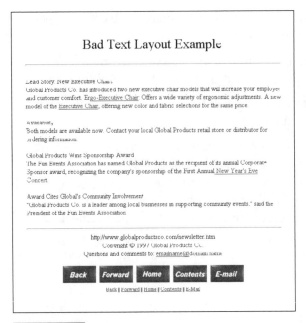

FIGURE 9.1 Insufficient white space.

Figure 9.2 illustrates the improved layout created with the Newsletter template.

Newsletter

Global Products Co.

In this Issue

Lead Story: New Executive Chairs

Global Products Co. has introduced two new executive chair models that will increase your employee and customer comfort.

- Ergo-Executive Chair. Offers a wide variety of ergonomic adjustments.
- A new model of the Executive Chair, offering ...
  ...tor and fabric selections for the same price.

Availability

Both models are available now. Contact your local Global Products retail store or distributor for ordering informatio...

BACK to contents

Global Products Wins Sponsorship Award

The Fun Events Association has named Global Products as the recipient of its annual Corporate Sponsor award, recognizing the company's sponsorship of the First Annual New Year's Eve Concert.

Award Cites Global's Community Involvement

"Global Products Co. is a leader among local businesses in supporting community events," said the President of the Fun Events Associa...

BACK to contents

http://www.globalproductsco.com/newsletter.ht...
Copyright © 1997 Global Products Co.
Questions and comments to: email:name@gl...

Back **Forward** **Home** **Contents** **E-mail**

Home | Executive | About | Contents | Search

FIGURE 9.2 Newsletter template.

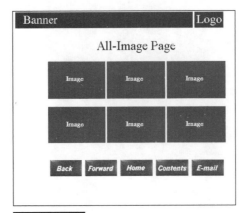

FIGURE 9.3 Graphics-only page.

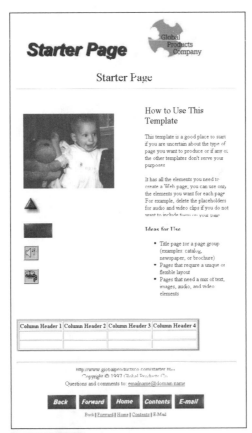

FIGURE 9.4 Starter template.

FIGURE 9.5 Too many links.

Graphics-Only Page

Figure 9.3 demonstrates the confusion when images are not supported by descriptive text. The Starter template, shown in Figure 9.4, is designed to present both content and navigation links in text, as well as to present images appropriately.

Too Many Links

Figure 9.5 shows the confusion that can overwhelm visitors when they view a page that contains too many and redundant text links. The Starter template shown in Figure 9.4 illustrates how the links for images, audio, and video can be improved with the use of graphical buttons. Additional techniques for implementing navigation links effectively are discussed in Chapter 8.

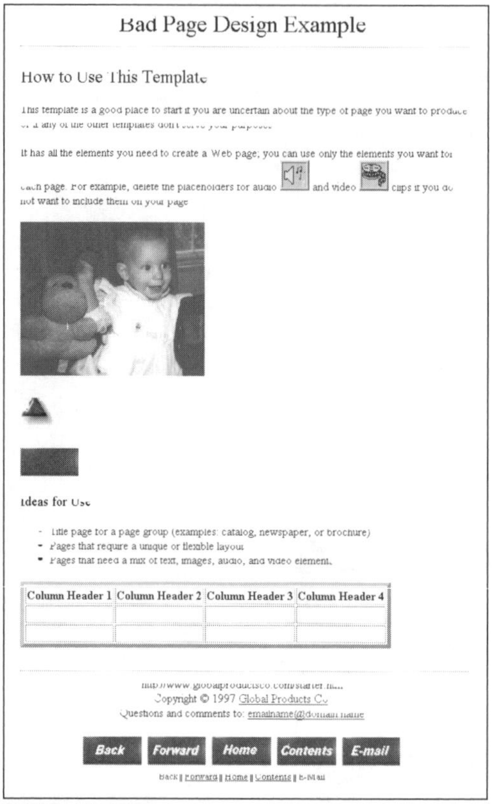

FIGURE 9.6 Poor page design.

Poor Page Design

Figure 9.6 presents an example of a poor page design and poor layout of text and images. Images that are interspersed in the text are ineffective for conveying your message and annoying for visitors to view. All templates on the CD-ROM are based on a clear and consistent page design, as illustrated by the Starter template (see Figure 9.4).

Poor Color Scheme

Figure 9.7 illustrates the reduced legibility that results from a poor color scheme on your site. Web pages are most effective when the color scheme permits a high contrast between the text and the background. As discussed in Chapter 7, black

FIGURE 9.7 Poor color scheme.

text on a white background is the easiest color scheme to read. Light-colored text on a light background, and colored text on a black background (called a "reverse"), can create Web pages that are dull in appearance and difficult to read. The templates on the CD-ROM use our recommended color scheme of black text on a white background.

CHAPTER TEN

SERVING IT WELL DONE: LEGAL AND INTERNATIONAL FACTORS FOR WEB PROMOTION

At this point, you have probably completed the plan for your site, gathered the content, and created at least a few Web pages. You're ready to "go live" with the site, loading your Web pages onto a server and making them available to visitors everywhere.

Before you do, verify that you have considered the many factors related to the subjects of this chapter: the legality of your content and promotional activities on the Web, and how well you are meeting the needs and interests of international visitors.

Legal Considerations

Because commercial uses of the Web are relatively recent and fast developing, the laws governing electronic marketing and sales activities have not yet fully emerged. You can expect that these laws will not only be enacted, but will vary among countries and local areas in terms of their requirements and constraints. You will want to work with an attorney who monitors development of laws governing the Internet and electronic commerce, review the resources listed in Appendix C, and monitor information on these laws yourself. Keywords to search: **Web + law** or **multimedia + law**.

This chapter presents an overview of the most common legal considerations for any type of promotional and sales activity that you conduct on the Web.

Who Owns What on Your Site?

You may assume that because you have created all content and programming that comprises your Web site—or paid someone else to create it for you—that you automatically own full rights to your site and everything on it. This could prove to be an inaccurate assumption for several reasons, including:

- Other people or companies may own the rights to specific portions of the text, images, or multimedia elements on your site. You must obtain a license or permission to use those elements in full or in part on your site, for a specified time period. Some content owners require you to pay a licensing or rights fee before they will grant this permission.

- Freelance writers, graphic designers, or agencies may retain the electronic rights to text or images they develop for printed materials that you now want to load into or adapt for a Web page.

- A Web site developer may retain the rights to scripts and other programming elements used to make your Web site fully operational. Many developers re-use programs for common tasks such as sending e-mail or processing forms, adapting these programs as necessary for the specific needs of your site.

In general, you own all rights if the content or programming work was developed by you or your employees as part of their work for your company or organization. If you contract for the services of external creative resources (e.g., writers or designers), you must obtain the copyright or appropriate usage rights for the content they create for your site.

When working with external resources, address these issues at the beginning of the project and confirm all arrangements in writing with a contract or letter of agreement. In addition, you may want to obtain a disk copy of all HTML code and other programs created for your site by an external Web developer.

Ownership and rights for Web sites is an evolving area of Internet law, so we recommend that you periodically search the Web for current information and guidelines.

Licenses and Permissions

Always assume that any content element you find in print material or on a Web site is covered by a copyright, even if no copyright notice appears. This includes clip-art images, geographic maps, and other elements that are marked as royalty-free, but in fact may come with restrictions on their commercial use. Also, specific images or recordings may be protected, even if the artwork, map, or music they present are in the public domain. Use the graphical or audio element only if an explicit notice appears with it to allow completely unrestricted use. Otherwise, you must contact the copyright owner to obtain a license or permission.

You must also obtain permission or usage rights for content that is created for you by consultants and other external creative resources (see Figure 10.1). Unless the terms of the contract explicitly transfer the ownership rights to you, the creative resource retains all rights beyond those for the specific project. This means you must obtain permission to use in a Web page any text or image from a printed document, any audio or video clip from a recording, or any multimedia element from a CD-ROM or other project.

Unless you obtain full copyright, the creative resource can use the element in other projects and grant permission to other companies to use or adapt it. While this may cause you to worry that the appealing image on your Web page may suddenly appear on many others, in practice this concern is usually invalid. And purchasing full rights can be expensive, so you may find it more cost-effective to give up some of the uniqueness of your site.

In general, it is less expensive to obtain only the specific rights you need, for a limited time period, than to purchase a complete set of all rights. For commercially published books, images, and multimedia elements, a rights agent can help you secure the licenses and permissions you need.

TIP:

Keywords to search: **multimedia + rights, multimedia + license, copyright + clearance, Web + intellectual + property**.

Element	Rights to License or Permissions to Obtain
Text	Rights to publish text that previously appeared in print material, in identical or adapted form on your Web site. If you plan to localize the text for international visitors, also purchase translation rights.
Images	Rights for use of the image itself and to apply animation to that image if appropriate. If the image includes recognizable people or celebrities, you must obtain permission for publicity.
Music	Rights for the music, for performance, and for the specific recording.
Other Audio	Permission for narration and translation of the text, rights from the narrator or actors to use their performances.
Video	Video and film elements present many of the same issues as music and audio elements, but can involve more people and organizations. For commercial videos or film clips, we recommend using a rights agent.

FIGURE 10.1 Licenses and permissions for Web content elements.

Element	Rights to License or Permissions to Obtain
Animations	Rights to add animation to all or part of an image or to reuse or adapt an existing animation.
Programs and Scripts	Rights to use and adapt HTML code, CGI scripts, and Java or other programming.

FIGURE 10.1 Continued

Site Programming

If you use the services of an external Web developer, the key question to ask is: "Will my business own all rights in the site, including all content and programming, or will we simply own the right to use this particular assembly of content and programming as our site?"[16] Owning only the right to use the site may be sufficient, depending on the nature of its programming and special features for forms processing or other visitor interaction.

The key to avoiding problems after your site has been developed is to state clearly all terms of the project and ownership rights in a contract or letter of agreement with the developer.

Linked Content

In terms of ownership rights, there is a difference between simply linking to another site and copying content from that site onto your own. While you generally do not need to obtain permission to link to another site, you *must* obtain permission from the site owner before copying any content, including text, images, multimedia elements, and any or all portions of the underlying HTML code.

Although no laws restrain your ability to link your site to any other, practice the courtesy of notifying the site owner or Webmaster when you create the link. Most site owners will welcome a link from your site as a new way to attract visitors. In turn, they may create a link to your site to foster a mutually beneficial relationship.

However, creating a reciprocal link is not automatic or obligatory for owners of other sites. We suggest that you ask for a reciprocal link by sending an e-mail message to the Webmaster or other contact for the external site.

Some organizations may not want a link from an external site because it may falsely imply an affiliation or endorsement of your product or organization, or create a negative association in the minds of their customers or members. Immediately remove a link to an external site if the owner objects.[17]

Check all external links on your site frequently. Because the nature and content of Web sites can change so quickly, you may find that a site no longer exists or has a new URL. You may find that a site is no longer relevant, or creates a negative association, and you will want to remove the link to that site before it gives a negative impression to your visitors.

Privacy Protection

When you publish a photo or illustration of a specific person, even an employee of your company, you must obtain permission from that person to use the image on your Web site. Most photographers use a standard form, called a model release, that will cover these rights. If a photograph shows a group of people, obtain a signed form from every person in the group.

Special limitations apply to the image, name, or other identifying characteristics of a celebrity, especially for an actual or implied endorsement of your organization or product. You cannot use any of these elements without obtaining permission or publicity rights from the celebrity or her estate. These restrictions apply to celebrities both living and dead and apply also to "lookalikes" or "soundalikes."

Another consideration is protecting the privacy of visitors as they interact with your site. Visitors will be concerned about the privacy of information they provide, and may view surveys and questions on other forms as too intrusive. If you collect any type of personal, financial, or other sensitive data from visitors, describe why you are requesting the information and what you will do with it. If appropriate, reassure the visitor about the confidentiality of the information as it is transmitted over the Internet via the security features supported on your Web server and in the visitor's browser.

In addition, commerce laws may restrict the types of data you may request from visitors. If in doubt, consult an attorney with specific expertise in these issues.

Copyright for Your Site

All content and programming on your Web site can be protected by copyrights. In countries that comply with the Berne convention for copyright laws, the text, images, and other elements on your Web site are protected in the same way as print materials. In other countries, copyright protection may be different.

To reinforce your copyright ownership, place a copyright notice on each page of your site and ensure that a copyright notice appears on all pages and documents printed from your site. Also place a copyright notice in each HTML file. An example of the correct form for a copyright notice is: "Copyright©*year* by *owner*."

⮑ Advertising and Commerce Laws

Advertising and commerce laws may apply to the information you publish or the types of sales activities you conduct on a Web site. For example, advertising laws in many countries outside of the United States are very restrictive about the types of direct comparisons you can make with competitive products. As another example, if you run a contest, sweepstakes, or giveaway on your site, it must comply with all national and local laws or you must limit who can enter.

Different commerce laws and government regulations may apply to issues such as sales terms, implied contracts created by orders made by customers via an e-mail message or Order Form on a Web site, sales transactions, warranty, and liability. And you must comply with laws and regulations that restrict the import or export of certain products in individual countries. Check the resources listed in Appendix C and discuss these issues with an attorney.

Prices and Offers

Information presented on your Web site for prices, product specifications, and other terms of sale must be current in order to comply with commerce laws. In addition, pricing information and sales offers can be subject to different legal considerations because your Web site is accessible to international users. The laws about these items can vary considerably among countries. You want to state clearly the countries in which prices and other sale terms are applicable and in which currencies. Another technique for handling these differences is to list country-specific contact information or link visitors to a separate Web page for international dealers or sales offices.

Indicate whether the stated prices include all applicable taxes and import or export duties. If these amounts are not included in the product price, list them separately or include a statement on all relevant Web pages that payment of these amounts is the responsibility of the purchaser. You may also want to create a separate page that lists all ordering and payment terms, warranty disclaimers, and other required information, linking to this page from all Brochure, Catalog, and Order Form pages on your site.

Trademarks

A trademark is a word, name, symbol—or a combination of these—that a company uses to distinguish a product from others. A service mark is the same as a trademark, except that it applies to nontangible services.

Use the correct trademark symbol on each appearance of a trademarked word or symbol on your Web pages. In the United States, these symbols are:

- ™ for an unregistered trademark

- ℠ for an unregistered service mark

- ® for a trademark or service mark that is registered with the U.S. Patent and Trademark Office.

Trademarks that are registered in other countries may be covered by different rules for notation.

In addition, acknowledge the trademark ownership with a statement at the bottom of each Web page where the trademark appears or create a separate page listing all trademark acknowledgments—for trademarks owned by your company and others, as appropriate.

Your ownership or registration of a trademark for a product or service does not automatically cover the same words when they are used as an Internet domain name. Conversely, registering a domain name does not give you an automatic trademark. However, most companies will make a legal challenge to any domain registration that appears to infringe on any of their trademarks.

Alteration of Images

When you use photo-manipulation or drawing software to create or work with scanned images, it is very tempting to "fix" or "improve" photographs, illustrations, or diagrams in order to enhance their appearance on the Web page. Before you do, remember the ethical implications and potential legal problems any alteration can create.

Certain minor modifications to images are acceptable, such as those made to correct presentation flaws or to improve clarity. However, extensive changes that substantially alter the proportions or appearance of a product may cause problems of misrepresentation or creation of a warranty condition that you may not want. And changes to images of people can cause a violation of their privacy rights.

International Considerations

With the reach of the Web truly worldwide, you can expect many international visitors to your site. As part of your planning, you may have defined whether and how you want to serve these visitors, both with information and electronic commerce capabilities. The discussion here will give you additional factors to consider, and ideas for making your site a welcoming and successful experience for visitors from outside of your home country.

To market successfully to an international audience, you must learn about—and respect—the differences in cultural, promotional, and business practices in each country or market. Market needs, visitor interests, buying factors, and sales cycles will vary, and you should reflect and accommodate these variations on your Web site.

Cultural Differences

Cultural factors can be extremely important if your site contains many images, audio, and video clips as well as text. You need to consider: "Will those elements be acceptable to an international audience? Will visitors interpret them correctly?" Remember that what may be appropriate in your culture may be totally offensive to someone in another part of the world. Avoid the assumption that if international customers want your product strongly enough they will accommodate themselves to the same information and marketing activities that are targeted to your domestic audience.

Appropriate images, symbols, and colors differ widely among cultures. Images of people that may be completely familiar in your culture may be puzzling or offensive in others. Formats for dates, measurements, telephone numbers, and addresses vary around the world. Consider how you will accommodate these differences in the content and interactivity on your Web site.

> **TIP:**
>
> Always include the name of the country in your address and the country code in your telephone number to facilitate offline contacts by international visitors to your Web site.

You may need to adapt the style and tone of your content to be more acceptable to the diverse preferences and sensitivities of an international market. In addition, watch for ambiguity or vagueness, as this can be compounded when the visitor tries to interpret and understand the text. Avoid local slang and references that will mystify visitors from other areas. And advertising laws in some countries do not allow the use of superlatives or broad comparisons of a product to others in its category.

Your dealers, sales representatives, or other business contacts in each country can give you valuable guidance on handling these cultural factors. Our recommended references are in Appendix C. In addition, the Web is a rich source of country-specific information; keywords to search: ***countryname + marketing*** or ***countryname + culture***.

Electronic Commerce around the World

Although you can reach a worldwide market with a Web site, you may choose to sell your product only in select countries or even only in your home country. Health, safety, and environmental laws may impact your ability to sell certain products in some countries, or specify how those products must be labeled and shipped.[18]

State clearly the markets where a product is available on all catalog and price list pages. If you market only to a single local, regional, or national audience, indicate this information on your home page to target only those visitors who can benefit from your site. Otherwise, visitors will assume that if you are promoting a product on the site, they will be able to buy it from you over the Web or through a local store or dealer.

It may also be the case that the product specifications or features are different in each country, and if so, you need to state that information clearly on the catalog page, price list, order form, and related pages. Indicate differences in product availability such as:

- Comparable product names or numbers.

- Variations in features, packaging, or specifications.

- Whether instruction booklets, labels, and other materials shipped with the product are available in the local language.

- List of stores or dealers by country.

- Differences in pricing, shipping, and payment terms.

The call to action on each relevant Web page should include detailed instructions on how to respond for each country, such as completing an online form or calling an in-country contact for more information. The templates in this book are designed with these features and others to serve international visitors.

Check with your bank or financial institution about accepting payments in local currencies or international credit cards (e.g., Eurocards or JCB cards). Clearly state the currencies, costs, and terms for product prices, payment methods, shipping procedures, and service programs for international customers. Indicate who is responsible for compliance with export and import laws and payments of taxes or duties.

Localized Content

English is the most common language for business and the most common on the Web. But your business may already have a significant market presence in one or more countries besides your own. Or, as you operate your Web site, you may find that it is attracting many visitors from certain countries. In either of these cases, you may want to develop local-language content on your site.

Consider whether you want to develop and maintain a local-language page for key information or if you want to maintain a complete, mirror site of localized content. For sites that are available in one or more alternate languages, place a link to each language version on each page. This is important for visitors who find a page on your site in one language as a result of a Web search, but who will want to view the page in one of the other available languages. For example, provide a link to a Spanish-language site on your English site and vice versa. Also place links to local-language sites at the top of your home page to allow visitors to immediately link to their preferred site.

Localizing the content on your Web site means more than simply translating the text. It means adapting the words, style, images, and overall presentation of the page to match the expectations and cultural considerations of each audience you want to reach. You will probably want to obtain the assistance of consultants or other resources to help you create an effective and appropriately targeted site.

TIP:

Many large, multinational corporations maintain several localized sites. Especially if you are fluent in one of the local languages, check those sites for ideas.

Creating localized Web content can require a significant investment of time and money. For this reason, you will want to work closely with your in-country contacts and translation resources to assure the best results.

CHAPTER ELEVEN

ADVANCED WEB POSSIBILITIES

In your explorations of the Web, you have probably seen many sites with impressive capabilities such as colorful graphics, flashy animation effects, a variety of audio and video clips, search and database features, a frame-based layout, even Java applets or a virtual reality environment. You may be wondering how you might use these capabilities to enhance your Web marketing, and how difficult and how expensive they are to implement. This chapter discusses advanced techniques for Web sites, giving you a general guide through the maze of ever-changing Web technology. Resources for many of these topics are listed in Appendix C.

Dazzling Graphics

While images, special buttons, and other decorative elements can substantially increase the visual appeal of your Web site, they can also substantially increase its development cost. A graphic designer who is experienced with Web technology and design can create effective and customized graphics for your site, although the expense may be more than you are willing or able to invest at the beginning of your Web marketing activity.

But can a Web site be effective without professionally designed graphics? Yes! You can use several techniques to add quality images and other graphical elements to your site. These techniques include:

- Scanning photographs of your products, employees, events, or other items that you are promoting. Many copy centers and photo developers offer scanning services for prints or slides. You can easily convert the scanned photograph file to a GIF or JPEG format suitable for use on the Web with utility software such as *Lview* (see Appendix C for source). This utility also allows you to crop the image and manipulate its colors, brightness, and contrast.

- Using images and logos from your print materials such as brochures and stationery. This technique has the added advantage of creating consistency between your printed materials and Web pages.

- Using any of the thousands of images that are available from clip-art collections on disk, CD-ROM, or the Web. However, make sure that you comply with any restrictions on the use of these images, including those that are marked as "royalty-free" (see Chapter 10).

 Image Maps

Image maps appear in the form of graphical maps, photos, or text and are used to show the organization and navigation within a site. An image map can contain multiple links, each leading to a different page in the same site or an external site. The browser reads the coordinates of the mouse cursor as it moves over the image map. When the visitor clicks on the image map, the browser loads the Web page specified for that area.

An image map consists of two files: the image itself, which is usually a GIF file identified as an image map by the <ISMAP> tag, and the corresponding MAP file. The map file contains a list of coordinate ranges to identify "live" areas within the image, and the URLs of the pages that correspond to each area. One of the best tools for creating an image map is *Mapedit* (see Appendix C).

> **TIP**
>
> An image map is conceptually different than a geographic map, which shows the street location of a retail store or office. However, geographic maps must be saved as images (usually in a GIF file) in order to appear on a Web page.

Frames

As described in Chapter 7, frames create separately active windows in the display area of a visitor's browser. Frames are an interesting feature of HTML, but one that has limited support from many Web designers. The primary problem with frames is the confusion they cause for the visitor when navigating the site:

- Clicking on a link in one frame of a multiple-frame Web page may cause the display in the other frame to change. Or an entirely new page may appear. Or the frame may activate a new copy of the browser program.

- Clicking on the Back button from a multiple-frame Web page does not always produce the results the visitor expects. Sometimes the visitor must use the right mouse button to navigate successfully. And the Location bar in the browser often shows the URL of the index frame, not the primary frame the visitor is viewing.

Frames are useful for displaying an index to your site in the browser window even when the visitor has clicked on a link to another site. If you offer links to external sites but want to ensure the visitor has a way back to your site, you can accomplish this with the proper use of frames.

Finally, frames were not in the original HTML standard, which means they are not supported by all browsers now in widespread use. If you decide to use frames but want your Web site to be viewable by all visitors, you will need to program and maintain non-framed pages in parallel with your framed versions. For all of these reasons, we cannot recommend the use of frames for most Web sites.

↳ Audio and Video Elements

It seems that everyone is talking about multimedia on the Web and the dynamic possibilities it will create for making Web sites more appealing to visitors. Instead of "boring" text and static images, music and video can make your pages seem more active.

You can use existing audio or video recordings created for your company, or license recordings produced by others (see

Chapter 10). To create a new recording for your Web site, you can work in a professional recording studio. Or you can use a microphone connected to a PC and audio or multimedia software to create audio files that can be placed on your Web site. You can also create video files using inexpensive products such as *QuickCam* (see Appendix C).

A drawback to audio, video, or multimedia files is their large size, even for short clips (see Chapter 7). Will your visitor want to wait several minutes to download an audio or video clip that lasts only a few seconds? Will you want to pay the increased server charges you will likely incur for this added Web transfer? We recommend answering these questions before investing time, money, and energy into creating multimedia elements for your site.

Many new technologies are emerging, such as streaming audio and video, that will allow faster and easier access to multimedia elements on Web sites. To find current information for these technologies on the Web, search with the keywords **audio + Web**, **video + Web**, and **multimedia + Web**.

Animation

Adding motion to Web pages can be done without spending a fortune for design studio fees or complex animation software. You can create impressive animated graphics, such as an active logo, using an animated GIF file (see the sample animation files on the CD-ROM). This file is created by taking a series of images and packing them into a single GIF file. When the visitor loads the page or primary image, the browser displays the component images sequentially, creating an illusion of motion. The animated GIF file can be constructed with commands for the browser to display the animation sequence once or repeatedly.

Animated GIF images are often effective substitutes for video on Web sites. Well constructed animated GIFs create a stream of motion that appears movie-like to the viewer. Additionally, the file size is small compared to the large file size and download requirements of digital video.

↳ Java and Javascript

Java is a computer programming language used on a Web site to create small, compiled application programs called *applets*. When a browser encounters an applet reference on a Web page, the browser loads the applet from the server onto the visitor's computer, then executes the applet.

Java's potential utility is enormous, but its acceptance has been slowed by security concerns, a lack of practical applications, and limitations on download and execution speed. For example, because a Java applet is executed by the browser, the possibility exists for attempted hacking by the author of the applet. Viruses are already spread on the Internet by downloading and executing infected programs; Java applets will increase the opportunities for viruses to spread in this way.

To be technically precise, a Java applet is interpreted, not executed, and controls in the Java language are meant to minimize the chances of creating an infectious applet. However, several well-publicized cases of security breaches have diminished public acceptance of Java. Many knowledgeable Web users now routinely disable Java in their browsers. As bandwidth increases and the Java software matures, its use will become more common and widespread.

Javascript is also an interpreted programming language, but it does not come in the form of applets. Instead, it is a script embedded in the Web page header. The browser executes this script when it encounters a reference to it in the body of the Web page.

Javascript is useful for many types of applications, from changing the background color of the page dynamically to checking a credit card number for correct syntax. Because the script is embedded in the HTML file for the page, Javascript executes faster than a Java applet while performing similar functions.

Many Java applications for business can be accomplished by using other, less costly techniques or a combination of tools such as searchable databases and scripts. While Java applets transfer much of the demand from the Web server to the visitor's computer, thus reducing your costs for data transfer, the additional development costs for site-specific Java applets may diminish or eliminate any real cost savings.

↳ Virtual Reality (VRML and Quicktime VR)

Virtual Reality Markup Language (VRML) creates a "virtual reality" environment on a Web site by creating a three-dimensional space that can be navigated by a correctly configured, high-end browser. VRML is a 3D programming language that has found limited practical use on the Web. In addition, VRML files are generally very large and slow to download. These limitations may change as available bandwidth increases for most visitors and VRML files become more universally accessible.

Another, more specialized virtual reality Web format is *Quicktime VR*, a technology developed by Apple Computer. Quicktime VR requires a special panoramic camera and software which creates a 360-degree virtual reality image in the browser, with the visitor appearing to be at the center of the image. The visitor can manipulate the view direction by clicking and dragging the mouse. The images are large and downloading is slow, but the results are impressive.

An example of commercial applications for VRML and Quicktime VR is a demonstration of an apartment or condominium interior. Or, a car buyer could experience the look and feel of a new automobile from a driver's-seat perspective.

↳ Common Gateway Interface (CGI) Scripts

CGI scripts are programs that reside on a Web server and are activated by the browser in response to a command from an HTML page. For example, when a visitor completes one of the forms templates and clicks on the Submit button, the browser calls the script *mailform.cgi*, which resides on your Web server. This script then calls the server's e-mail program to send the visitor's input to you in the form of an e-mail message.

Processing the inputs entered on an online form is a typical use of a CGI script. But scripts can do more. For example, the *mailform.cgi* script checks the format of the e-mail address entered by the visitor and produces an error message if it is not valid. A similar script could validate the format of credit card numbers. As another example, scripts generate the visitor counter (often called "hit counter") that appears on many Web sites.

A script could be written to enter data automatically into selected fields on a form, based on a visitor's choices in previous fields or even on different Web pages. For example, the script could automatically enter event details if it was programmed to capture the visitor's selection. This automation saves the visitor from needing to enter the information twice.

CGI scripts can be as simple or as complex as needed, based on the application. They can also provide entire database applications for electronic commerce or online customer service activities.

In most cases, scripts must reside in a special directory on the Web server. Consult with your Internet Service Provider about where to store the scripts for your site.

Perl is a widely used CGI script language and Perl interpreters are common on UNIX servers. Writing Perl scripts usually requires a fair amount of programming knowledge, but many sample scripts are available as shareware. One of the best sources is *Matt's Script Archive* (see Appendix C).

↳ Search Capabilities

If your site encompasses many pages, you may want to implement a simple search script to enable a visitor to quickly find specific information or pages. The script resides on your server and responds to keywords entered by the visitor on a Web page that presents a search form. The script can search through all HTML pages on your site and return a page of links to every page that contains the keyword(s).

Database Applications

If you intend to offer visitors a large number of choices for products or other information, you may want to consider using a database application on your Web site. In this application, a database containing product information resides on your Web server, with a database program. The program interacts with the choices made by visitors and accesses your product database to present the requested information.

The advantage of this approach for presenting a catalog is that a database program can create HTML pages "on the fly." For example, when a visitor clicks on a "Wonder Products" link on a Catalog Contents page, the database program will actually create one or many HTML pages showing the product selections and present these pages to the visitor's browser for display.

Catalog and mail-order companies may use database search tools to help the visitor locate products quickly and easily without scrolling through each item. As another example, companies with many employees can provide searchable databases on Web pages that make it simple to find a specific employee.

A database capability allows you to avoid creating individual HTML pages in advance for each product or other items in your database. It also makes it simpler to maintain your Web site because you can update your database more easily than updating individual HTML pages. To create scripts, you can use shareware database programs such as MSQL ("Mini SQL"), which run as Perl scripts and can be implemented by someone with limited Perl knowledge.

Password Controls

You may want to protect access to pages that contain sensitive or proprietary data. Or you may want to control access to digitized merchandise, such as software or books, that is available for download from your Web server. A simple way to implement this protection is to establish passwords for those directories.

To implement password controls, place a special text file in the same directory, containing pairs of username/password text strings. When the server encounters this file in a directory, it causes the browser to display a form requiring the visitor to enter a valid username/password pair before the server will display the protected page or file. Consult your Internet Service Provider for detailed instructions.

PART III

WEB

MARKETING

RESOURCES

GUIDE TO THE CD-ROM

The CD-ROM that accompanies this book contains the Web page templates described in Chapter 3 and their associated files. It also includes a variety of software that will help you develop a promotional Web site quickly and easily. This appendix presents information on the CD-ROM content and instructions for working with the different types of files and tools. See Appendix B for instructions on actually implementing your Web site.

CD-ROM Contents

The CD-ROM contains the files listed in Figure A.1, organized in the directory structure shown in Figure A.2. Use the Windows File Manager or Explorer program to view the complete directory and file structure on the CD-ROM.

The template files with the .HTM extension are HTML files. We used the .HTM file extension instead of .HTML to make the files compatible with the range of personal computers—Windows 3.1, Windows 95, and Macintosh—as well as Web servers (including Windows NT and UNIX operating systems).

You can view the templates in your browser without a live Internet connection. To do this, choose the browser command for opening a local file and select the file *cdhome.htm* in the root directory of your CD-ROM drive. *cdhome.htm* is a top-level Web page that will lead you on a guided tour of all files on the CD-ROM. We have sized the elements on these pages for the default window size in both Netscape Navigator and Microsoft Internet Explorer; if you have a different window size, the elements may not appear as pictured in this book.

File Type	File Name	Description
Templates	*.RTF, *.HTM	*.RTF are Rich Text Files for the templates that you can load into a word processor for editing. *.HTM are text-only files for the templates that you can edit with a word processor or HTML editor
Buttons and banners	*.GIF, *.JPG	Image files for the navigation buttons and banners that appear on the templates. You can edit the banner text with a paint program.
Image and Multimedia Placeholders	*.GIF	Image files that appear on the templates as placeholders and which you replace with real images on your Web pages.
Scripts	*.CGI, *.TXT	Script files that you place on your Web server or embed in your Web pages for execution.
Tools	*.EXE or *.ZIP	Useful software tools for developing a Web site.

FIGURE A.1 Content of the CD-ROM.

Directory	Contents
root	Top-level Web pages describing the contents of the CD-ROM.
\template	All HTML files and images for the templates in this book.
\tools	Shareware programs that you may use for building your own Web site.
\makeover	The "makeover" examples described in Chapter 9.
\ingreds	Individual elements to use when adapting the templates.
\writespk	The pages for www.writespark.com described in Appendix B.

FIGURE A.2 Directory structure of the CD-ROM.

Hardware and Software Requirements

The template and image files on the CD-ROM are compatible with any Windows or Macintosh personal computer. Specific hardware and software requirements include the following:

- HTML files: Open in any word processor, text editor, or HTML editor.

- Image files: Open with the *Lview* program (see Appendix C) or any browser. To edit, open in any paint program that supports import and modification of bit-mapped images.

- The HTML editors: Run on any 386 or higher computer running Windows 3.1 or Windows 95.

- Other programs in the TOOLS directory may have different requirements. For details, check the *readme.txt* or similar file which may appear when you install the tool.

↳ Working with the Template Files

You can create actual Web pages from the templates on the CD-ROM by following these general steps:

1. Copy the files for the templates and associated elements to your computer.
2. Modify the templates by adding your own text, images, multimedia elements, and links. The tools on the CD-ROM will help you with these tasks.
3. Create and test a master copy of your Web site on your computer (see Appendix B for instructions).

Appendix B also contains a case study on the complete process for developing and maintaining a Web site, including examples of modified templates.

Copying the Templates to Your Computer

To copy the template files from the CD-ROM to your computer, do the following:

1. Create a subdirectory (Windows-based systems) or folder (Macintosh systems) called WEBPAGE (or something similar) on the hard disk of your computer.
2. Copy all files in the TEMPLATE subdirectories on the CD-ROM to the WEBPAGE subdirectory or folder on your hard disk. Verify that you have copied all files you need for each template by checking the contents of your hard-disk subdirectory or folder against Figure A.3.

NOTE

All templates use the following files for the navigation buttons: *back.gif, forward.gif, home.gif, contents.gif, email.gif, bluearrow.gif.*

Template	Text *.RTF and *.HTM	Image and Multimedia Files	Script Files
Advertisement	No HTML file needed	ad.jpg	
Article	article.htm	artban.jpg, wmclogo.jpg, catitm1.gif	
Brochure	brochure.htm	broban.jpg, glblogo.jpg, chair.gif	
Catalog Contents	catalog.htm	contban.jpg, catlogo1.jpg, catitm1.jpg	
Catalog Page	catitm1.htm	catban.jpg, catlogo1.jpg, catitm1.jpg	
Company Profile	coprof.htm	coban.jpg, glblogo.jpg, building.jpg	
Contents Page	contents.htm	globan.jpg, glblogo.jpg	
Coupon	coupon.htm	coupban.jpg, catlogo1.jpg, coup.gif, order.gif	
Event Calendar	calendar.htm	calban.jpg, fealogo.jpg, music.gif, palette.gif tickets.gif, register.gif	
Event Registration Form	eventfrm.htm	eventban.jpg, fealogo.jpg	mailform.cgi
Event Registration FAX Form	eventfax.htm		
FAQ Page	faq.htm	faqban.jpg, catlogo1.jpg	

FIGURE A.3 Templates and associated files.

Template	Text *.RTF and *.HTM	Image and Multimedia Files	Script Files
Locator	locator.htm	locban.jpg, glblogo.jpg, store.jpg	
Newsletter	newsltr.htm	newsban.jpg, glblogo.jpg, chair.gif, music.gif	
Press Release	pressrel.htm	pressban.jpg, fealogo.jpg, pressrel.gif	
Price/Parts List	pricelst.htm	priceban.jpg, glblogo.jpg	
Product Inquiry Form	inquiry.htm	inqban.jpg, glblogo.jpg	mailform.cgi
Product Order Form	order.htm	ordban.jpg, catlogo1.jpg	mailform.cgi
Profile	exprof.htm	execban.jpg, wmclogo.jpg, king.jpg, audio.wav, audio.gif	
Selection Guide	guide.htm	guideban.jpg, fealogo.jpg	mailform.cgi
Seminar Description	seminar.htm	semban.jpg, wmclogo.jpg, catitm1.gif, jim.avi, video.gif	
Services List	services.htm	serban.jpg, wmclogo.jpg, servs.gif	
Starter Page	starter.htm	startban.jpg, glblogo.jpg, catitm1.jpg, audio.au, soundbtn.gif, video.avi, filmbtn.gif	
Visitor Registration/ Survey Form	survey.htm	survban.jpg, glblogo.jpg	mailform.cgi
What's New Page	whatsnew.htm	whatban.jpg, fealogo.jpg, new.gif	

FIGURE A.3 Continued

Modifying the Templates

You can modify the templates to incorporate your own text, logos, images, multimedia elements, and links. Follow the procedures in this section, and see the case study in Appendix B for more ideas and guidelines on adapting the templates.

To modify the text, follow these steps:

1. Open the *<template>.rtf* or *<template>.htm* file in a word processor or text editor (some programs do not support the RTF format). While you can change any aspect of the text or HTML commands in the template files, the RTF version uses the color red to display text you will want to change first. You can also open the .HTM file in an HTML editor (see Appendix C).

2. To adapt the templates for your own Web pages as quickly as possible without knowing anything about HTML, just replace our sample text with your own. However, be careful to avoid changing any HTML tags (the characters between the < and >brackets) that surround the text. If you don't want to use some of the material on a template, you can delete it along with the enclosing HTML tags. If you want to add material, look for a block that has the format you want and just copy its style in the place on the page where you want that element to appear. Even though HTML coding is easy to learn by example, you may want to purchase a basic HTML reference book for specific guidance.

3. When you have completed all modifications to the template, save it in text format with the name: *<filename.htm>*. You may want to change the filename at this point to avoid overwriting the template file itself and to give it a name that will be more meaningful to you. If you use a Windows 95 or Macintosh computer, remember to use all lowercase letters for the filename.

To modify the banners, image placeholders, or buttons, you need a good paint program that can import and manipulate bit-mapped graphics. If you do not have one of the commercial products, we recommend the shareware program

Paintshop Pro (see Appendix C). Open one of our sample banner GIF files inside the paint program and check the program's online help file to determine if you can change it.

NOTE

The filename *dummy.htm* that appears as a remote hyperlink in many of the templates is a placeholder for the actual links you may want to create from that page. For example, the Article template contains the *dummy.htm* placeholder in several places in the page footer. One of these references is for the "Web Marketing Consultants Co." link. On your page, replace this reference with a link to your company's home page (usually *index.htm*). Wherever the *dummy.htm* placeholder appears, you should either delete that link or replace it with the correct link to another page on your site or to an external site. Also remember to reference the correct page for the navigation buttons and associated text links that appear in the footer of each template.

To find other navigation buttons to use on your pages, check the site http://www.cum.qc.ca/images/Images.html, a good "freeware" library of buttons and icons for Web pages. If you find an image you want to use, click the right mouse button to save the image on your computer's hard disk.

To add images or multimedia elements to a template, follow these steps:

1. Images must be in a .GIF or .JPG file format (see Chapter 7 for a description). GIF is the preferred format for simple images (a maximum of 256 colors). For complex images or photographs of people, the JPG format gives better definition and more colors, although in a larger file size. Most scanner software can create files in either of these formats. The resolution of the images need not be greater than "Low" 72 DPI (dots per inch) because that is the resolution of most monitors.

2. Place the image on the Web page by wrapping the file in an HTML image tag: `<a href img src="filename. gif" width=xxx height=yyy alt="Description of image">`. Using the height and width tags on all images

will allow the browser to display all text on the page before it starts loading the images. This will allow visitors to read your message while the images load.

The procedures for adding video and audio files to a page are similar, but each type of file has its own unique file extension. The most common multimedia file types are .AVI (audio/video) and .WAV (audio). These file types can be played by Windows operating system utilities as well as the browsers themselves. Other file types may require special helper programs or plug-ins for the browser, which are usually available at no charge. Check the online help in your browser or contact the browser vendor for more information.

HTML Coding Examples

This section presents instructions for coding several common HTML elements contained in the templates. Refer to this information when you want to adapt the template for use in your own Web pages. Learning these elements will help you develop pages more quickly and resolve coding problems more easily. The example elements shown here are incorporated in the Seminar Description template (see Figure 3.41).

For more extensive modifications to the templates, we recommend that you seek guidance from a reference book on HTML, use one of the Web publishing products, or work with a Web developer.

Tables

The TABLE tag organizes information on the page in columns and rows. Each row in the table is bracketed by `<TR></TR>` pairs. Headers in each column are bracketed by `<TH></TH>` pairs. Data items in each cell are bracketed by `<TD></TD>` pairs. See Figure A.4.

Date/Time	Location
07 May	Festival Hotel
10 June	Home University

FIGURE A.4 Table element.

```
<TABLE border=2 width=80%>
<TR><TH>Date/ Time</TH><TH>Location</TH></TR>
<TR><TD>07 May</TD><TD>Festival Hotel</TD></TR>
<TR><TD>10 June</TD><TD>Home University</TD></TR>
</TABLE>
```

Links

Figure A.5 shows an example of a link to another page on the same site and in the same directory as the current page.

```
<b>Instructor/Leader:</b> <a href="profile.htm">Expert
Consultant</a>
```

If the *profile.htm* page is located in directory "abc" one level down from the site's root directory, it would be referenced as `/abc/profile.htm`. If *profile.htm* is in the root directory of an external site (domain name *xyz.com*), it would be referenced as `http://www.xyz.com/profile.htm`.

Bullet and Numbered Lists

For a list of items that you want to highlight with bullets, use the `<ul></ul>` tags to surround your list and `<li>` before each list item.

```
<b>Learning Objectives:</b>
<ul>
<li> Understand promotional activities on the Web
<li> Create an effective Web site for marketing
<li> Learn about selling products and services online
</ul>
```

To create a numbered list, use the `<ol></ol>` tags instead of `<ul></ul>`. The `<li>` tag is the same for both bullet and numbered lists. See Figure A.6.

Instructor/Leader: Expert Consultant

FIGURE A.5 Navigation link.

Learning Objectives:

- Understand promotional activities on the Web
- Create an effective Web site for marketing
- Learn about selling products and services online

FIGURE A.6 Bullet list.

Video and Audio Elements

This section describes the HTML coding for a video element, but it also applies to audio elements. A reference to a video clip is coded as follows:

```
<a href="video.avi"><img src="filmbtn.gif" width=40
height=40 align=right border=0 alt="Video Clip"></a>
<p><br><p align=right><a href="video.avi">Seminar Video
Clip</a>
</p>
```

The *video.avi* reference is to the actual video file residing in the same directory as the current page. The file *filmbtn.gif* contains the film reel button, and it resides in the same directory. This tag specifies the width and height of the button (always a good idea) and the "alt=" tag presents descriptive text when the image is not displayed in a visitor's browser.

By making the button a link, the browser will load and play the video.avi file when a visitor clicks on that button. The third line of the code is a text link that performs the same function.

To adapt this code for an audio element, substitute the name of the audio file in place of *video.avi*, reference *soundbtn.gif* for the audio button, and change the descriptive text for the "alt=" tag. See Figure A.7.

FIGURE A.7 Video element button and link.

Page Footer

The first three lines of the page footer are coded as follows:

```
<center>http://www.webmarketco.com/seminar.htm
<br>Copyright &copy; 1997 <a href="dummy.htm">Web
Marketing Consultants Co.</a>
<br>Questions and comments to:
<a href="mailto:emailname@domain.name">emailname@domain.
name</a>
```

The first line of code is simply the URL of this page. It is a good idea to include the complete URL in case a visitor prints the page from the browser. Visitors will be able to find your site again from the URL on the printed page.

The second line is a link to the Web Marketing Consultants Co. home page (here coded as *dummy.htm*). The third line is an e-mail link, which is coded so that when the visitor clicks on *emailname@domain.name* the browser will open an e-mail message that is pre-addressed. Remember to substitute your correct e-mail address for every occurrence of *emailname@domain.name* within the HTML code. See Figure A.8.

 # Working with the Tools

You need only a few tools to build a Web site: a browser, a word processor or HTML editor (optional, but very helpful), and an FTP (File Transfer Protocol) program to upload your pages from your PC to a Web server. Other useful tools include an image manipulation program such as *Lview Pro* and a paint program such as *Paintshop Pro*. (See Appendix C.)

> http://www.webmarketco.com/seminar.htm
> Copyright © 1997 Web Marketing Consultants Co.
> Questions and comments to: emailname@domain.name

FIGURE A.8 Template footer.

As you gain experience in developing Web pages, you may want to explore other, more sophisticated tools. An excellent online source for tools is http://www.shareware.com.

You may also edit and create HTML files in your word processor with add-on Web publishing tools. Contact the vendor of your word processing program for information on features and availability of these tools.

Tools on the CD-ROM are versions for Microsoft Windows 3.x or Windows 95. Versions for Macintosh or UNIX operating systems also may be available; contact the vendor for information. A brief description and vendor contact information are available in the *readme.txt* or similar file in the directory for each tool on the CD-ROM.

Understand that these tools are distributed as shareware. Shareware (also known as user-supported software) is a means of distributing software created by individuals or companies too small to make inroads into conventional retail distribution networks. The authors of shareware retain all rights to the software under the copyright laws while still allowing free distribution. This gives you the chance to freely obtain and try out the software before purchasing it. Shareware should not be confused with public-domain software even though they are often obtained from the same sources.

If you continue to use any of the shareware programs on the CD-ROM after the specified trial period (typically 30 days), you are expected to register your use of the product with the author or vendor and pay a registration fee. Some shareware programs will stop working at the end of the trial period unless you register that copy.

Instructions for the registration process are usually presented in a *readme.txt* file or similar file, or an initial screen within the program. When you purchase a shareware product, the vendor may provide a printed manual, free updates, telephone support, and other services. But perhaps more importantly, your purchase encourages further development of useful products by independent vendors—products that aren't always offered by major companies in the industry.

Installing the Tools

All programs in the TOOLS directory are delivered either in the form of self-extracting executable files (file extension .EXE) or zipped files (file extension .ZIP). To install a particular tool on your Windows 3.x or Windows 95 computer, follow the general instructions below. You should also follow the installation instructions included in the *readme.txt* file (if any), located in the same subdirectory as the tool.

To install a self-extracting executable file (file extension .EXE), follow the example procedure described here:

1. Use either the Explorer or File Manager program to create a new (empty) directory on your hard disk for the program you want to install.

2. Copy the file <PROGRAM>.EXE from the TOOLS directory on the CD-ROM to the new directory.

3. Run <PROGRAM>.EXE from Windows. If using Windows 95 or Windows NT with the NewShell, use the menu Item Run from the task bar. For Windows 3.x, from either File Manager or Program Manager, select the menu command File|Run.

4. The program may display a message that your system is not prepared to run the software, and it may explain why. Possible reasons are that your computer is running Windows NT version 3.50 or older, or that your computer is running Windows 3.1 without Win32 extensions. The message will offer suggestions for resolving the problem; contact the vendor if you need additional assistance.

5. If the software can be installed, the program will prompt you to select an installation directory and other installation options. Click on OK to proceed with the installation. After the setup program terminates, use the Explorer or File Manager to delete the installation directory and all files in it. Your system will then be ready to run the program.

To install a "zipped" file (one with file extension .ZIP), you need an "unzip" program. The .ZIP file extension indicates the file has been compressed using one of the PKZIP compression programs. To use the file, you must first uncompress it, then install it. We have included *Winzip* on the CD-ROM, one of the best Windows utilities for this purpose. You can install *Winzip* on your PC by following the procedure described above.

After installing *Winzip*, you can install a zipped file (file extension .ZIP), following the procedure described here:

1. Use either the Explorer or File Manager program to create a new (empty) directory on your hard disk for the program you want to install.

2. Copy the file <PROGRAM>.ZIP from the TOOLS directory on the CD-ROM to the new directory.

3. Double-click on the <PROGRAM>.ZIP filename. If you have a correctly installed "unzip" program, it will be invoked to decompress the file. Follow that program's instructions to extract the files into the new directory.

4. Run <PROGRAM>.EXE from Windows. If using Windows 95 or Windows NT with the NewShell, use the menu Item Run from the task bar. For Windows 3.x, from either File Manager or Program Manager, select the menu command File I Run.

5. If the software can be installed, the program will prompt you to select an installation directory and other installation options. Click on OK to proceed with the installation. After the installation program terminates, use the Explorer or File Manager to delete the installation directory and the files in it. Your system will then be ready to run the software.

Other programs on the CD-ROM are installed in a similar manner. If you encounter any problems during the installation process, contact the vendor for assistance. Contact information is available in the *readme.txt* file for the program or in the software itself.

The software accompanying this book is provided as is without warranty or support of any kind. Should you require basic installation assistance, or if the CD-ROM is defective, contact Wiley product support at +01 212 850-6194, Monday-Friday, 9:00 a.m. to 4:00 p.m. Eastern time or via e-mail at: wprtusw@wiley.com.

IMPLEMENTING AND MAINTAINING A WEB SITE

If you have little or no experience in developing a Web site, you may be wondering whether you have the required technical knowledge and skill. As you will discover by reading this appendix, implementing and maintaining a simple Web site are tasks that can be learned quickly. You will gain even more insight by reading the case study at the end of this appendix, which describes how author Janice King planned and implemented her Web site based on the ideas, templates, and procedures in this book.

Creating a Web Site

You have completed your plans for Web marketing, and you have adapted the templates in this book for the actual Web pages on your site. To implement the site you will need to complete these tasks:

- Choose an Internet Service Provider (ISP) to host your Web site and determine whether you want to register a domain name.
- Install and test your Web pages on the ISP's server computer.
- Promote your site in Web directories and search engines.
- Maintain the site by periodically adding new content and retesting all links.

Working with an ISP

Most small businesses and nonprofit organizations do not have the financial or technical resources to purchase and maintain a dedicated computer to use as a Web server. Instead, they rent server space and capabilities from an ISP, a company that provides Web hosting and sometimes Internet access services. Most ISPs offer a choice of packages for Web hosting services, with pricing based on a monthly account fee.

When choosing an ISP to host your Web site, carefully consider the factors described in this section. But first you should understand that your Web site does not need to reside with your dial-up service provider (the company that provides your telephone connection to the Internet). Your Web site can be hosted anywhere on the Internet because both you and visitors can access it by entering the site's assigned URL. Because of the interconnectedness of the Internet, it does not matter whether the host ISP for your Web site is located in your town, across the country, or in another part of the world. Also for this reason, it does not matter whether your Web site is hosted by a different ISP than the one that provides your dial-up access to the Internet.

While your dial-up service provider may offer Web site hosting services, we recommend that you compare the offerings of several ISPs to find the exact combination of services you need and the most competitive pricing. You can find a list of ISPs on the Web with the search keywords **Internet service provider**. All ISPs maintain a Web site that describes their services and prices as well as the equipment and communication facilities that support those services.

When comparing the offerings of different ISPs, consider these factors:

1. *Domain name service*. Does the price for the service package or account you want include the cost of servicing a domain name for your business (e.g., www.widgets.com)? Servicing domain names requires fixed resources from an ISP, but many ISPs include the charge for this service in the monthly account price.

2. *Disk storage*. Your Web pages and images will need to reside on the ISP's Web server (typically a UNIX-based computer) to be available to the Internet 24 hours a day. At a minimum, 5 megabytes of disk storage should be included in the monthly account fee. Your site may require more disk space initially (especially if you include numerous images or multimedia elements on your pages) or as it grows over time. Check the ISP's price for additional storage space, or

for an option to upgrade in the future to a service plan that includes a greater amount of storage. To determine how much disk space you will need, look at the total disk space used by all the files for your Web pages on your computer. This number will be easy to identify if you have stored all files in a single directory; just check the total for that directory.

3. *Data transfer*. When a visitor to your site accesses one of your Web pages, the page is transferred as data from the server to the Internet. This data transfer creates an expense for your ISP in the form of communications equipment and usage charges for the links from the server to the Internet. The ISP passes on these costs to you in the form of a monthly data-transfer charge. Most monthly account fees include a specified amount of data transfer, typically 500 megabytes per month, which is adequate for most sites. If your site contains numerous images and multimedia elements, or if you experience a large number of visits, your data transfer rate may be higher. In this case, verify that the charges are reasonable for additional amounts of transfer over your monthly allocation.

4. *Fast Internet access*. How fast your Web pages load in a visitor's browser depends on a number of factors, but one of the most important is the speed of your ISP's connection to the Internet. A full T1 (in North America) or E1 (in other parts of the world) connection is a minimum, with a T3 or E3 connection preferable. The ISP also should maintain at least one backup connection to the Internet in case the primary connection develops a problem. Also check the type of server equipment the ISP is using; at a minimum, a Pentium-class computer is required for acceptable responsiveness. Because traffic load on the entire Internet can affect responsiveness at any given moment, you may also want to access the ISP's Web site at different times of the day to verify speed.

5. *CGI scripts*. You want the ability to run CGI scripts in your own directories on the ISP's server. Some ISPs do not allow this configuration, and as an alternative, they give you access to all the scripts you may need from a "public" directory on the server, typically named the *cgi-bin* directory. Examples of scripts you may want to use from an ISP's public directory include an e-mail form (similar to the *mailform.cgi* script included on the CD-ROM), image mapping, a guest book, a page "hit" counter (number of times the page is accessed by visitors), and credit-card verification. Confirm with the ISP whether these scripts are available and whether they are adequate for your needs.

6. *E-mail forwarding*. If you use one ISP for Web hosting and a different ISP for dial-up access, you may need an e-mail forwarding capability that will send e-mail from visitors on your Web site (maintained by your Web hosting ISP) to your e-mail account (maintained by your dial-up ISP). For example, you may want mail sent to *sales@widgets.com* listed on your Web site to be forwarded to your dial-up Internet access account (e.g., *myname@dialup.net*). This capability enables you to direct specific types of e-mail to different people within your company without needing to change your Web pages each time you change the employee assignment. When evaluating this capability from an ISP, you will want the flexibility of several e-mail forwarding addresses as a standard feature for your account. The ISP also may offer e-mail boxes in addition to or instead of e-mail forwarding.

7. *E-mail auto responder*. Successful promotion on the Web requires that you respond very quickly to every e-mail message, product order, inquiry, or other contact from visitors on your site. In most cases, visitors expect a response within 24 hours, and responding in just a few hours can give your company a competitive advantage. However, consider whether you will be able to

answer every e-mail inquiry from the site within this time frame.

To simplify e-mail handling, you may want to implement an automatic-response capability for all or selected types of inquiries from visitors to your site. For example, you may want an e-mail message that a visitor sends to *info@widgets.com* to automatically receive a sort of electronic form letter, explaining the services and products you provide. The response is sent automatically and immediately by the ISP's "auto responder" capability. The automated response provides immediate feedback to the visitor while allowing you to follow-up with an additional, personalized e-mail message at a later, convenient time. Automatic responses are especially valuable if your site attracts a large number of international visitors, where time zone differences may make it impossible for you to respond within a few hours.

8. *Password protection of directories.* You may want to restrict visitor access to confidential or valuable information on your Web site, such as content that you sell from the site or a price list. One way to restrict access is to place the information in a password-protected directory on the server, giving the password only to visitors who have purchased the content or subscribed to your service, or to authorized visitors such as dealers and employees (see Chapter 11). Your ISP account should allow you to implement password protection on any of your directories.

9. *Anonymous FTP.* You may want to provide information on your Web site in the form of downloadable files that a visitor can access by a process known as "anonymous FTP" (file transfer protocol). If you need this feature, verify that the ISP provides it as either a standard or add-on feature of your account.

10. *Secure service.* If you intend to accept credit-card transactions on your Web pages, you will need access

to a secure server maintained by the ISP. A secure server can communicate with the encryption features in the visitor's browser to protect credit-card numbers and other sensitive data. (See Chapter 4 for a discussion of security issues for electronic commerce.) Even if you do not plan to sell products online when first implementing your Web site, you will want to ensure that the ISP offers this service as a future option, for a reasonable additional charge on your monthly account.

11. *Data backup.* Verify that the ISP makes a regular back-up to tape or disk of all files associated with your Web pages. Also determine whether the ISP maintains a "hot spare" server, one that is standing by with current copies of your Web pages in case the primary server fails. These factors are important for avoiding the situation where visitors would not be able to access your site because the ISP's server is not working. Remember that if visitors experience a problem in accessing your site, they may assume that it no longer exists and may not try to access it again.

12. *Access to statistics.* You will want to know which of your pages are the most popular among visitors, where your visitors are located (by domain and country), and how your visitors find your site (that is, which Internet sites they visit before they come to your site). The Web server software tracks this information in logs, which the ISP should make available to you as part of your service program.

13. *Other services.* If your Web pages include audio and video elements or advanced techniques such as VRML, you must determine if the ISP supports these capabilities and the associated costs you will incur. In addition, evaluate how the ISP keeps pace with emerging Web technologies if these will be important to implement on your site.

ISP or a Web Developer?

Depending on the size and complexity of your site, you may need to work with both an ISP and a Web developer. Most ISPs provide only hosting services, not the programming and design capabilities offered by a Web developer. Some ISPs have a Web development division or will recommend developers for you.

Look to the ISP for basic technical support on uploading and maintaining files on the server. Look for a LISTSERV or chat group and help files (technical support FAQ file) on the site to determine the ISP's responsiveness to customer requests.

Obtaining a Domain Name

Registering and maintaining a unique domain name for your Web site is a decision you will want to make before implementing your Web marketing activities. You will need to understand the concept of a domain, the marketing and implementation trade-offs, and the procedures and costs associated with maintaining your own domain.

A domain on the Web has two aspects. The first is the exclusive right to use a unique set of characters as an address on the Internet (e.g., www.widgets.com). The second aspect is the practical matter of maintaining and supporting the domain, a task that must be performed by your ISP.

You can register your own domain name (www.widgets.com) or use a domain name provided by your ISP (www.ispdomain.com/widgets). Both of these approaches have advantages and limitations for both marketing goals and implementation activities.

Marketing and Implementation Trade-offs

Registering a unique domain name for your Web site offers several marketing advantages:

- The site name can correspond to your company, organization, or brand name and reinforce your overall promotional efforts.

- The URL for a site with a unique domain name is usually shorter and easier to remember than nondomain URLs.

- Many visitors try to find sites simply by typing the company name in their browsers, for example, www.company.com.

In addition, registering your own domain name enables you to change ISPs in the future without the need to notify visitors of your new location or reprint materials that contain the URL for your Web site. The domain name will move with you to the new ISP; this is not the case if you use an ISP's domain name.

The most significant drawback of maintaining a unique domain name for many small businesses is the associated costs. You must be prepared to pay the monthly domain service fee for the life of your Web site. You also must pay the annual domain registration fee to the responsible InterNIC agency. If you stop either of these fees, the ISP will stop servicing your domain name and your Web site will not be available to visitors. If you are uncertain about your long-term commitment to Web marketing, you can start by placing your site under an ISP's domain name, then implement your own domain at a later time.

Implementing a Domain Name

While your ISP will handle most of the steps for you, it is important to understand the process for registering and maintaining a unique domain name for your Web site. In general, the process includes these steps:

1. You must determine that the domain name you want is available, that is, it is not being used by anyone else. Even though an exact match to your company name or preferred domain name may not be available now or later, variations on your desired domain name may

work just as well to communicate your company, products, and services.

2. You must register the domain name with the responsible InterNIC agency and pay the current annual registration fee.

3. The domain must be administered by your ISP, which may offer varying degrees of support at dramatically different prices. Usually maintenance is based on a flat monthly fee billed to a credit card. Domain maintenance is necessary because each server connected to the Internet can handle only a finite set of domain protocols. Each domain serviced by the ISP requires that traffic be routed from one Internet address to another each time a visitor accesses your Web site or sends e-mail to an address in your domain. In short, servicing an individual domain is more complicated and uses more of the server's total capacity than sites that reside under the ISP's domain name. As a result, most ISPs charge a monthly fee for this service.

⤷ Installing and Testing Web Pages

The best way to create a Web site is to create an exact copy (called a "mirror") of the site on your own computer first. This copy should be contained in a directory structure identical to the one you will use on the server. An identical directory structure will allow you to completely test and verify all links among pages on your site without placing it on the server and accessing it from a live connection on the Internet.

This testing activity is essential for ensuring that visitors have a positive experience as they navigate your site. While you will be eager to implement your site as quickly as possible, remember that if your site attracts visitors before you are ready, they may not come back again. Resist the temptation to unveil an incomplete site or one that is finished but not fully tested and debugged.

Uploading Files to the Server

After you have tested and verified that all elements of your site work correctly on your own computer, upload the files to your ISP's Web server using an FTP program. An FTP program is included on the CD-ROM, or a similar capability may be available in your Internet access software (most browsers do not include an FTP program). A good FTP program provides an interface that resembles that of the File Manager or Explorer programs in Microsoft Windows.

Even though transferring files with FTP is a simple process, obtain specific instructions from your ISP. In general the process includes these steps:

1. Open the FTP program and enter the Internet address or name of your Web server. Then enter the name of the directory on your computer that contains the files to upload. Finally, enter the name of the directory on the Web server where your files will reside.

2. After FTP establishes a connection with your server, copy the files from your computer to the server.

3. Verify that all files have been transferred completely by comparing the file list on the server with the directory on your computer.

Implementing Subdirectories

The number of subdirectories you need to create under the main root directory of your user space on the Web server depends on the size and organization of your site. If your site contains a large number of HTML and other files (more than 30), creating subdirectories will make it easier for you to find and maintain specific pages in the future. If your site uses fewer than 30 files for pages, images, and other elements, you will find it simpler to store all files in the main directory of your user space on the server. A good FTP program will automatically copy your computer's subdirectory structure for your Web site onto the server.

> **NOTE**
>
> Servers assume the file for your home page is named *index.htm* or *index.html*. This allows visitors to find your home page just by typing your domain name (for example, http://www.widgets.com). If your home page has a different filename, the visitor will see only a directory listing for your user space on the server.

Testing on the Server

After transferring all files, test all pages and links on your site by using your dial-up account to establish a connection to the Web, then type the URL of your site into your browser. Navigating your site as if you are a visitor, verify the following items in your testing:

- All pages on your site are available on the server and load with all associated images and multimedia elements.

- All navigation links work correctly, both within the site and to external sites.

- All scripts operate correctly, and any forwarded e-mail is sent to the correct address. Test the forwarding capability by sending an e-mail to yourself from an e-mail link on one of your Web pages.

If you encounter any problems, check the following:

- Missing files

- Wrong file extension

- Files in the wrong directory or the directory reference is wrong

- Case-sensitivity (safest is always to use lowercase letters in filenames)

- The settings of permissions for file access (check with your ISP for assistance)

If you find a problem in the page content or links, correct the files on your computer first, test the correction, then upload the corrected files to the server.

Installing and Testing CGI Scripts

CGI scripts will not work correctly on your computer because the server executes the scripts, not the browser. The only place to test scripts is on the server after you have uploaded all files for your site.

Ask your ISP where to store script files on the server. Some ISPs require that all scripts be stored in a special directory under the ISP's control or in a specially named subdirectory in your server space.

Remember to transfer the script files in ASCII mode, not binary mode. After the script files are in place on the server, you may need to change the access permissions for these files to allow access from your Web pages. Changing permissions can be done with an FTP program, but ask your ISP for assistance and specific instructions for this task.

NOTE

UNIX-based Web servers are sensitive to the case of letters in filenames, treating any variation in the case as a reference to a different file. This can create a problem for visitors who directly access a specific page on your site by typing its complete URL. Always use lowercase letters in your filenames.

Promoting the Web Site

How will visitors find your site on the Web? This question is frequently asked by marketers, even those who are experienced Web users. It is a valid question because there are a number of ways for visitors to find your Web site, from search engines and directories on the Web to print materials to advertising.

We recommend proactively publicizing the URL for your Web site at every opportunity, using tools available on the Web as well as traditional advertising and marketing tools. Effectively promoting your Web site (generating traffic to the site) requires a conscious commitment to the process, which is open-ended and demands both imagination and diligence.

Web Directories

One of the most common ways to promote your site is through the free directories and search engines (also called search sites) on the Web. One of the oldest and largest of the directories is Yahoo! (www.yahoo.com), which lists Web sites by category and subcategories. Other popular sites are Lycos, Web Crawler, Infoseek, AltaVista, and Excite (see Appendix C). The directory sites are cross-linked, making them easy to find on the Web.

There are hundreds of other directories and search engines on the Web, most of which are free, but some charge a listing fee. Although there are more than enough free directories available to market almost any site, you may not want to rule out a paid directory listing if it matches your product or service, and if the directory operators are credible and have a good history of delivering business and traffic to Web sites.

> **TIP**
>
> The directories and search engines aren't the only means for promoting your site on the Web. See Chapters 1, 4, and 7 for discussion of site promotion through links on other sites and in advertisements and other printed marketing materials.

The primary difference between directories (such as Yahoo!) and search engines (such as Lycos) is that directories will not list your URL unless you submit it. Each directory has its own criteria for submitting the URL and related information about the site. Check the directory sites for instructions on submitting a listing for your site. Although the Web directories do not have an obligation to accommodate a particular company or organization, they generally strive for fairness and accuracy in their listings.

Each directory posts individual business or organization listings at different speeds. Some postings happen within minutes while others may take more than a month, depending on the volume and rate of submittals to the particular directory.

In most cases, a Web directory is subdivided into categories, and businesses or organizations are listed in only one or two categories. Not every category is defined in every directory, so it is typically up to the submitter to choose the best category for the listing.

We recommend that rather than trying to perfectly match the submittal requirements for each directory, you focus instead on general guidelines and post to as many directories and search engines as possible. The key to a good general submittal is to ensure that your Web site is titled descriptively, placing words that describe the subject or product category in the document title. Also, place strong, descriptive copy and keywords in the first paragraph of text on the page to help the search engines find and display the essential information about your site.

A great shortcut for listing your site on multiple directories and search engines is to use Web-based programs that make automated submissions. A number of these utilities are available on the Web, and they can shorten the process significantly. Most of these programs do not charge a fee for submissions to the dozen or so key directories. They will charge a fee for extra submissions, sometimes offering hundreds of directories from which to choose for targeted marketing.

Web Search Engines

Search engines on the Web use automated robots or spiders, which are powerful forms of indexing software, to create listings based on identifying the keywords that appear on a Web page. The robots and spiders continuously search the Web for new or updated pages by following links from one page to another. The goal of the search engines is to identify and catalog every URL on the Web.

The automated robots and spiders may record the complete text from each page and follow any external links within the text. Unless a Web site is specifically excluded from the robot searches, it will eventually be found and cataloged by a search engine. Most search engines also allow you to submit the URL for your site; this will shorten the time required for the search engine to find and list your site.

Some people try to improve their listings on the search engine sites by inserting dozens or even hundreds of keywords at the bottom of each Web page. While this may improve the chances that the page will be found for a handful of searches, many directories and search engines exclude these deliberately redundant keywords altogether. Any short-term gains with search engines using redundant key word gimmicks will be forfeited when the Web site is submitted to the directories. Again, we recommend accuracy and clarity in the title and text on all Web pages as the best way to improve both listings and service to visitors.

Maintaining the Web Site

Much of the discussion about Web marketing implies that you need to change your site almost continually. For most small organizations, this is both unnecessary and too costly in terms of time and resources. You should plan to update your site periodically as you offer new products, events, or services and as you implement Web promotions. You may also want to add new pages that reflect new print materials, such as brochures and press releases. The What's New template is an easy way to add new information to your site and encourage frequent repeat visits.

When you are ready to update your site, the following procedures will help you to simplify the task and avoid problems:

1. Remember always to maintain "master" copies of your Web pages on your own computer as a mirror of your

live site. If something happens to those copies (such as a hard disk failure), you can download the versions from the Web server back to your computer.

2. When you need to change a Web page on your site, change the master copy first and test the modified page thoroughly on your computer *before* you upload it to the server.

3. *Never* upload an untested page to your server, no matter how minor the change. One small mistake can create significant problems when a visitor's browser attempts to display that page or navigate from it to another page or site. While you can sometimes correct problems directly in the files stored on the server, this approach can create more problems than it solves. *Always test every change thoroughly on your computer before uploading it to your live site.*

4. After you upload a modified file to the server, *always test the affected pages again on the server*. Although the page may display and operate correctly on your computer, this does not mean it will work correctly on the server. Perform all tests listed earlier in the section "Testing on the Server" whenever you upload a new file to your site.

Verifying Links to External Sites

If you have implemented links to external sites on any of your pages, regularly test those links to verify that they still work as expected. To test, access your site as if you are a visitor, then click on the links and determine if they lead to the site that you expect, and to the type of content you want visitors to see. Software tools are also available for checking links automatically, a capability that is especially valuable for large sites with many external links. To find these tools, search the Web with the keywords **link+checker**. Chapters 5 and 8 present additional guidelines for implementing links to external sites.

↳ Case Study: Cooking Up a Web Site

To demonstrate the validity of our approach to Web marketing, I (Janice King) used the templates and procedures covered in this book to develop a Web site for my small consulting business. This section describes how I approached this project, the decisions I made during development, and the lessons I learned. The illustrations show how I adapted the templates for my Web pages; you can see the latest versions by checking my Web site at http://www .writespark.com. (Check http://www.say64k.com for my co-authors, Paul Knight and Jim Mason.)

Getting Started

I followed these steps in developing my site:

1. I used the guidelines in Chapters 4 and 5 to plan the structure for the site and determine how to conduct online sales. I completed the Site Plan Worksheet from Chapter 5 (see Figure B.1), deciding what I wanted to implement on my site now and what information and activities could wait until a future time.

2. I gathered my print materials to use as input in choosing and adapting templates. I also located printed copies of my business logo, portrait photo, and the cover of my book *Writing High-Tech Copy That Sells*. I noted the location on my computer for existing text files that could be adapted and identified the new text I would need to create for the Web pages.

3. I chose the templates I wanted to adapt and marked up printouts for each to show the types of changes I would need to make. This activity gave me a list of pages for the site. From this list, I planned the navigation within the site, creating a navigation flowchart as described in Chapter 5 (see Figure B.2).

Site Plan Worksheet

Goal:

To reach new prospects with information on my services, books, and resources.

Description of Target Audience:

Primary audience is marketing communication and public relations managers in high-tech companies. Secondary audience is other marketing and technical writers.

Visitor Expectations for Site:

Useful information about my qualifications and services. Information on how to contact me by phone, fax, or e-mail. For books, an online order form or capability.

Site Content and Activity:

Initially will be a small and simple site to gain feedback on visitor interests. Present basic information on my services and resources, and encourage visitors to request additional information by submitting a Visitor Registration form, sending an e-mail message to me, or calling me.

Design Principles:

Adapt the templates from The Web Marketing Cookbook, maintaining a consistent look among all pages on the site. Minimize the use of images and multimedia elements to assure fast loading times.

Security or Access Considerations:

None.

Roles and Resources:

Adapt the templates myself. Use the services of a graphic designer to scan and size the images. Check with my ISP for instructions on registering my domain name and loading my files onto the server.

Completed by: Janice King   Date: March 1997

FIGURE B.1 Site Plan worksheet for www.writespark.com.

Adapting the Templates

With all my planning complete and all input collected, I was ready to transform the templates into Web pages by modifying the HTML code. I had no knowledge of HTML or Web

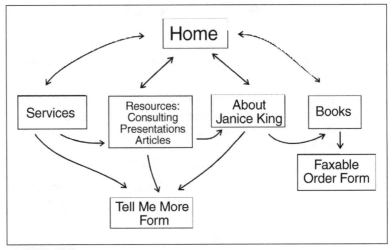

FIGURE B.2 Navigation flowchart for www.writespark.com.

development before I began to work with the templates, although I have used other markup languages in the past. As a result, by looking at the templates I found it easy to figure out the structure of the HTML tags and how to modify them. However, if I want to develop more complex pages, I would purchase a thorough reference book on HTML or work with a Web developer.

I loaded the template files into my word processor and made changes by typing in my own text, and copying and modifying the HTML tags, following the instructions in Appendix A. I found this approach easiest to use because my changes were fairly minimal, and I was modifying only a few templates. However, as I expand my site, I plan to use an HTML editor to simplify this task.

Figures B.3 through B.18 show the results of my work, both as pictures of the actual Web pages and the underlying HTML files. The remainder of this section describes the decisions and changes I made when creating these pages.

All Pages

For all pages on my site, I implemented these items:

- I deleted the Contents button and link from the standard navigation buttons at the bottom of the page because my site isn't big enough to require a Contents page.

- I changed the Back and Forward buttons and links in the footer to cycle through all pages on my site in a circular fashion. I simply entered the appropriate page reference in each file. For an example, see item 3 in the description for Figure B.3.

- I changed the <TITLE> and <ALT> tags on each page to incorporate descriptive text about my company and services, which will improve the site's listings in the Web directories and search engines.

- I used links to encourage exploration on the site, adapting the specific links to each page. In addition, I created a link from my name in the copyright (located in the footer) to the Profile page (*profile.htm*).

FIGURE B.3 Home page on www.writespark.com.

- I replaced all references to emailname@domain.name with my e-mail address: janice@writespark.com.

- I changed the text in the page banners in Paintshop Pro, resizing the height and width to reflect the size of my company logo.

- I changed all references to images to match the actual filenames, for example, *king.jpg* for my photo that appears on the Profile page.

- I added links to guide visitor exploration on the site. The Tell me more: link is designed to encourage the visitor to complete the Visitor Registration/Survey form (*visreg.htm*) and is the call to action for several pages on the site.

Home Page

I used the Starter template as the basis for this page, deleting the text and associated HTML tags for all elements I did not need. See Figures B.3 and B.4.

1. Several items on the bullet list point to the Resources page (*resource.htm*) with targets for linking to particular points on that page.

2. The link to the 64k Internet Marketing site shows an example of coding a link to an external site. Here I don't mind if visitors link to the 64k site, because Paul and Jim have created a reciprocal link, meaning visitors can easily return to my site.

3. I deleted the Back and Home buttons and links in the footer because they do not make sense for this page. I kept the <p> and <br> tags when I removed navigation buttons and links in the footer because these tags control the layout of these buttons on the page.

4. I saved this file with the name *index.htm*; the server will display this page when a visitor types only the URL http://www.writespark.com.

```
<html><head><title>Janice King & WriteSpark(TM): Expert
Resources for High-Tech Copywriting</title></head>

<body bgcolor="#ffffff">
<IMG SRC="home.jpg" WIDTH=350 HEIGHT=50 ALT="Home Page"> <IMG
SRC="logo.gif " WIDTH=146 HEIGHT=90 ALT="Logo">
<p>
<center>

<font size=+2>Expert Resources for Marketing Writing</font>
<p>
</center>
Welcome to WriteSpark(TM) resources for marketing special-
ists, public relations staff, product managers, copywriters—
anyone who markets a product, service, or company via print
or online.
<p>
You'll learn about my copywriting and consulting services,
training programs, books and publications. If you need a
workshop or presentation for your staff or group, you can
review my topics and contact me from this site.
<p>
Please take a moment to complete the <a
href="visreg.htm">Tell me more</a> form. It will help me
address your specific questions and improve the site's con-
tent.
<p>
Many new offerings are in the works here at
<b>writespark.com</b>; you'll want to bookmark this site and
return often to see the latest!
<center>
<p>Regards,
<p><i>Janice King</i></center>

<br><hr size=3 >
<br><font size=+1>WriteSpark: Expert Resources from Janice
King</font>
<ul>
<li> <a href="services.htm">Copywriting services</a>
<li> <a href="books.htm">Books & publications</a>
<li> <a href="resource.htm">Consulting & training
services</a>
```

FIGURE B.4 HTML code for home page on www.writespark.com.

```
<li> <a href="resource.htm#present">Presentations</a>
<li> <a href="resource.htm#article">Articles</a>
<li> <a href="profile.htm">About Janice King</a>
<li> <a href="visreg.htm">Tell me more!</a>
</ul>
<br>
<p>The pages on this site were developed using templates
from my new book, <a href="books.htm"><i>The Web Marketing
Cookbook</i></a>, written with my co-authors Paul Knight and
James H. Mason. Paul and Jim offer expert Web development
services through their company, <a
href="http://www.say64k.com">64k Internet Marketing Inc.</a>
<br><hr size=3>
<center>
http://www.writespark.com/index.htm
<br>Copyright &copy; 1997 <a href="profile.htm">Janice M.
King</a>
<br>WriteSpark is a trademark of Janice M. King.
<br>Questions and comments to: <a href="mailto:janice@writes-
park.com">janice@writespark.com</a>
<p>
<a href="services.htm"><img src="forward.gif" width=80
height=40 border=0></a>
<a href="mailto:janice@writespark.com"> <img src="email.gif"
width=80 height=40 border=0></a>
<br>
<a href="services.htm">Forward</a> ||
<a href="mailto:janice@writespark.com">E-Mail</a></font>
</body>
</html>
```

FIGURE B.4 Continued

Services Page

I adapted this page from the Services template to describe my
primary business: copywriting services. See Figures B.5 and B.6.

1. I decided not to link to client sites (even to pages that
   show some of my work) because I don't want to lose
   visitors before they have fully explored my site. In addition, when a visitor requests more information on my
   services, I want to tailor the materials and samples I send
   to the prospect's specific project needs and interests.

2. I added links to encourage visitors to explore the other
   pages on my site. Whether or not they are interested

in my copywriting services, they may be interested in my other products and services.

3. The call to action on this page encourages visitors to telephone or use the "Tell me more" page or e-mail as the means to initiate a dialogue. I copied the setup of

FIGURE B.5 Services page on www.writespark.com.

```
<HTML><HEAD><TITLE>Janice King, Copywriter: Marketing
Communication and Public Relations Services</TITLE></HEAD>

<BODY BGCOLOR="#ffffff">
<IMG SRC="services.jpg" WIDTH=350 HEIGHT=50 ALT="Services
Page"> <IMG SRC="logo.gif " WIDTH=146 HEIGHT=90 ALT="Logo">
<CENTER>
<P>
<FONT SIZE=+3> Janice King</FONT>
<BR><FONT SIZE=+2> Copywriter</FONT>
</CENTER>
<HR SIZE=3>
<TABLE CELLPADDING=5 CELLSPACING=5 BORDER=0>
<TR>
<TD VALIGN=TOP>
<P><FONT SIZE=+1>Services offered . . .</FONT>
<UL>
<LI> Concept Development
<LI> Program Planning
<LI> Research
<LI> Interviewing
<LI> Copywriting
<LI> Editing
<LI> Diagrams
<LI> Project Management
<LI> Reviews
</UL>
</TD>
<TD VALIGN=TOP>
<P><FONT SIZE=+1>Ideal for . . .</FONT>
<UL>
<LI> Brochures and Data Sheets
<LI> White Papers
<LI> Press Releases and Backgrounders
<LI> Trade Magazine Articles
<LI> Case Studies and Application Notes
<LI> Customer Newsletters
<LI> Sales Guides and Dealer Materials
<LI> Conference and Trade Show Materials
<LI> World Wide Web Content
</UL>
</TD>
</TR>
<TR>
```

FIGURE B.6 HTML code for services page on www.writespark.com.

```
<TD VALIGN=TOP>
<P><FONT SIZE=+1>Special expertise in . . .</FONT>
<UL>
<LI> Voice and data communications
<LI> PBX, ACD, and Central Office systems
<LI> Voice processing systems
<LI> Call centers
<LI> Cellular and PCS
<LI> WAN and LAN technologies
<LI> SONET, ATM, Frame Relay, SMDS, ISDN
<LI> Host connectivity products
<LI> SNA and multiprotocol networks
</UL>
</TD>
<TD VALIGN=TOP>
<P><FONT SIZE=+1>Representative Clients . . .</FONT>
<UL>

<LI> ADC Kentrox
<LI> Ameritech Corporation
<LI> Attachmate Corporation
<LI> Boole & Babbage
<LI> Cisco Systems
<LI> Digital Systems International
<LI> Hewlett-Packard
<LI> Make Systems
<LI> Nortel
<LI> Omnipoint
<LI> Sprint
<LI> Tektronix
<LI> US WEST
</UL>
</TD>
</TR>
</TABLE>
<CENTER>


<TABLE BORDER=0><TR>
<TD WIDTH=50% VALIGN=TOP><FONT SIZE="+1">
To learn how Janice King can help you achieve outstanding
results for your marketing communications and public rela-
tions materials, contact her today!
</FONT>
```

FIGURE B.6 Continued

```
</TD>
<TD WIDTH=50% VALIGN=TOP>
<P><A HREF="visreg.htm"><IMG SRC="bluearrow.gif" ALIGN=MIDDLE
BORDER=0>Tell Me More!</A>
<P><A HREF="resource.htm"><IMG SRC="bluearrow.gif" ALIGN=MID-
DLE BORDER=0>More Resources</A>
<P><A HREF="books.htm"><IMG SRC="bluearrow.gif" ALIGN=MIDDLE
BORDER=0>Books</A>
<P><A HREF="profile.htm"><IMG SRC="bluearrow.gif" ALIGN=MID-
DLE BORDER=0>About Janice King</A>


</TD>
</TR></TABLE>

<P>
Janice King
<BR>MarkeTech
<BR>1075 Bellevue Way NE, Suite 486
<BR>Bellevue, WA   USA 98004
<BR>Tel: 206 828 9179 Fax: 206 827 4067
<BR>e-mail:<A HREF="mailto: janice@writespark.com">
janice@writespark.com</A>
</CENTER>

<P><BR><HR SIZE=3>
<CENTER>
http://www.writespark.com/services.htm
<BR>Copyright &copy; 1997 <A HREF="profile.htm"> Janice M.
King</A>
<BR>Questions and comments to: <A HREF="mailto:
janice@writespark.com"> janice@writespark.com </A>
<P><A HREF="index.htm"><IMG SRC="back.gif" WIDTH=80 HEIGHT=40
BORDER=0></A>
<A HREF="resource.htm"><IMG SRC="forward.gif" WIDTH=80
HEIGHT=40 BORDER=0></A>
<A HREF="index.htm"> <IMG SRC="home.gif" WIDTH=80 HEIGHT=40
BORDER=0></A>
<A HREF="mailto: janice@writespark.com"> <IMG SRC="email.gif"
WIDTH=80 HEIGHT=40 BORDER=0></A>
<BR><FONT SIZE=-1><A HREF="index.htm">Back</A> ||
<A HREF="resource.htm">Forward</A> ||
<A HREF="index.htm">Home</A> ||
<A HREF="mailto: janice@writespark.com">E-Mail</A></FONT>
</BODY>
</HTML>
```

FIGURE B.6 Continued

these links from the Catalog Page template
(*catitm1.htm*).

Books Page

I adapted this page from the Catalog Page template, listing both of my books on the same page. In the future, if I offer additional publications for online sale, I may create a separate page for each item, again adapting the Catalog Page template. See Figures B.7 and B.8.

1. I kept only the "Order this Item" link because all books I offer for sale are described on the page.

2. Here is how I handled a product that wasn't ready for sale yet, but for which I wanted to generate pre-publication interest and inquiries.

Faxable Order Form

I adapted the Event Registration Fax Form template to incorporate information specific to book sales from the Books page. Because this is a form that visitors will print and mail to me, I didn't need to worry about placing my site on a secure Web server or implementing a script to process orders. To ensure that purchasers obtain current information before placing an order, I included this reference to my Web site. See Figures B.9 and B.10.

Resources Page

I adapted the Starter template for this page, again deleting the text and HTML elements I did not need. See Figures B.11 and B.12.

1. I will adapt the Seminar Description, Event Calendar, and Event Registration Form templates as I schedule public workshops in the future.

2. I may create links to these organizations on a separate Links page. A separate page will allow me to provide a description of why I recommend a visit to each site,

Books

Books by Janice King

Writing High-Tech Copy That Sells

The first and only guide to writing powerful, persuasive promotional materials for high-tech products. This trailblazing book is both a superb tutorial for novices and an indispensable working reference for established professionals, arming you with

- Valuable insights and practical advice on writing clear, compelling promotional materials for high-tech products or services
- Proven techniques that will improve the copy in all the materials you write
- Superb ideas you can use every day for brochures, direct mail packages, press releases, sales guides, and more
- Helpful tips for using electronic media such as CD-ROM brochures, online advertising, and fax-on-demand
- Vital information on adapting your materials for the growing international marketplace

Contents

- Planning for High-Tech Marketing Communication: Success Starts Here
- The High-Tech Audience: Targeting Your Materials
- Message, Objective, and Purpose: The Essentials for On-Target Communication
- Creative Issues: Developing the Best Ideas, Styles, and Methods
- Document Elements: Packaging Your Information for Greater Impact
- Content Types: Presenting High-Tech Information Effectively
- Text Techniques: Adding Power to Your Copy
- Legal and Ethical Issues: Avoiding Problems in Your Materials
- International High-Tech Marketing Communication: Adapting Your Materials to the Global Market
- Sales Materials: Reaching Prospects and Customers
- Press Materials: Reaching Journalists and Analysts
- Alliance Materials: Reaching Dealers and Partners
- Marketing Communication in Electronic Media: Expanding Your Horizon
- Copywriting Checklist
- Glossary
- Bibliography and Resources
- References

Reader and Reviewer Comments

"What makes this book particularly appealing to me is that it's not just some dry textbook. It's a clear guide for anyone who writes marketing or press materials in high-tech."

"It's an excellent resource for anyone who's ever been asked to produce promotional materials for a technical product. I've broken the spine reading and re-reading it, propping it up by my keyboard while composing brochures on the fly."

"This is the first book I've seen that really aligns itself specifically with the sort of work we're doing, whether it's direct mail, press releases, data sheets, white papers, or online publications."

"Janice King's book is meant to be read and then kept close by for easy reference while you write your marcom project."

"This one text could easily replace half a dozen others on a writer's bookshelf."

"An indispensable book for those seeking to advance their knowledge and skill in this growing aspect of professional communication."

Item: Book01 **Price:** US$17.95 paper, US$39.95 cloth **Shipping:** US$3.00 ea to US, US$4.50 ea to Canada, US$10.00 ea elsewhere

Order this Item

The Web Marketing Cookbook

Co-authored with Paul Knight and James H. Mason. Available March 1997; here is a preview.

Contents

- Web Marketing: Entrée or Appetizer?
- Web Communications by Industry
- Web Marketing Templates
- Cooking Up Riches with Web Commerce
- Planning Your Menu
- Text Ingredients
- Visual and Multimedia Ingredients
- Navigation: Guiding Visitors Through Your Buffet
- Guidelines and Makeovers
- Serving it Well Done: Legal and International Factors for Web Promotion
- Advanced Web Possibilities
- CD-ROM with ready-to-go Web page templates, individual ingredients, and tools for fast Web development!

Back | Forward | Home | E-mail

Back | Forward | Home | E-Mail

FIGURE B.7 Books page on www.writespark.com.

```
<HTML><HEAD><TITLE>Janice King & WriteSpark: Books for
Marketing, Copywriting, and Public Relations</TITLE></HEAD>

<BODY BGCOLOR="#ffffff">

<IMG SRC="books.jpg" WIDTH=350 HEIGHT=50 ALT="Books Page">
<IMG SRC="logo.gif " WIDTH=146 HEIGHT=90 ALT="Logo">
<CENTER>
<P>
<FONT SIZE=+3>Books by Janice King </FONT>
</CENTER><P><BR>
<TABLE CELLSPACING=5 CELLPADDING=5 BORDER=0>
<TR><TD WIDTH=30% VALIGN=TOP ALIGN=CENTER>
<IMG SRC="book1.jpg" WIDTH=216 HEIGHT=334 ALIGN=LEFT
ALT="Cover">
</TD>
<TD WIDTH=70% VALIGN=TOP>
<P><FONT SIZE=+1>Writing High-Tech Copy That Sells </FONT>
<P><B>The first and only guide to writing powerful, persua-
sive promotional materials for high-tech products.</B> This
trailblazing book is both a superb tutorial for novices and
an indispensable working reference for established profes-
sionals, arming you with:
<UL>
<LI> Valuable insights and practical advice on writing
clear, compelling promotional materials for high-tech prod-
ucts or services
<LI> Proven techniques that will improve the copy in all the
materials you write
<LI> Superb ideas you can use every day for brochures,
direct mail packages, press releases, sales guides, and more
<LI> Helpful tips for using electronic media such as CD-ROM
brochures, online advertising, and fax-on-demand
<LI> Vital information on adapting your materials for the
growing international marketplace
</UL>
</TD>
</TR>
</TABLE>

<P><FONT SIZE=+1>Contents</FONT>
<UL>
<LI> Planning for High-Tech Marketing Communication: Success
Starts Here
```

FIGURE B.8 HTML code for books page on www.writespark.com.

```
<LI> The High-Tech Audience: Targeting Your Materials
<LI> Message, Objective, and Purpose: The Essentials for On-
Target Communication
<LI> Creative Issues: Developing the Best Ideas, Styles, and
Methods
<LI> Document Elements: Packaging Your Information for
Greater Impact
<LI> Content Types: Presenting High-Tech Information
Effectively
<LI> Text Techniques: Adding Power to Your Copy
<LI> Legal and Ethical Issues: Avoiding Problems in Your
Materials
<LI> International High-Tech Marketing Communication:
Adapting Your Materials to the Global Market
<LI> Sales Materials: Reaching Prospects and Customers
<LI> Press Materials: Reaching Journalists and Analysts
<LI> Alliance Materials: Reaching Dealers and Partners
<LI> Marketing Communication in Electronic Media: Expanding
Your Horizon
<LI> Copywriting Checklist
<LI> Glossary
<LI> Bibliography and Resources
<LI> References
</UL>
<P><FONT SIZE=+1>Reader and Reviewer Comments</FONT>
<P><CENTER><I>"What makes this book particularly appealing to
me is that it's not just some dry textbook. It's a clear
guide for anyone who writes marketing or press materials in
high-tech."
<P> "It's an excellent resource for anyone who's ever been
asked to produce promotional materials for a technical prod-
uct. I've broken the spine reading and re-reading it, prop-
ping it up by my keyboard while composing brochures on the
fly."
<P> "This is the first book I've seen that really aligns
itself specifically with the sort of work we're doing,
whether it's direct mail, press releases, data sheets, white
papers, or online publications."
<P> "Janice King's book is meant to be read and then kept
close by for easy reference while you write your marcom pro-
ject."
<P> "This one text could easily replace half a dozen others
on a writer's bookshelf."
<P> "An indispensable book for those seeking to advance
```

FIGURE B.8 Continued

```
their knowledge and skill in this growing aspect of profes-
sional communication."</CENTER></I>
<P><B>Item:</B> Book01 <B>Price:</B> US$17.95 paper, US$39.95
cloth <B>Shipping: </B>US$3.00 ea to US, <BR>US$4.50 ea to
Canada, US$10.00 ea elsewhere
<P><BR>
<CENTER>
<A HREF="orderfax.htm"><FONT SIZE="+2">Order this Item
</FONT></A>
</CENTER>
<PRE>



</PRE>
<P><FONT SIZE=+1>The Web Marketing Cookbook</FONT>
<P>Co-authored with Paul Knight and James H. Mason.
Available March 1997; here is a preview:
<P><FONT SIZE=+1>Contents</FONT>
<UL>
<LI> Web Marketing: Entree or Appetizer?
<LI> Web Communications by Industry
<LI> Web Marketing Templates
<LI> Cooking Up Riches with Web Commerce
<LI> Planning Your Menu
<LI> Text Ingredients
<LI> Visual and Multimedia Ingredients
<LI> Navigation: Guiding Visitors Through Your Buffet
<LI> Guidelines and Makeovers
<LI> Serving it Well Done: Legal and International Factors
for Web Promotion
<LI> Advanced Web Possibilities
<LI> CD-ROM with ready-to-go Web page templates, individual
ingredients, and tools for fast Web development!
</UL>

<P><HR SIZE=3>
<CENTER>
http://www.writespark.com/books.htm
<BR>Copyright &copy; 1997 <A HREF="profile.htm">Janice M.
King</A>
<BR>Questions and comments to: <A HREF="mailto:
janice@writespark.com"> janice@writespark.com </A>
<P><A HREF="profile.htm"><IMG SRC="back.gif" WIDTH=80
HEIGHT=40 BORDER=0></A>
```

FIGURE B.8 Continued

```
<A HREF="services.htm"><IMG SRC="forward.gif" WIDTH=80
HEIGHT=40 BORDER=0></A>
<A HREF="index.htm"> <IMG SRC="home.gif" WIDTH=80 HEIGHT=40
BORDER=0></A>
<A HREF="mailto: janice@writespark.com "> <IMG SRC="email.gif"
WIDTH=80 HEIGHT=40 BORDER=0></A>
<BR><FONT SIZE=-1><A HREF="profile.htm">Back</A> ||
<A HREF="services.htm">Forward</A> ||
<A HREF="index.htm">Home</A> ||
<A HREF="mailto: janice@writespark.com">E-Mail</A></FONT>
</BODY>
</HTML>
```

FIGURE B.8 Continued

and it also will encourage visitors to explore my site
fully before linking to other sites.

Profile Page

I adapted this page from the Profile template, which is
designed for presenting the credentials of consultants as well
as company employees. See Figures B.13 and B.14.

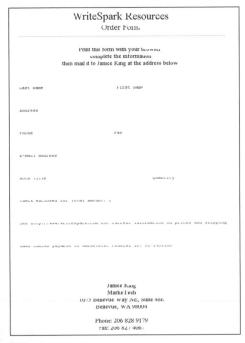

FIGURE B.9 Order form on www.writespark.com.

```
<html><head><title>Janice King & WriteSpark: Order
Form</title></head>

<body bgcolor="#ffffff">

<center>

<p>

<font size=+3>WriteSpark Resources</font>

<font size=+2><br>Order Form</font>

<hr size=3>

<p><font size=+1>Print this form with your browser, <br>com-
plete the information,<br> then mail it to Janice King at
the address below.</font>

</center>

<pre>

Last Name_____ First Name _____

Address_____

Phone_____ Fax _____

E-mail address_____

Book Title _____ Quantity _____

Check enclosed for Total Amount: $ _____

See http://www.writespark.com for current information on
prices and shipping fees.

Make checks payable to MarkeTech. Federal ID: 91-1489108

</pre>

<center>

<font size=+1>

<p>Janice King

<br>MarkeTech

<br>1075 Bellevue Way NE, Suite 486

<br>Bellevue, WA  98004

<p>Phone: 206 828 9179

<br>Fax: 206 827 4067

</font>


</body>

</html>
```

FIGURE B.10 HTML code for order form on www.writespark.com.

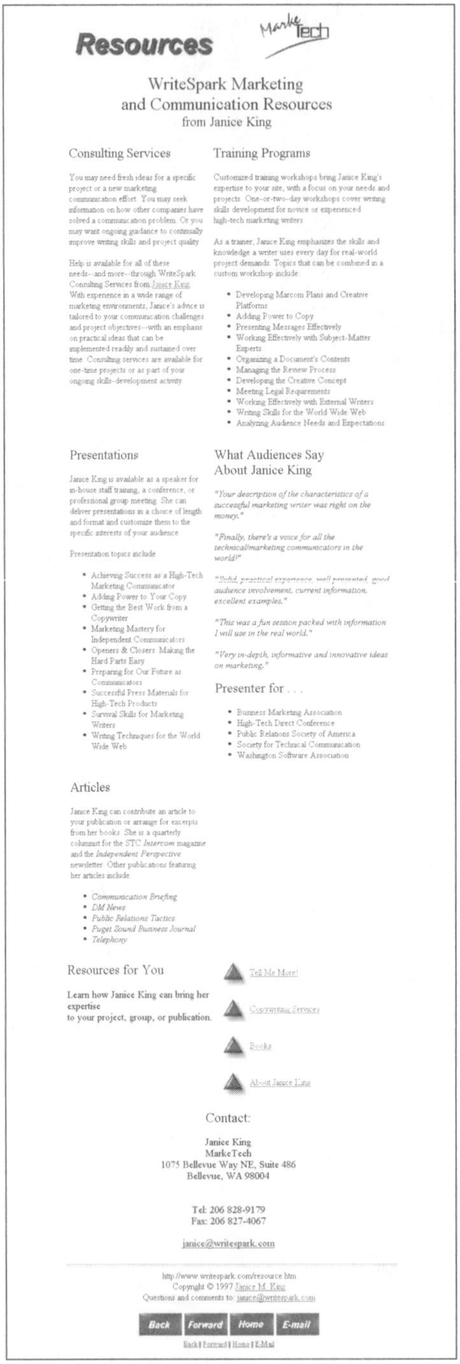

FIGURE B.11 Resource page on www.writespark.com.

```
<HTML><HEAD><TITLE>Janice King & WriteSpark: Marketing &
Copywriting Resources Page</TITLE></HEAD>

<BODY BGCOLOR="#ffffff">
<IMG SRC="resource.jpg" WIDTH=350 HEIGHT=50 ALT="Resources
Page"> <IMG SRC="logo.gif " WIDTH=146 HEIGHT=90 ALT="Logo">
<P>
<CENTER>

<FONT SIZE=+3>WriteSpark Marketing <BR>and Communication
Resources</FONT>
<BR><FONT SIZE=+2> from Janice King</FONT>
<P>


<TABLE CELLPADDING=5 CELLSPACING=5 BORDER=0>
<TR>
<TD VALIGN=TOP WIDTH=40%>
<FONT SIZE=+2>Consulting Services</FONT>
<P>
You may need fresh ideas for a specific project or a new
marketing communication effort. You may seek information on
how other companies have solved a communication problem. Or
you may want ongoing guidance to continually improve writing
skills and project quality.
<P>
Help is available for all of these needs—and more—through
WriteSpark Consulting Services from <A
HREF="profile.htm">Janice King</A>. With experience in a wide
range of marketing environments, Janice's advice is tailored
to your communication challenges and project objectives—with
an emphasis on practical ideas that can be implemented read-
ily and sustained over time. Consulting services are avail-
able for one-time projects or as part of your ongoing
skills-development activity.
<P>
<A NAME="training"></A>
</TD>
<TD VALIGN=TOP WIDTH=60%>
<FONT SIZE=+2>Training Programs</FONT>
<P>Customized training workshops bring Janice King's exper-
tise to your site, with a focus on your needs and projects.
One-or-two-day workshops cover writing skills development for
novice or experienced high-tech marketing writers.
<P>
As a trainer, Janice King emphasizes the skills and knowl-
edge a writer uses every day for real-world project demands.
```

FIGURE B.12 HTML code for resource page on www.writespark.com.

```
Topics that can be combined in a custom workshop include:
<UL>
<LI> Developing Marcom Plans and Creative Platforms
<LI> Adding Power to Copy
<LI> Presenting Messages Effectively
<LI> Working Effectively with Subject-Matter Experts
<LI> Organizing a Document's Contents
<LI> Managing the Review Process
<LI> Developing the Creative Concept
<LI> Meeting Legal Requirements
<LI> Working Effectively with External Writers
<LI> Writing Skills for the World Wide Web
<LI> Analyzing Audience Needs and Expectations.
</UL>
</TD>
</TR>
<TR>
<TD VALIGN=TOP>
<P>
<A NAME="present"></A>
<FONT SIZE=+2>Presentations</FONT>
<P>
Janice King is available as a speaker for in-house staff
training, a conference, or professional group meeting. She
can deliver presentations in a choice of length and format
and customize them to the specific interests of your audi-
ence.
<P>
<FONTSIZE=+1>Presentation topics include . . .</FONT>

<UL>
<LI> Achieving Success as a High-Tech Marketing Communicator
<LI> Adding Power to Your Copy
<LI> Getting the Best Work from a Copywriter
<LI> Marketing Mastery for Independent Communicators
<LI> Openers & Closers: Making the Hard Parts Easy
<LI> Preparing for Our Future as Communicators
<LI> Successful Press Materials for High-Tech Products
<LI> Survival Skills for Marketing Writers
<LI> Writing Techniques for the World Wide Web
</UL>
<P>
</TD>
<TD VALIGN=TOP>

<FONT SIZE=+2>What Audiences Say <BR>About Janice King</FONT>
```

FIGURE B.12 Continued

```
<BR>
<I>
<P>"Your description of the characteristics of a successful
marketing writer was right on the money."
<P>"Finally, there's a voice for all the technical/marketing
communicators in the world!"
<P>"Solid, practical experience, well presented, good audi-
ence involvement, current information, excellent examples."
<P>"This was a fun session packed with information I will
use in the real world."
<P>"Very in-depth, informative and innovative ideas on mar-
keting."

</I>


<P>
<FONT SIZE=+2>Presenter for . . .</FONT>
<UL>
<LI> Business Marketing Association
<LI> High-Tech Direct Conference
<LI> Public Relations Society of America
<LI> Society for Technical Communication
<LI> Washington Software Association
</UL>
<P>
</TD>
</TR>
<TR>
<TD VALIGN=TOP>
<A NAME="article"></A>
<FONT SIZE=+2>Articles</FONT>
<P>
Janice King can contribute an article to your publication or
arrange for excerpts from her books. She is a quarterly
columnist for the STC <I>Intercom</I> magazine and the
<I>Independent Perspective</I> newsletter. Other publications
featuring her articles include:
<UL>
<LI> <I> Communication Briefing
<LI> DM News
<LI> Public Relations Tactics
<LI> Puget Sound Business Journal
<LI> Telephony</I>
</UL>
```

FIGURE B.12 Continued

Implementing and Maintaining a Web Site

```
</TD>
</TR>
</TABLE>

</CENTER>
<TABLE BORDER=0><TR>
<TD WIDTH=50% VALIGN=TOP><FONT SIZE=+2>Resources for
You</FONT>
<FONT SIZE=+1>
<P> Learn how Janice King can bring her expertise <BR>to your
project, group, or publication.

</TD>
<TD WIDTH=50% VALIGN=TOP>
<P><A HREF="visreg.htm"><IMG SRC="bluearrow.gif" ALIGN=MIDDLE
BORDER=0>Tell Me More!</A>
<P><A HREF="services.htm"><IMG SRC="bluearrow.gif"
ALIGN=MIDDLE BORDER=0>Copywriting Services</A>
<P><A HREF="books.htm"><IMG SRC="bluearrow.gif" ALIGN=MIDDLE
BORDER=0>Books</A>
<P><A HREF="profile.htm"><IMG SRC="bluearrow.gif" ALIGN=MIDDLE
BORDER=0>About Janice King</A>


</TD>
</TR></TABLE>


<CENTER>


<P>
<FONT SIZE="+2">Contact:</FONT>
<P>
<FONT SIZE="+1">Janice King
<BR>MarkeTech
<BR>1075 Bellevue Way NE, Suite 486
<BR>Bellevue, WA  98004
<P>
<BR>Tel: 206 828-9179
<BR>Fax: 206 827-4067
<BR><P><A HREF="mailto:janice@writespark.com">
janice@writespark.com</A>
</FONT></CENTER>

<BR><HR SIZE=3>
```

FIGURE B.12 Continued

```
<CENTER>
http://www.writespark.com/resource.htm
<BR>Copyright &copy; 1997 <A HREF="profile.htm">Janice M.
King</A>
<BR>Questions and comments to: <A HREF="mailto:janice@writes-
park.com">janice@writespark.com</A>
<P><A HREF="services.htm"><IMG SRC="back.gif" WIDTH=80
HEIGHT=40 BORDER=0></A>
<A HREF="profile.htm"><IMG SRC="forward.gif" WIDTH=80
HEIGHT=40 BORDER=0></A>
<A HREF="index.htm"> <IMG SRC="home.gif" WIDTH=80 HEIGHT=40
BORDER=0></A>
<A HREF="mailto:janice@writespark.com"> <IMG SRC="email.gif"
WIDTH=80 HEIGHT=40 BORDER=0></A>
<BR><FONT SIZE=-1><A HREF="services.htm">Back</A> ||
<A HREF="profile.htm">Forward</A> ||
<A HREF="index.htm">Home</A> ||
<A HREF="mailto:janice@writespark.com">E-Mail</A></FONT>
</BODY>
</HTML>
```

FIGURE B.12 Continued

1. My portrait photo was scanned into JPEG format
   (*king.jpg*).

2. The link to the Books page gives visitors more information and encourages purchases.

3. I removed the button and link for the audio clip, but if
   I wanted to link to an audio element, I would have
   replaced the reference with the correct file name for
   the audio file.

4. I removed the link from my name in the copyright
   notice because that link on other pages points to this
   Profile page.

Tell Me More Form

I used the structure of the Visitor Registration/Survey template with very few modifications. I simply changed the text
on the form to fit my needs, including the text for the questions and the items that appear in the pull-down list. See
Figures B.15 and B.16.

FIGURE B.13 Profile page on www.writespark.com.

1. The "Tell Me More!" title matches the link text that appears on other pages.

2. I inserted my e-mail address, which is required by the script to send a completed form to me as an e-mail message.

3. I changed the URL in the *thnx.htm* file, which the script displays as an acknowledgment when a visitor submits the "Tell Me More" form (see Figures B.17 and B.18).

4. I changed the labels for the form items that will be processed by the script to match what appears on the form. This will also make it easier to understand the

```
<HTML><HEAD><TITLE>About Janice King</TITLE></HEAD>

<BODY BGCOLOR="#ffffff">

<TABLE>
<TR>
<TD NOWRAP>
<IMG SRC="execban.jpg"  WIDTH=350 HEIGHT=50 ALT="Executive
Profile">
<IMG SRC="logo.gif " WIDTH=146 HEIGHT=90 ALT="Logo">
</TD>
</TR>
</TABLE>

<P>
<TABLE BORDER=0 CELLSPACING=5 CELLPADDING=5>
<TR>

<TD VALIGN="Top" WIDTH="30%">
<IMG SRC="king.jpg" WIDTH=144 HEIGHT=206 >
</TD>

<TD VALIGN="Top" >
<BR><FONT SIZE=+3>About Janice King</FONT>
<BR><FONT SIZE=+2>MarkeTech</FONT>
<P><BR><FONT SIZE=+1>Freelance Copywriter and Author</FONT>
<HR SIZE=3>
<P><B>Professional Experience:</B> Janice King provides copy-
writing services to leading companies in the telecommunica-
tions, networking, and software industries throughout North
America. Janice is also an expert on the subject of market-
ing writing for technology products who frequently speaks
and publishes on these topics. Her background encompasses
more than 15 years of professional communication and market-
ing management experience.

<P><B>Specialization:</B>Copywriting for marketing public
relations materials in the telecommunications and networking
industry.

<P><B>Education: </B>B.A. Economics and Russian Studies, The
Evergreen State College

<P><B>Memberships and Affiliations: </B> Public Relations
Society of America, Society for Technical Communication,
Washington Software Association.
```

FIGURE B.14 HTML code for profile page on www.writespark.com.

```
<P><B>Awards and Honors: </B> International Association of
Business Communicatiors, Society for Technical Communication.

<P><B>Publications:</B> Author, <I>The Web Marketing
Cookbook</I> (Wiley 1997) and <I>Writing High-Tech Copy That
Sells</I> (Wiley 1995) Columnist, "Marketing Writing for
Technical Products," STC <I>Intercom.</I> Numerous articles
on marketing and communication.

 <P><B>Speeches, Seminars, and Presentations: </B>Frequent
speaker at conferences, trade shows, and seminars on market-
ing writing, especially for high-tech products.

</TR></TABLE>
<CENTER>

<P><B>Contact Information:</B>
<P>Janice King
<BR>MarkeTech
<BR>1075 Bellevue Way NE, Suite 486
<BR>Bellevue, WA USA 98004
<BR>Tel: 206 828 9179
<BR>e-mail:<A HREF="mailto: janice@writespark.com">
janice@writespark.com </A>
</CENTER>

<P><BR><HR SIZE=3>
<CENTER>
http://www.writespark.com/profile.htm
<BR>Copyright &copy; 1997  Janice M. King
<BR>Questions and comments to: <A HREF="mailto:
janice@writespark.com"> janice@writespark.com</A>
<P><A HREF="resource.htm"><IMG SRC="back.gif" WIDTH=80
HEIGHT=40 BORDER=0></A>
<A HREF="books.htm"><IMG SRC="forward.gif" WIDTH=80 HEIGHT=40
BORDER=0></A>
<A HREF="index.htm"> <IMG SRC="home.gif" WIDTH=80 HEIGHT=40
BORDER=0></A>
<A HREF="mailto: janice@writespark.com"> <IMG SRC="email.gif"
WIDTH=80 HEIGHT=40 BORDER=0></A>
<BR><FONT SIZE=-1><A HREF="resource.htm">Back</A> ||
<A HREF="books.htm">Forward</A> ||
<A HREF="index.htm">Home</A> ||
<A HREF="mailto: janice@writespark.com">E-Mail</A></FONT>
</BODY>
</HTML>
```

FIGURE B.14   Continued

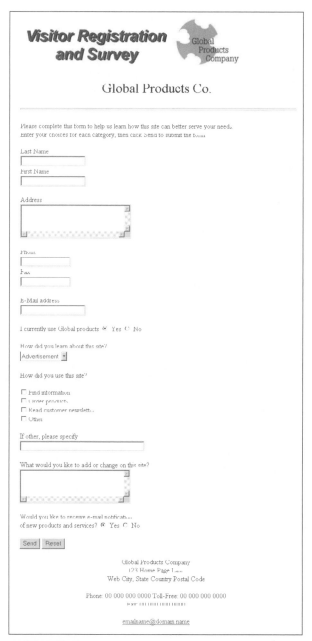

FIGURE B.15 Visitor survey page on www.writespark.com.

form. This will also make it easier to understand the responses the script sends to me as an e-mail message.

```
<html><head><title>Janice King & WriteSpark: Visitor
Survey</title></head>

<body bgcolor="#ffffff">
<IMG SRC="survban.jpg" WIDTH=350 HEIGHT=100 ALT="Visitor
Registration/Survey"> <IMG SRC="logo.gif " WIDTH=146
HEIGHT=90 ALT="Logo">
<center>
<p>
<font size=+3>Tell Me More! </font>
<p>
</center>
<hr size=3>
<p>Please complete this form to learn more about how Janice
King can better serve your needs for copywriting, marketing
communication, and public relations resources.
<br> Enter your choices for each category, then click Send
to submit the form.

<FORM ACTION="/cgi-local/mailform.cgi" METHOD="POST">
 <INPUT TYPE="hidden" NAME="mailformFromEmail" VALUE="Website
Visitor">
 <INPUT TYPE="hidden" NAME="mailformFromName" VALUE="Website
Visitor">
 <INPUT TYPE="hidden" NAME="mailformToEmail"
VALUE="janice@writespark.com">
 <INPUT TYPE="hidden" NAME="mailformToName" VALUE="Your
Name">
 <INPUT TYPE="hidden" NAME="mailformSubject" VALUE="Visitor
Survey">
 <INPUT TYPE="hidden" NAME="mailformURL"
VALUE="http://www.writespark.com/thnx.htm ">
 <INPUT TYPE="hidden" NAME="mailformBcc" VALUE="">
<p>Last Name <INPUT TYPE="text" NAME="1-lastname" SIZE="20">
        First Name <INPUT TYPE="text" NAME="1a-firstname"
SIZE="20">
<p> Address <br><TEXTAREA NAME="2-address" ROWS="3"
COLS="30"></TEXTAREA>
<p>Phone <INPUT TYPE="text" NAME="3-phone" SIZE="15"> Fax
<INPUT TYPE="text" NAME="4-fax" SIZE="15">
<p>E-Mail address <INPUT TYPE="text" NAME="5-email"
SIZE="20">
<p>I would like to receive more information on Janice King's
services and products
<INPUT type=radio NAME="6-UseProducts" value="Yes" CHECKED>
```

FIGURE B.16 HTML code for visitor survey page on
www.writespark.com.

```
Yes
<INPUT type=radio NAME="6-UseProducts" value="No"> No
<p>How did you learn about this site?<br>
<SELECT NAME="7-FoundUs">
<OPTION VALUE="Advertisement">Advertisement
<OPTION VALUE="Newsletter">Newsletter
<OPTION VALUE="SearchTool">Search Tool
<OPTION VALUE="Salesperson">Salesperson
<OPTION VALUE="AnotherUser">Another User
</SELECT>
<p>How did you use this site?<br>
<br><INPUT TYPE=CHECKBOX NAME="8-EvalServices"
VALUE="1">Evaluate services
<br><INPUT TYPE=CHECKBOX NAME="8-OrderProducts"
VALUE="1">Order products
<br><INPUT TYPE=CHECKBOX NAME="8-ContactJanice"
VALUE="1">Contact Janice King
<br><INPUT TYPE=CHECKBOX NAME="8-Other"  VALUE="1">Other
<br>If other, please specify <INPUT TYPE="text" NAME="8-
OtherUse" SIZE="40">

<p>What are your specific interests or needs?
<br><TEXTAREA NAME="9-AddChange" ROWS="3"
COLS="30"></TEXTAREA>
<p>Would you like to receive e-mail notification of new
products and services?
<INPUT type=radio NAME="a-EmailNotice" value="Yes" CHECKED>
Yes
<INPUT type=radio NAME="a-EmailNotice" value="No"> No

<p>
<INPUT TYPE="SUBMIT" VALUE="Send"> <INPUT TYPE="RESET"
VALUE="Reset">
 </FORM>




<center>
<p>              Janice King
<br>             MarkeTech
<br>             1075 Bellevue Way NE, Suite 486
<br>             Bellevue, WA  USA 98004
<p>              Phone: 206 828 9179
<br>             Fax: 206 827 4067
<p><a href="mailto: janice@writespark.com">janice@writes-
park.com</a>
</center>
```

FIGURE B.16 Continued

```
<br><hr size=3>
<center>
http://www.writespark.com/survey.htm
<br>Copyright &copy; 1997 <a href="profile.htm">Janice M.
King</a>
<br>Questions and comments to: <a href="mailto:
janice@writespark.com"> janice@writespark.com</a>
<p><a href="index.htm"> <img src="home.gif" width=80
height=40 border=0></a>
<a href="mailto:janice@writespark.com"> <img src="email.gif"
width=80 height=40 border=0></a>
<br>
<a href="index.htm">Home</a> ||
<a href="mailto:janice@writespark.com">E-Mail</a></font>
</body>
</html>
```

FIGURE B.16 Continued

5. I dropped the Back and Forward links because they don't make sense on this page. I would like the visitor to go back to the home page.

Implementing the Web Site

I followed the procedures listed earlier in this Appendix for establishing an account with an ISP, registering my domain name, and uploading my files with an FTP program. All of this activity proceeded smoothly, increasing my confidence for maintaining and expanding my Web site in the future.

Lessons Learned

While I found the templates easy to modify and test, here are a few hints that will help your development activity:

- Spell-check and proofread the HTML files while you are working with them in a word processor or HTML editor. When you load the HTML file for testing in your browser, print the displayed page and proofread it again.

- Remember to save the HTML file as plain ASCII text, not in the word processor's native document format

FIGURE B.17 Response page on www.writespark.com.

(e.g., a Microsoft Word *.DOC file) or in RTF format. If you save in document format inadvertently, the browser will be able to load your pages in most cases, but garbage characters may appear on the page.

- Working with the .RTF files in a word processor is very helpful for learning the difference between editable text and the HTML tags. When you have saved the modified template as an .HTM file in text format, use that file to make future edits. The replaceable text will no longer appear in red because text files do not save that type of formatting. However, after you have practiced with a few templates, you should be able to easily distinguish your text from HTML coding.

- Because I do not have experience in working with image files, I sought help for scanning and sizing the logos and images on my pages. You may want to work with a graphic designer, desktop publisher, or Web developer for this task. In addition, I would work with a Web developer if I needed any additional scripts or other complex HTML coding for my site.

- Testing is critical! Follow the procedures recommended earlier in this Appendix for testing your pages before and after uploading them to your Web server. Even on a

```
<html><head><title>Janice King & WriteSpark: Thank You
Page</title></head>

<body bgcolor="#ffffff">

<img src="books.jpg" width=350 height=50 alt="Books Page">
<img src="logo.gif " width=146 height=90 alt="Logo">
<center>
<p>
<font size=+3>Thanks from Janice King </font>
<br><hr size=3 >
<br><font size=+2>Thanks for sending your inquiry. I'll be
in touch soon.</font>

<p><hr size=3>

http://www.writespark.com/books.htm
<br>Copyright &copy; 1997 <a href="profile.htm">Janice M.
King</a>
<br>Questions and comments to: <a href="mailto:
janice@writespark.com"> janice@writespark.com </a>
<p><a href="home.htm"><img src="home.gif" width=80 height=40
border=0></a>
<a href="mailto: janice@writespark.com "> <img
src="email.gif" width=80 height=40 border=0></a>
<br><font size=-1><a href="home.htm">Home </a> ||
<a href="mailto: janice@writespark.com">E-Mail</a></font>
</body>
</html>
```

FIGURE B.18 HTML code for response page to vistor survey on www.writesprk.com.

small site like mine, there is a significant amount of interactivity among the pages to be coded and tested.

Future Plans

I plan to update my site regularly, as I add new services and resources. Here are some of my ideas:

- Use the Seminar Description template to present information on my workshops.

- Investigate my ISP's secure ordering capability and adapt the Product Order Form template to accept online orders for books and seminar registrations on my site.

- Register my site with the Web search engines and directories, running searches myself to determine if visitors can find my site and to identify ways to improve its content for better indexing.

RESOURCES

We have found these resources helpful for developing effective content and implementing a promotional Web site. Any references to URLs in this appendix were current as of late 1996, but may have changed or no longer be valid when you try to reach them.

Many of the tools listed here are included on the CD-ROM. Load the *cdhome.htm* page from the CD-ROM into your browser to find detailed information on accessing the tools.

↳ HTML and Web Development Tools

- *Image collections*. Corel Web.Gallery: Corel Corporation, http://www.corel.com. And, Sandra's Clip Art Server: http://www.cs.yale.edu/HTML/YALE/CS/HyPlans/ loosemore-sandra/clipart.html.

- *Image maps. Mapedit*: http://www.boutell.com/mapedit. This site offers an extremely easy-to-use tool that enables you to define the clickable areas on an image map simply by dragging your mouse.

- *Animated GIF files*. An excellent shareware source for creating animated images is *GIF Construction Set* from Alchemy Mindworks, Inc., located online at http://www.mindworkshop.com. A tutorial for creating animated GIFs can be found at http://www6.uniovi.es/gifanim/gifmake.htm.

- *Java and Javascript*. Shareware Java applets can be found at *Gamelan*, http://www.gamelan.com/index.shtml. Javascript shareware is offered by the *Javascript Planet* at http://www.geocities.com/SiliconValley/7116/.

- *VRML*. A good starting point for gaining an understanding of VRML is Netscape's *VRML Resources* page at http://www.netscape.com/comprod/products/ navigator/live3d/vrml_resources.html.

- *Quicktime VR*. Visit the Apple Computer site at http://qtvr.quicktime.apple.com/dev/dev.html.

- *Search scripts*. An easily implemented search script can be found at *Matt's Script Archive* at http://worldwidemart.com/scripts/.

- *Shopping cart software*. A good source for a shopping cart script is *Selena's Scripts* at http://kragar.eff.org/~erict/Scripts/.

- *Quickcam*. A low-cost, digital video camera and software package are available at http://www.connectix.com.

- *Image Editing*. *Lview* is an excellent, shareware image-editing program, available at http://world.std.com/~mmedia. We also recommend *Paintshop Pro* at http://www.shareware.com.

- *Mini-SQL (mSQL)*. A lightweight, relational database engine is available as shareware at http://Hughes.com.au/product.

 # World Wide Web Marketing

Web Sites

- Directories and search engines: Yahoo!: http://www.yahoo.com, Lycos: http://www.lycos.com, Web Crawler: http://www.webcrawler.com, Infoseek: http://www.infoseek.com, AltaVista: http://www.altavista.com, Excite: http://www.excite.com. Also, check these resources for sites related to Web marketing in your industry.

- List of e-mail marketing discussion lists: http://nsns.com/MouseTracks.

- Web marketing info center: http://www.wilsonweb.com.

- Advertising law Internet site: http://www.webcom.com/~lewrose.

Additional resources are listed on the *resources.htm* page on the CD-ROM.

Books

Carter, Mary E. *Electronic Highway Robbery*. Berkeley, CA: Peachpit Press, 1996.

Dowling, Paul J. Jr., Thomas J. Kuegler Jr., and Joshua O. Testerman. *Web Advertising and Marketing*. Rocklin, CA: Prima Publishing, 1996.

Hoft, Nancy. *International Technical Communication*. New York: John Wiley, 1995.

Horton, William. *Designing and Writing Online Documentation: Hypermedia for Self-Supporting Products*. New York: John Wiley, 1994.

Horton, William, Lee Taylor, Arthur Ignacio, and Nancy L. Hoft. *The Web Page Design Cookbook*. New York: John Wiley, 1996.

Judson, Bruce. *NetMarketing: How Your Business Can Profit from the Online Revolution*. New York: Wolff New Media, 1996.

King, Janice M. *Writing High-Tech Copy That Sells*. New York: John Wiley, 1995.

Sterne, Jim. *World Wide Web Marketing*. New York: John Wiley, 1995.

Smedinghoff, Thomas J. *Online Law: The SPA's Guide to Doing Business on the Internet*. Reading, MA: Addison Wesley Developers Press, 1996.

Magazines

The following publications are available in both print and Web versions:

Internet World: http://www.mecklerweb.com.
NetGuide: http://techweb.cmp.com.
New Media: http://www.macromedia.com.
Wired: http://www.hotwired.com.

R E F E R E N C E S

Note: Any references to URLs in this appendix were current as of late 1996, but they may have changed or no longer be valid when you try to reach them.

1. Mason, David and Mary Johnston Turner. "Not All Web Site Visitors Will Be Customers." *Communications Week*, September, 2, 1996.

2. Willms, Paul. "Average Hit Counts." 64k White Paper, June 1996.

3. Knepper, Kim. "Newsflash: Affluent People Really Do Use the Internet." *Public Relations Tactics*, September 1996.

4. Hoffman, Donna and Thomas Novak. "Intelligent Agent." *HotWired*, August 29, 1996.

5. Barron, Kelly. "Catalogs Get Haute." *The Orange County Register*, September 11, 1996.

6. Yokell, Larry. "Convergence Strategies." *Byte*, September 1996.

7. Wladawsky-Berger, Irving. "Hot Seat: E-Mail Buyers Beware." *InfoWeek*, August 26, 1996.

8. Sterne, Jim. *World Wide Web Marketing: Integrating the Internet Into Your Marketing Strategy*. New York: John Wiley, 1995.

9. Dimick, Sharlyn A., Thomas G. Acree, Leslie K. Gasser, Jeffrey T. Penka, and Matthew K. Wise.

"Developing and Maintaining a Successful Web Site: How to Keep Visitors Coming Back." In *Proceedings of the 43rd Annual Conference*. Seattle, WA: Society for Technical Communication, 1996. 281-286.

10. Degener, Jutta. *What Is Good Hypertext Writing?* (http://kbs.cs.tuberlin.de/~jutta/ht/writing.html).

11. Taylor, Dave. "The Medium Is Not the Message." *Marketing Computers*, June 1996.

12. Nielsen, Jakob. "International Usability." *Alert Box*, August 1996 (http://www.sun.com/columns/alertbox/9608.html).

13. Horton, William, Lee Taylor, Arthur Ignacio, Nancy L. Hoft. *The Web Page Design Cookbook*. New York: John Wiley, 1996.

14. Morris, Mary E. S. and Randy J. Hinrichs. *Web Page Design: A Different Multimedia*. Mountain View, CA: SunSoft Press, 1996.

15. Nielsen, Jakob. "Top Ten Mistakes in Web Design." *Alert Box*, May 1996 (http://www.sun.com/columns/alertbox/9605.html).

16. Hoffman, Ivan. *Internet Law Simplified*. (http://home.earthlink.net/~ivanlove).

17. O'Mahoney, P. J. Benedict. *World Wide Web Issues*. (http://www.benedict.com/webiss.htm).

18. Hoft, Nancy L. *International Technical Communication*. New York: John Wiley, 1995.

Applet A small, compiled application program that is interpreted by a browser.

Authentication A process for verifying the identity of a visitor or credit card, especially for an electronic commerce transaction.

Bookmark Similar to a bookmark placed in a book, a bookmark is a function of a Web browser that saves the URL and name of a specific Web page, enabling the visitor to return quickly to that page in the future.

Browser Software that allows a user to navigate the Web, view Web pages, and follow links to other sites and documents.

Call to Action A sentence or phrase, usually at the end of a marketing document, that motivates the reader to buy the product, contact a dealer, request more information, or take another action in the sales process.

Callout A line of text that points to a detail in a diagram, illustration, or photograph.

CGI *Common Gateway Interface* is used by Web server software to allow programs to interact with Web documents. CGI scripts control functions such as interactive forms and sending an e-mail message from a Web page.

Cross-Sell Promoting an accessory or related product as part of the sale of a base product.

Digital Cash Also called cybercash. A form of electronic currency for making purchases on the Web.

Encryption A process for transforming sensitive data into a protected, unreadable form before sending it over the Internet.

FAQ *Frequently Asked Questions*, a Web page of questions and answers commonly asked about a product, company, organization, or topic.

Formatting Device Changes in type style, use of a different color, use of punctuation, or changes in copy layout that are made to highlight key messages in the text.

FTP *File Transfer Protocol*, the underlying software method for transferring files between computer systems over the Internet.

GIF *Graphics Interchange Format*, a common file format for images, icons, and graphical symbols that appear on Web pages. Compare to JPEG.

Home Page The first page or entry point for visitors to a Web site. A home page may be the only page on the site, or it may serve as an index to other pages on the site.

HTML *HyperText Markup Language*, a formatting language for creating Web pages. HTML allows Web designers to create online documents that include text, images, and links to related documents or elements within the same site or on other Web sites.

HTTP *HyperText Transport Protocol*, the most commonly used method for transferring data on the Web that enables users to navigate among Web sites and display Web pages.

Internet Phone A technology that enables users to conduct voice conversations over an active link on a Web page. This technology allows visitors to click on a designated link and initiate a voice call to a company representative.

Involvement Device A checklist, quiz, worksheet, game, or other text element that prompts a reader to pause and become involved with the document.

Java A computer programming language used (among other things) to create small, compiled application programs for use on Web pages. See also *applet*.

JPEG *Joint Photographic Experts Group*, a common compressed format for image files, especially photographs and video. Compare to GIF.

Keyword A name, word, or phrase that is used by search tools to find Web sites with content that contains the keyword.

Link A connection from one Web page to another, or to an image, audio file, or video clip.

Marquee A line of text that scrolls across the display window of the visitor's browser. Typically used to promote specific products or topics on a Web site. Some browsers cannot display marquees.

Multimedia The use of any combination of text, images, sound, video, and animation on a Web page.

Offer The buying terms for a product or service, including price, payment options, delivery terms, time limitations, and purchase incentives.

Overline A line of text that appears over a main headline to serve as a lead-in. An overline is an alternative way to present a secondary idea in a headline (the other way is to state the secondary idea after the main headline).

PDF *Portable Document Format*, a file format for preserving the layout and pagination of a printed document when it is transferred in electronic form. One of the formats typically offered for documents that a visitor can download from a Web site for printing offline.

Positioning The market perception of a product, service, or company; often a statement of the perception that the company wants to create.

Postscript A programming language used by compatible printers. One of the formats typically offered for documents that a visitor can download from a Web site for printing offline.

Pull Quote A statement or quotation that appears in a boxed area within the body of a brochure or article. A pull quote is a technique for emphasizing a very positive quotation or key message, especially for readers who quickly review the text.

Script A program that processes forms or performs other functions for displaying information or interacting with visitors on a Web site.

Search Engine Also called a search tool or search site. A software program that searches Web pages for content that matched keywords entered by the user.

Server A computer that stores the pages for a Web site and makes them accessible to visitors over the Internet.

Testimonial A quote, case study, or other information from a customer that endorses a product, service, or company.

Up-sell Promoting a bigger, higher-function, or more expensive model as part of the sale of a base product.

URL A *Uniform Resource Locator* is an address that specifies the exact location of a Web site.

VRML *Virtual Reality Markup Language*, a programming language that creates a realistic, graphical environment on a Web page.

Web Page A single file of content within a Web site. May contain text, images, and multimedia elements and be the equivalent of one or more printed pages.

Web Site A collection of Web pages developed for a company, organization, or person.

World Wide Web Also known as the Web. A collection of sites that are stored on numerous computers around the world, and all linked to the Internet. Web sites use HTTP for navigation and communication with a visitor's browser and may use tools such as HTML, CGI, and Java for displaying content and interacting with visitors.

Press Release template, 137–138

Price/Parts List template, 140–142

Product Inquiry Form template, 145–147

Product Order Form template, 151–153

Profile template, 157–159

Selection Guide template, 163–165

Seminar Description template, 169–171

Services List template, 174–176

Starter Page template, 178–180

Visitor Registration/Survey Form template, 183–185

What's New Page template, 189–190

HTML coding examples, 330

humor, 244

I

icons, 254, 257

image maps, 272, 311

images, *See also* graphics
 altering, 305
 captions, 260
 clarity, 260
 clip art, 311
 editing, 65
 file size, 259
 guidelines, 253, 257–260, 291
 ideas, 310

modifying, 328

index page, 350

industries
 agriculture, 21, 34
 automotive, 21, 35
 creative professionals, 22, 36–38
 education, 23, 39–40
 every business, 32–33
 financial, 23–24, 41–42
 health care, 24, 43
 manufacturing, 24, 44
 media and publishing, 25, 45
 nonprofit organizations, 25–27, 46–48
 personal, family and home, 27–28, 49–51
 professional services, 28–29, 52–54
 real estate, 29–30, 55
 retail, direct mail, online, 30, 56
 service providers, 33
 travel, 30–31, 57–59

information
 needs, 211
 security, 218

inquiry forms, 11, 143

installing pages, 348

intelligent agents, 203

interacting with visitors, 212, 216, 279

international, 305–308
 colors, 256
 electronic commerce, 306
 forms, 264
 online sales, 12, 86, 191–203, 307

writing techniques, 244
Internet Service Providers (ISPs), 340, 346
Internet telephones, 200, 203

J

Java, 210, 215, 221, 226, 263, 314
Javascript, 263, 314
jobs, 218–222
journalists, 210
JPEG, 65, 257

K

keyword searches, 197
kiosks, 203

L

laws
    attorney, 220
    commerce, 202
    legal considerations, 105, 296–305
    marketing to children, 209
layout guidelines, 252–265
leads, 208
licenses, 297–299
lines, divider, 233
links, 254
    defining, 243
    embedded, 272
    external sites, 217
    guidelines, 273–279, 291
    HTML coding, 331
    legal factors, 300
    testing, 274
    text, 277–279
    types, 270, 272
    verifying, 355
    visitor expectations, 269
links, ideas for
    agriculture, 34
    automotive, other vehicles, and equipment, 35
    creative professionals, 36–38
    education, 39–40
    every business, 32–33
    financial, 41–42
    health care, 43
    manufacturing, 44
    media and publishing, 45
    nonprofit organizations, 46–48
    personal, family and home, 49–51
    professional services, 52–54
    real estate, 55
    retail, direct mail, online industries, 56
    service providers, 33
    travel, 57–59
lists, 244–245, 331
loading times, 232, 252, 258, 262
local-area marketing, 197
localized content, 308
location indicators, 246, 254
Locator template, 21–31, 125–128, 196
logos, 257
loyalty, sustaining, 208

M

magazines, 5, 10
mailform.cgi, 116, 216
maintaining the site, 354
makeovers, 287–294

manufacturing, 24, 44
maps
   geographic, 126
   image, 272
   site, 214, 272
market research, 181
marketing, dialogue, 13
marquees, 263
media
   combining, 7–8
   ROI, 9
   traditional, 5, 9, 14
media and publishing industry, 25, 45
META tags, 246
MIDI, 261
mistakes, 286
modifying images, 328
modifying templates, 328–330
MPEG, 262
multicolumn layout, 235, 254–255
multimedia
   developers, 220
   elements, 215, 217, 252, 260–263
   legal factors, 297
multiple page content, 232–237, 235

N

narrowcasting, 13
navigation, 267–281
   buttons, 254, 271, 329
   flowchart, 225
   in a site, 274
   to other sites, 275–277
Newsletter template, 21–31, 129–134, 236, 240

newspapers, 5, 10, 14
nonprofit organizations, 9, 25–27, 46–48, 193, 197

O

offers, 303
office, 125, 196
offline sales, 196
online documents, 230
online sales, 4–5, 191–203, 208, 275–276, 344
   international, 12, 307
   legal, 105, 149, 303
   security, 195
ordering online, 200–202, *See also* Product Order Form
overlines, 245
ownership usage rights, 297

P

page layout, 252–265, 285, 292
pages
   banner, 246
   footer, 247
   installing, 348
   single vs. multiple, 232–237
   testing, 348
paint programs, 328
passwords, 218, 317, 344, *See also* security
patterned background, 256
payment, 202
permissions, 297–299
personal, family and home industries, 27–28, 49–51
photographs, 257

T

tables, 235, 246, 254, 257, 330
television, 5, 6, 10
templates, 21–31, 61–190
  adapting, 62–64, 356–389
  Advertisement, 65–68
  Article, 69–74, 236
  Brochure, 75–80, 236
  Catalog Contents, 81–84, 239
  Catalog Page, 85–90, 236, 239
  Company Profile, 91–96
  Contents Page, 97–104
  copying, 325
  Coupon, 105–108
  Event Calendar, 109–114, 236
  Event Registration Form, 115–120, 200
  FAQ Page, 121–124
  Locator, 125–128, 196
  Newsletter, 129–134, 236, 240
  modifying, 328–330
  Press Release, 135–138
  Price/Parts List, 139–142
  Product Inquiry Form, 143–148, 200, 280
  Product Order Form, 149–154, 200–201, 240
  Profile, 155–159
  Selection Guide, 161–166, 280
  Seminar Description, 167–171
  Services List, 173–176
  Starter Page, 177–180
  Visitor Registration/Survey Form, 181–186, 200, 211, 280
  What's New Page, 187–190
testing, 227–228
  links, 274
  pages, 348
  server, 350, 355
text
  guidelines, 285
  links, 272, 277
  vs. graphics, 214
text-only version, 215
thank you page, 116
TIFF file, 65
tone, 249
tools, 333–337
trademarks, 304
traffic, measuring, 8, 10
transfer, data, 342
travel industry, 30–31, 57–59
trends, electronic commerce, 202

U

underlines, 244
uploading files, 349
up-selling, 76, 86, 194
URLs, 279, 347
  notation, 248
  promoting, 198
usage rights, 299

V

video, 261, 312, 332
Virtual Reality, 315
Visitor Registration/Survey Form template, 21–31, 181–186, 200

SOFTWARE LICENSE FOR QUICKTIME

Please read this license carefully before using the software. By using the software, you are agreeing to be bound by the terms of this license. If you do not agree to the terms of this license, promptly return the unused software to the place where you obtained it and your money will be refunded.

1. License. The application, demonstration, system, and other software accompanying this License, whether on disk, in read-only memory, or on any other media (the "Software") the related documentation and fonts are licensed to you by John Wiley & Sons. You own the disk on which the Software and fonts are recorded but John Wiley & Sons and/or John Wiley & Sons's Licensor(s) retain title to the Software, related documentation and fonts. This License allows you to use the Software and fonts on a single Apple computer and make one copy of the Software and fonts in machine-readable form for backup purposes only. You must reproduce on such copy the John Wiley & Sons copyright notice and any other proprietary legends that were on the original copy of the Software and fonts. You may also transfer all your license rights in the Software and fonts, the backup copy of the Software and fonts, the related documentation and a copy of this License to another party, provided the other party reads and agrees to accept the terms and conditions of this License.

2. Restrictions. The Software contains copyrighted material, trade secrets and other proprietary material. In order to protect them, and except as permitted by applicable legislation, you may not decompile, reverse engineer, disassemble or otherwise reduce the Software to a human-perceivable form. You may not modify, network, rent, lease, loan, distribute, or create derivative works based upon the Software in whole or in part. You may not electronically transmit the Software from one computer to another or over a network.

3. Termination. This License is effective until terminated. You may terminate this License at any time by destroying the Software, related documentation and fonts, and all copies thereof. This License will terminate immediately without notice from John Wiley & Sons if you fail to comply with any provision of this License. Upon termination you must destroy the Software, related documentation and fonts, and all copies thereof.

4. Export Law Assurances. You agree and certify that neither the Software nor any other technical data received from John Wiley & Sons, nor the direct product thereof, will be exported outside the United States except as authorized and as permitted by the laws and regulations of the United States. If the Software has been rightfully obtained by you outside of the United States, you agree that you will not re-export the Software nor any other technical data received from John Wiley & Sons, nor the direct product thereof, except as permitted by the laws and regulations of the United States and the laws and regulations of the jurisdiction in which you obtained the Software.

5. Government End Users. If you are acquiring the Software and fonts on behalf of any unit or agency of the United States Government, the following provisions apply. The Government agrees: (i) if the Software and fonts are supplied to the Department of Defense (DoD), the Software and fonts are classified as "Commercial Computer Software" and the Government is acquiring only "restricted rights" in the Software, its documentation and fonts as that term is defined in Clause 252.227-7013(c)(1) of the DFARS; and (ii) if the Software and fonts are supplied to any unit or agency of the United States Government other than DoD, the Government's rights in the Software, its documentation and fonts will be as defined in Clause 52.227-19(c)(2) of the FAR or, in the case of NASA, in Clause 18-52.227-86(d) of the NASA Supplement to the FAR.

6. Limited Warranty on Media. John Wiley & Sons warrants the diskettes and/or compact disc on which the Software and fonts are recorded to be free from defects in materials and workmanship under normal use for a period of ninety (90) days from the date of purchase as evidenced by a copy of the receipt. John Wiley & Sons's entire liability and your exclusive remedy will be replacement of the diskettes and/or compact disc not meeting John Wiley & Sons's limited warranty and which is returned to

John Wiley & Sons or a John Wiley & Sons authorized representative with a copy of the receipt. John Wiley & Sons will have no responsibility to replace a disk/disc damaged by accident, abuse, or misapplication. Any implied warranties on the Diskettes and/or compact disc, including the implied warranties of merchantability and fitness for a particular purpose, are limited in duration to ninety (90) days from the date of delivery. This warranty gives you specific legal rights, and you may also have other rights which vary by jurisdiction.

7. Disclaimer of Warranty on Apple Software. You expressly acknowledge and agree that use of the Software and fonts is at your sole risk. The Software, related documentation and fonts are provided "AS IS" and without warranty of any kind and John Wiley & Sons and John Wiley & Sons's Licensor(s) (for the purposes of provisions 7 and 8, John Wiley & Sons and John Wiley & Sons's Licensor(s) shall be collectively referred to as "John Wiley & Sons") expressly disclaim all warranties, express or implied, including, but not limited to, the implied warranties of merchantability and fitness for a particular purpose. John Wiley & Sons does not warrant that the functions contained in the software will meet your requirements, or that the operation of the software will be uninterrupted or error-free, or that defects in the software and the fonts will be corrected. Furthermore, John Wiley & Sons does not warrant or make any representations regarding the use or the results of the use of the software and fonts or related documentation in terms of their correctness, accuracy, reliability, or otherwise. No oral or written information or advice given by John Wiley & Sons or a John Wiley & Sons authorized representative shall create a warranty or in any way increase the scope of this warranty. Should the software prove defective, you (and not John Wiley & Sons or a John Wiley & Sons authorized representative) assume the entire cost of all necessary servicing, repair or correction. Some jurisdictions do not allow the exclusion of implied warranties, so the above exclusion may not apply to you.

8. Limitation of Liability. Under no circumstances including negligence, shall John Wiley & Sons be liable for any incidental, special or consequential damages that result from the use or inability to use the software or related documentation, even if John Wiley & Sons or a John Wiley & Sons authorized representative has been advised of the possibility of such damages. Some jurisdictions do not allow the limitation or exclusion of liability for incidental or consequential damages so the above limitation or exclusion may not apply to you. In no event shall John Wiley & Sons's total liability to you for all damages, losses, and causes of action (whether in contract, tort [including negligence] or otherwise) exceed the amount paid by you for the Software and fonts.

9. Controlling Law and Severability. This License shall be governed by and construed in accordance with the laws of the United States and the State of California, as applied to agreements entered into and to be performed entirely within California between California residents. If for any reason a court of competent jurisdiction finds any provision of this License, or portion thereof, to be unenforceable, that provision of the License shall be enforced to the maximum extent permissible so as to effect the intent of the parties, and the remainder of this License shall continue in full force and effect.

10. Complete Agreement. This License constitutes the entire agreement between the parties with respect to the use of the Software, the related documentation and fonts, and supersedes all prior or contemporaneous understandings or agreements, written or oral, regarding such subject matter. No amendment to or modification of this License will be binding unless in writing and signed by a duly authorized representative of John Wiley & Sons.